The Clausewitz Myth

Or the Emperor's New Clothes

The Clausewitz Myth

Or the Emperor's New Clothes

Azar Gat

London, UK
Washington, DC, USA

CollectiveInk

First published by Chronos Books, 2024
Chronos Books is an imprint of Collective Ink Ltd.,
Unit 11, Shepperton House, 89 Shepperton Road, London, N1 3DF
office@collectiveinkbooks.com
www.collectiveinkbooks.com
www.chronosbooks.com

For distributor details and how to order please visit the 'Ordering' section on our website.

Text copyright: Azar Gat 2023

ISBN: 978 1 80341 621 2
978 1 80341 630 4 (ebook)
Library of Congress Control Number: 2023942790

A CIP catalogue record for this book is available from the British Library.

Design: Lapiz Digital Services

UK: Printed and bound by CPI Group (UK) Ltd, Croydon, CR0 4YY
Printed in North America by CPI GPS partners

We operate a distinctive and ethical publishing philosophy in all areas of our business, from our global network of authors to production and worldwide distribution.

Other Books by Azar Gat:

The Origins of Military Thought: From the Enlightenment to Clausewitz. Oxford University Press. 1989. ISBN 9780198229483.

The Development of Military Thought: The Nineteenth Century. Oxford University Press. 1992. ISBN 978-0198202462.

Fascist and Liberal Visions of War: Fuller, Liddell Hart, Douhet, and Other Modernists. Oxford University Press. 1998. ISBN 9780198207153.

British Armour Theory and the Rise of the Panzer Arm: Revising the Revisionists. Palgrave Macmillan. 2000. ISBN 9780312229528.

A History of Military Thought: From the Enlightenment to the Cold War. Oxford University Press. 2001. ISBN 9780199247622.

War in Human Civilization. Oxford University Press. 2006. ISBN 9780199236633.

Victorious and Vulnerable: Why Democracy Won in the 20th Century and How it is Still Imperiled. Rowman & Littlefield Publishers. 2010. ISBN 9781442201149.

Nations: The Long History and Deep Roots of Political Ethnicity and Nationalism. Cambridge University Press. 2012. ISBN 9781107400023.

The Causes of War and the Spread of Peace: But Will War Rebound? Oxford University Press. 2017. ISBN 9780198795025.

War and Strategy in the Modern World: From Blitzkrieg to Unconventional Terrorism. Routledge. 2018. ISBN 9781138632561.

Ideological Fixation: From the Stone Age to Today's Culture Wars. Oxford University Press. 2022. ISBN 9780197646700.

Contents

1

Introduction: Clausewitz the 'Absolute' — and the Real One

Carl von Clausewitz (1780–1831) is by far the most celebrated military theorist, whose reputation has reached new heights. This book is as much about the Clausewitz phenomenon as it is about his ideas. It argues that many of his interpreters, struggling to make sense of his work, have not admitted – to themselves, no less than to their readers – that they did not quite figure it out. Hence, 'the emperor's new clothes.' Indeed, the problems of understanding have magnified Clausewitz's reputation, as they have widely been interpreted as a sign of his profundity. This has been the case since the posthumous publication of his work in 1832–1835 and as his reputation reached its first pinnacle in the decades before World War I. During our times, Clausewitz's fame has enjoyed a towering renaissance, reaching new, stratospheric, heights, most notably in the English-speaking world. Remarkably, this current wave has involved quite opposite emphases than those of earlier times. A new book proposing to present Clausewitz's work to the lay reader appears almost every year. Ambitious doctoral students seek to try their hand at one of the most prestigious topics in the field. Senior professors wish to crown their careers by sticking their flag on this ostensibly commanding peak. Cohorts of officers in military schools and colleges are delivered proverbs from Clausewitz as the supreme wisdom of the profession. University students are treated to a scarcely less critical diet.

Since there is no smoke without fire, people naturally tend to assume that there must be a genuine reason for this intense preoccupation and unrivalled celebrity. There is a snowball

1

effect involved. Clausewitz's major work, *On War*, is revered as a classic and is commonly referred to as the 'masterpiece', with Clausewitz lauded as the great 'philosopher of war'. Every field has its classics and masterpieces, right? Clausewitz's work is widely proclaimed as the one in the study and theory of war. He has occasionally been referred to as the Adam Smith of military theory.

While I chose the title of this book deliberately, to make the point that Clausewitz's stock is in bubble territory and that his interpreters have greatly contributed to this situation, the book is anything but a case for the prosecution. There is nothing more remote from my interests. On the contrary, my objective is to portray a clear scholarly picture of what Clausewitz was all about; what gave his ideas their particular form and trajectory; which of them still possess a 'lasting' value; which are simply wrong; and which are those whose significance is hugely inflated in the current discourse. Clausewitz had a lot going for him as a thinker and a man. He had a very powerful inquisitive mind. He was highly intelligent – though, in my humble opinion, not a genius. He was an authentic person of absolute integrity, honest and honourable, very serious in both his practical and intellectual pursuits, fully dedicated to his work, and committed to searching for the truth. Not uncommonly among authors, he had a very high opinion of his life's work, believing it was going to create a revolution in the study of war – which it has, at least in terms of the great resonance it has had. In this sense, Clausewitz himself, like the protagonist in Hans Christian Andersen's tale, played his part in the Emperor's New Clothes no less than the onlookers.

What then is the source of the discrepancy between the 'absolute' and 'real' Clausewitz? (To those unfamiliar: I am paraphrasing two of his much-discussed concepts.) As noted, interpreters, while often not admitting it, have not been quite sure of what exactly Clausewitz's work meant. In the last years of his life, after most of *On War* had already been drafted, he experienced a crucial intellectual turning-point which transformed his entire theory of war. He concluded that this would necessitate a radical revision of his manuscript, which would alter his fundamental, life-long concept of war. But he died before he was able to complete the revision, leaving behind a draft that incorporated both his old and new ideas, at odds with each other – the *On War* that we know today. Moreover, how he tried to reconcile his old and new ideas was and has remained, enigmatic. Thus, although this development has become increasingly recognised, some interpreters have denied that such a radical change in Clausewitz's thought occurred. The majority in recent decades have accepted that it did, but many of them have grasped neither its full nature nor how radical it was. They have hesitated as to what it actually entailed. Paradoxically, as already mentioned, this break in Clausewitz's thought and the ambiguity it created have only contributed to his image of profundity. Moreover, the question of the intellectual, philosophical, and cultural influences of the great era of European and German thought in which Clausewitz lived on the shaping of his work has added to both the obscurity and sense of profundity surrounding it.

These intrinsic obscurities, together with the dominant outlook and general drift of our times, have produced an uncritical reverence for Clausewitz's work for commentators. For many, he simply could not be wrong. From such a perspective, those in past generations who admired his work for very different reasons than today have been regarded as having been ridiculously mistaken. Similarly, his critics over the centuries have been brushed aside for having been guilty of ignorant misunderstandings. No less importantly, lingering uncertainties as to what exactly Clausewitz stood for have made many of the books professing to render his work accessible to the ordinary reader little more than extended paraphrasing which scarcely clarifies anything. Failing to identify the forest, they have attempted to explain each tree, often tediously, and, not infrequently, incorrectly.

I have written about much of this in my *The Origins of Military Thought: From the Enlightenment to Clausewitz* (1989), incorporated into the omnibus edition of my three-part work, *A History of Military Thought from the Enlightenment to the Cold War* (2001). Still, even though the book has become standard, many of those working on Clausewitz have been careful not to express an opinion on – either accept or object to – the picture of Clausewitz's intellectual background and core ideas unfolded in the book. As explained in the following chapters, it seems many have felt ill-equipped to engage with the former and hesitant with respect to the significant revision of the image of Clausewitz which the latter involved. To a considerable degree, this revision ran against the current.

In returning to the subject after thirty-five years, I had to consider both those who have not read my earlier book and those who have. For the benefit of the former, it has been necessary to incorporate much of what I wrote there, albeit in a condensed form. For those who have read my earlier book, this new one will serve as an updated, much expanded, and significantly augmented edition, focusing on the Clausewitz part of the older book. It addresses some of the extensive literature which has appeared over the last thirty-five years and which in the main only enhanced the adulation and sanctification of Clausewitz and his work. It emphasises more sharply the gap between the image of what I call the 'absolute' Clausewitz – the Clausewitz who could not be wrong – and the real one. It takes account of new writings by Clausewitz, in both German and English, which have come to light since my earlier book came out, and which mostly reinforce my interpretation of his core ideas and development. In the process, this book develops some major themes that did not receive full attention at the time. Finally, in this volume, I am not as oblique on the significant deficiencies in Michael Howard and Peter Paret's immensely successful English translation of *On War* (1976) as I was when writing my doctorate under Howard's very generous tutelage. If, over the last thirty-five years since the publication of my first book on the subject, the lionisation and sanctification of Clausewitz has only increased, there would seem to be a need for a stronger statement, incorporating all the above, which would seek to fundamentally change the terms of the discourse. Indeed, a stronger dose of medicine may be called for to halt and reverse the sweeping tide.

It is only natural that the book might be received with hostility by those heavily invested in the current trend. Indeed, I end this introduction with an apology. If this book is sometimes harsh in its criticisms of other commentators on Clausewitz, please remember that this comes with the territory. As everybody familiar with Clausewitz knows all too well, he was highly critical and often scathing in his judgements on many of his contemporaries – all in the service of knowledge. I can only wish that readers will address and weigh the evidence alone and in a spirit of unalloyed dedication to scholarship. Hopefully, Clausewitz's view of war and its theory presented here will make his thought clearer, if less profound and of a more chequered record of validity.

2

Clausewitz's Unrecognized Intellectual Setting

Clashing Climates of Ideas and Military Theory

To understand what Clausewitz's work was all about and how his main ideas in the field of military theory were shaped, it is first necessary to realise that he did not conceive them on an Olympus of abstract timeless thought, in the way we often imagine famous theorists cut in marble. Rather, he was very much the product and proponent of two epoch-making revolutions that were sweeping Europe during his lifetime: one cultural-intellectual-ideological, the other military. We begin with the former.

Although philosophical influences on Clausewitz's ideas and many mystifying writings have been assumed ever since the publication of his work, their exact nature has remained somewhat vague. Given the typical composition of his readership, this is unsurprising. The great majority of his readers, either military men or students of military affairs, have not been familiar with the intellectual background that informed Clausewitz's work. Moreover, they naturally tended to believe that whatever these intellectual influences might have been, they ultimately mattered little for the final product and for the subject at the centre of Clausewitz's work and of their own interest: war and military theory. They thus assumed, and hoped, that such external influences could safely be disregarded. While many of those who have written on Clausewitz, most of them military historians, have shared this attitude, others have made greater efforts to unravel the philosophical influences on his work. Furthermore, among Clausewitz scholars, there have also been some trained in philosophy who were better equipped to address the issue.

However, the problem was that the intellectual influences that shaped Clausewitz's thought and work did not come purely from 'philosophy'. Philosophers were certainly involved and influential, but unless their ideas are interwoven into much broader cultural-political-public trends, these ideas, as most people suspect, remain confined to the few. Broad cultural-political-public trends are labelled ideologies, climates of ideas, and comprehensive worldviews. The beginning of the nineteenth century saw a massive, sweeping clash between two such broad trends, which engulfed educated public opinion throughout Europe and Germany. This was the clash between the worldview of the Enlightenment which had dominated since about the middle of the eighteenth century and a powerful reaction against it which emerged later in that century. From around 1800 it became a tidal wave in response to the challenges posed by the French Revolution and Napoleonic imperialism. In the absence of a better name, this counter-movement is often referred to under the designation given to some of its aspects at the time, Romanticism, which does not quite convey the breadth and depth of its messages; or under a retrospective title, the Counter-Enlightenment, coined in our own times by the eminent student of ideas, Isaiah Berlin.[1]

To demonstrate the wide differences between philosophical doctrines, which remain confined to the initiated in the profession, and broad, sweeping public ideologies, climates of ideas, or comprehensive worldviews, here are a couple of examples. The clash between liberalism-capitalism and socialism/communism which raged during the nineteenth and twentieth centuries certainly involved the ideas of great philosophers and thinkers. Adam Smith, J. S. Mill and Karl Marx are but a few names. However, the immense public salience of liberalism and socialism, the passions they stirred, and the intense conflict between them did not arise from the number of people who read these thinkers' works. As is well known, very few did. It was rooted in the unrivalled public, political, and social significance of the questions involved for the masses of people and, indeed, in class identities and the interests in question. Another example: the rift between progressives and conservatives currently ripping apart the American public is not primarily attributable to the ideas of philosophers. To be sure, some brand-name philosophers and thinkers have articulated ideas central to the debate on both sides. However, most of the questions professional philosophers debate among themselves remain confined to the obscurity of their university departments. The current stormy clash raging in the United States between conservative and progressive 'philosophies' emanates from their public, political, and social significance for the masses of people, with their respective identities, interests, and views of life.

Much the same applies to the all-encompassing clash between the Enlightenment and the so-called Counter-Enlightenment which broke out among the educated public at large as a highly charged cultural-political phenomenon around 1800, at the very time Clausewitz reached maturity. While famous philosophers, thinkers and publicists were involved on both sides, these sweeping movements and respective climates of ideas were an expression of much broader trends nonreducible to professional 'philosophy'. Shaping all spheres of Western consciousness, they profoundly affected military theory as well. We now proceed to explain them both.

The Enlightenment and Military Theory

The all-powerful intellectual climate or worldview known as the Enlightenment swept across Europe and dominated educated public opinion from around the middle of the eighteenth century. While its most glittering centre was France and the

Paris salons of the *philosophes*, its proponents were as significant and its impact as profound and transformative throughout the continent (and across the Atlantic). Again, the great majority of the so-called *philosophes* were not philosophers in the ordinary sense of the word of working within the traditional fields of the discipline, and certainly not in academia. They came from a large variety of intellectual occupations – publicists, social commentators, dramatists, art critics, and some scientists – all figuring as public intellectuals (or men of letters, as they were then called). The central, resounding message of the movement was the supreme sovereignty of human reason as the instrument for understanding the world, both the natural and the social. Up until then, they charged, human history had mostly comprised a dark record of superstitions, prejudices, and unverified traditions. Sanctified as the word of God by the clergy and enforced by political authorities, they were used to perpetuate ignorance, bad institutions, and social injustice. However, once the rule of reason was established and allowed free rein, a new bright era of Progress would commence. Orderly disciplines of investigation in each field would discover the underlying laws governing the natural and social worlds and extend human control over them, thereby setting in motion a steady improvement of the human condition. Notably, much of this intellectual platform was to be astoundingly realised over the following centuries.

But what was the basis for this new, unbound optimism? A major impetus for the Enlightenment was the spectacular success of the Scientific Revolution of the seventeenth century, from Galileo to Newton. With Newton's *Philosophiae Naturalis Principia Mathematica* (1687) the entire field of mechanics, from the movements of the stars and planets in the heavens to those of earthly bodies, was captured by three natural laws of mathematical precision. Nothing like this had even remotely been achieved before. Most thinkers of the Enlightenment, not themselves scientists, were not interested in physics as such and did not delve into the mathematical subtleties of science. For them, Newtonian science was a striking demonstration and symbol of the potency and promise of the scientific method for the foundation of all human knowledge and activity on an enduring basis of critical empiricism and reason. At the same time, they did not hold that the rigorous mathematical accuracy and logic of the natural sciences applied to every other field, certainly not to the same degree. What they believed in was the possibility and necessity of establishing orderly disciplines and sound theories in what we now term the social sciences and humanities. Each such discipline would discover the underlying patterns and general regularities observed in, and generalised from, experience in their particular fields. Mathematical tools and rigour in these fields of inquiry were desired where applicable. This is the approach guiding the social sciences to this day.

Thus, following in Locke's footsteps, Condillac developed associationist psychology in his *Essai sur l'origine des connaissances humaines* (1746), *Traité des systemes* (1749), and *Traité des sensations* (1754). Helvétius carried it in a hedonist direction and towards utilitarian ethics in his *De l'esprit* (1758). Society and politics were governed by principles that arose from the nature of things; Montesquieu's *De l'esprit des lois* (1748) expounded this in a manner that drew general admiration throughout Europe. Political economy was launched as a distinct science in the 1750s with the activity of the physiocrats headed by Gournay, Quesnay, and Turgot. Adam Smith's *The Wealth of Nations* (1776) formulated the principles which constitute the basis of economics to this day. La Mettrie's *L'Homme machine* (1747) and Holbach's *Système de la nature* (1770) offered a materialist explanation of man and nature. Rousseau wrote his prize-winning essay *Discours sur les sciences et les arts* for the Academy of Dijon in 1749–50, his *Du contrat social* appeared in 1762, and his *Émile* (1762) laid the ground for modern educational theory. The *Grande Encyclopédie* edited by Diderot and D'Alembert first came out in 1751. Symbolising the period, all spheres of human life and all natural phenomena were to be subjugated to intellectual domination, and war was no exception.

Furthermore, in addition to the sciences and less rigorous disciplines, there were both the fine and the practical arts. These involved creative work to achieve an effect in the world. Here the model that dominated the Enlightenment stemmed from the highly influential legacy of late seventeenth and early eighteenth-century neo-classicism in the arts. The neo-classicists, taking their cue from Aristotle's *Poetics*, formulated a set of rules and principles for the construction and critique of artistic creation. They held that every art had universal, immutable rules and principles embodied in the great creations of both the past and the present, often referred to as the 'mechanical' or scientific part of the art. However, and no less importantly, they maintained that these universal rules and principles then required application to individual creations by the free, indeterminant working of inspired genius, the 'sublime' part of the art. This dual framework, originally developed for the dramatic arts, expanded to all other arts, including the art of war.

The military thinkers of the Enlightenment, practically without exception serving officers, absorbed these all-powerful cultural messages of their time and applied them to their professional field. From the late 1740s onward, a new theoretical enterprise, unprecedented in scope and sense of mission, emerged in a whole series of military works. War, their authors complained, was ruled by 'arbitrary traditions', 'blind prejudices', and 'disorder and confusion'. These had to be replaced by critical analyses and orderly systems which the men of the period understood in definitive and universal terms, largely overriding circumstantial differences and historical change. The organisation of armies and the conduct of war would thus be grounded in a theory consisting of universal rules and principles, to be applied by great generals to specific campaigns and battles.

Marshal-General of France Maurice de Saxe's opening statement in his *Reflections on the Art of War*, published posthumously in 1756, is only one famous example. He echoed the archetypal worldview of the Enlightenment word for word: 'War is a science covered with shadows in whose obscurity one cannot move with an assured step. Routine and prejudice, the natural result of ignorance, are its foundation and support. All sciences have principles and rules; war has none.'[2] True, as de Saxe wrote, there were widely read and much-admired military tracts from classical antiquity and the Renaissance. But all in all, they did not amount to a universal theory of war in the sense that the people of the Enlightenment now understood it. The idea that such a theory existed or should be formulated was the creation and legacy of the Enlightenment. From the middle of the eighteenth century onward, there was a line of military thinkers embarking on this intellectual mission, invariably expressing the same overriding messages. They tried their hand at formulating a universal theory for the art of war – an orderly 'system' of rules and principles that would guide its conduct.

Readers might ask themselves what military officers had to do with such lofty concerns such as the Enlightenment's worldview, cultural-philosophical messages, and the theory of art. The military of today is in many ways a world apart, with officers busy in their units and professional schools, dedicated to their vital practical mission of national defence. Philosophers, intellectuals, and art critics are looked at as inhabiting a separate world and as being very much secluded in their ivory towers. Little interaction seems to exist between the two worlds.

However, things were very different in the eighteenth century. Officers came almost exclusively from the ranks of the nobility in continental Europe, or the social class of 'gentlemen' in Britain and the new American republic (hence the phrase 'an officer and a gentleman'). They shared the same education and moved in the same social circles as their peers. Moreover, the nobility was a class of leisure. They were almost obligated *not* to work. And the officers among them were no exception. While valour in war was part of their class requirements, they were not expected to do much in peacetime. The day-to-day training and handling of the troops was entrusted to the NCOs. Experts in leisure time, the officers indulged in a variety of familiar pastimes: riding, hunting, gambling, drinking, 'whoring', and of course the much more delicate courting of women of society in the province in which their unit was stationed. We are all familiar with this from period dramas. However, on top of all that, some of them, probably a small, yet significant minority, had genuine intellectual interests and orientation.

Going further, how are we to understand the connection between the military and the theory of art, not to mention the dramatic arts? What affinity could there possibly be between officers and the rather exclusive world of the theatre? Needless to say, there were no televisions or movies at the time. Royal courts, above all the glittering court of Versailles, home to thousands of members of the nobility, and also the aristocratic palaces around the country, required entertainment during the long evenings. There were banquets, parties, dancing, musicians and, indeed, theatrical performances. It is not a coincidence that the reign of the Sun King Louis XIV is also known as the classical age of French drama, featuring such great names as Corneille, Moliere, and Racine. It was not that there was something in the water that produced such a concentration of geniuses. There was simply a huge demand, and royal patronage, for their merchandise. (The same would apply to the fields of classical music and opera at the Habsburg Viennese court a century later.) Furthermore, by the middle of the eighteenth century, the theatre was a favourable pastime for, and the talk of the day among, the more affluent classes in the capitals of Europe. And it was only these classes that counted in the public sphere.

Echoing the messages of the Enlightenment and applying them to their own field, the military thinkers of the Enlightenment emphasised the notion that it was possible and necessary – indeed, essential – to study the military occupation theoretically, at school, and from professional tracts. This was a novelty, for in practically all armies, with very rare exceptions, initiation into the military profession had been carried out through practical experience: by joining a unit, learning from the veterans, and picking up things with time. It was in accordance with this novel yet powerfully resonating idea of military education that officers' academies were established in rapid succession by all the great powers, as well as by smaller states, throughout the West from the late 1740s onward. West Point was established last, in 1802, in the young American Republic by no other than President Thomas Jefferson, the leader of the party that opposed a centralised state and regular armies. This apparent paradox is resolved when one recalls that Jefferson was also one of the leading proponents of the American Enlightenment.

The second half of the eighteenth century also saw a steep rise in the publication of military books and periodicals, similarly spurred by the deep conviction that the military profession could and should be studied theoretically and, indeed, that it was in dire need of what was now termed 'theory'. There was a close interplay between the proliferation of military academies and schools and the emergence and expansion of a community of officers who advocated the idea of military science and education and who regarded the formulation of a general theory of war as a most pressing need.

Thus, adopting the neo-classical framework, the military thinkers of the Enlightenment maintained that the art of war, like all arts, was susceptible to systematic formulation and called for orderly 'systems' based on rules and principles of universal validity. They held that these rules and principles had been uniformly revealed in the campaigns of the great generals of history, from classical antiquity to the present. It was noted that some branches of the art of war – like fortifications and artillery, and in the future perhaps also aspects of field warfare – were susceptible to mathematical formulation. In the same breath, however, the military thinkers of the Enlightenment maintained that the art of war and its theory, again as with all arts, escaped complete formalisation, with its rules and principles always requiring circumstantial application by the creative genius of the general.

In the wake of the Seven Years' War, the military thinkers of the Enlightenment, preoccupied with the relative advantages and disadvantages of the infantry line and column, focused their efforts on devising a system for the formation and conduct of troops on the battlefield. This is the sphere for which they revived the Greek term 'tactics'. Overriding technological and other historical changes, the theory of tactics, they believed, should comprise universal and immutable rules and principles. By the final decades of the eighteenth century, their interest switched to devising a theory for the conduct of armies in the theatre of operations, and to discovering the universal rules and principles that secured victory in a campaign. They variably designated this field 'grand tactics', 'operations', or 'strategy' – the latter being the term that would gain greater currency by the nineteenth century.

Among the many military thinkers of the Enlightenment, some were especially influential. Colonel Jacques Antoine Hippolyte Count de Guibert (1743–1790) moved into the Paris salons of the *philosophes* and aspired to make a great name for himself in a variety of intellectual and artistic pursuits. His wide-ranging and ambitious *Essai général de tactique* (1770, 1772) became the subject of a poem by none other than the patriarch of the French Enlightenment, Voltaire. Guibert's book may not have fulfilled its author's burning desire to formulate a general theory of tactics, and war, based on universal principles. Nonetheless, it put forward a new tactical system that combined the flexibility of the column with the firepower of the line. Guibert also advocated mobile, offensive operations. Adopted by the French royal army during the final years of the *ancien régime*, his combination of the column and the line was to give the Revolutionary and Napoleonic armies a decisive advantage.[3]

The Welshman Henry Humphrey Evans Lloyd (c. 1718–1783), a soldier of fortune and spy, serving a number of European powers, was another influential military thinker of the era. Deeply steeped in the literature of the Enlightenment, he applied it to study the psychology of the troops and the relationship between military and political and social institutions in his *History of the Late War between the King of Prussia and the Empress of Germany and her Allies* (2 vols., London, 1766, 1781), (meaning, the Seven Years' War), otherwise known as Lloyd's *Memoirs*. He also devised a method for measuring the power of states, based on their demographics and national income, which is scarcely inferior to any such method applied today for the same purpose. However, Lloyd's most influential concept was the lines of operations connecting armies in the field with their supply bases. He believed the key to the art of manoeuvre between opposing armies in a theatre of operations lay in this concept.[4]

A Prussian officer Adam Heinrich Dietrich von Bülow (1757–1807), with great fanfare, made this concept the cornerstone of a fanciful geometrical and supposedly scientific system of strategy in his *Geist des neuern Kriegssystems* (1799) [*The Spirit of the Modern System of War*]. More significantly, Antoine Henri

Jomini (1779–1869) adapted Lloyd's concept of the lines of operation to Napoleonic warfare, strikingly laying bare the emperor's principles of operations. He became an immediate pan-European celebrity when his *Traité des grandes opérations militaires* appeared in six volumes in 1804–1809. Indeed, his work informed the counter-strategies adopted by the coalition against Napoleon in the years of his fall, 1813–1815. Jomini remained by far the pre-eminent military theorist during much of the nineteenth century. Generations of officers, educated at military academies on Jomini's theoretical works and monumental campaign histories, treated him with the admiration reserved for classic authors. Willisen and Rüstow in Germany, Napier and Hamley in Britain, and Dennis and Alfred Mahan in the United States were only some of his most prominent disciples. In the United States, the generals who led both sides in the Civil War implemented his operational principles, which they had studied at West Point, in some of the most brilliant campaigns of the war. His concepts of the 'central position' and 'interior lines' remain useful to this day. Many other military theorists were widely read during the second half of the eighteenth century, all propounding the vision of the Enlightenment to formulate a theory of war based on universal rules and principles.

As Jomini put it in his *Treatise*: 'The fundamental principles upon which rest all good combinations of war have always existed... These principles are unchangeable; they are independent of the nature of the arms employed, of times and places... For thirty centuries there have lived generals who have been more or less happy in their application.'[5] 'Genius has a great deal to do with success, since it presides over the application of recognized rules, and seizes, as it were, all the subtle shades to which their application is susceptible. But in any case, the man of genius does not act contrary to these rules.'[6]

Notably, the great masters of war during the same period shared this vision and outlook. In addition to the instructive works that he circulated among his officers and the seminars that he conducted for them, Frederick the Great, the hero of the *philosophes*, established the *Académie militaire* (1765), the Prussian officer academy. He sent its broad programme of studies to his correspondent, the co-editor of the *Encyclopédie* D'Alembert, for his assessment. As the 'philosopher of sans-souci', the way the king referred to himself, wrote: 'Every art has its rules and maxims; they must be studied. Theory facilitates practice... In the profession of war, the rules of the art are never transgressed without punishment from the enemy.'[7]

Similarly, the ambitious young cadet at the French military school at Brienne, Napoleon Bonaparte, still in his teens, read all the military theorists of the Enlightenment, as well as every work of military history.[8] As he would later put it: 'All great captains have done great things only by *conforming* to the rules and natural principles of the art... They have succeeded only by thus conforming, whatever may have been the audacity of their enterprises and the extent of their success. They have never ceased to make war a *veritable science*.'[9] The following passage could just as well have been written by Jomini: 'Gustavus Adolphus, Turenne and Frederick, as also Alexander, Hannibal and Caesar have all acted on the same principles. To keep your forces united, to be vulnerable at no point, to bear down with rapidity upon important points – these are the principles which ensure victory.'[10]

Napoleon's opponent on the Austrian side, the highly respected general and military theorist Archduke Charles, wrote in the same spirit: 'The principles of the science of war are few and unchanging. Only their application is never the same and can never be the same. Every change in the conditions of armies: in their arms, strength and position, every new invention, involves a different application of these rules.'[11]

The above quotations from Napoleon are particularly interesting. They show that while new intellectual trends, to which Clausewitz would give expression, emphasized the general's genius, modelled on Napoleon, and rejected the concept of universal principles, Napoleon himself – like Jomini and most of his contemporaries – interpreted war and his own conduct as a general differently. In line with the military thinkers of the Enlightenment, he viewed them through the dual concept of universal principles, on the one hand, and their application by genius, on the other.

For a fully detailed and extensively documented description of the intellectual background, outlook, and doctrines of the military thinkers of the Enlightenment, the interested reader is referred to the first half of my *The Origins of Military Thought: From the Enlightenment to Clausewitz* (incorporated into my *A History of Military Thought from the Enlightenment to the Cold War*).

The Counter-Enlightenment and the German Cultural Scene

As pointed out by Berlin, the fierce and wide-ranging opposition to the ideas of the Enlightenment was as old as the Enlightenment itself. However, in addition to government censorship, and sometimes persecution, the opposition came primarily from traditional, mostly religious elements outside the intellectual circles, with whom there was no common ground for genuine communication. This situation changed with the Counter-Enlightenment. The opposition now came from within the intellectual elite, developed from the legacy of the Enlightenment itself, and challenged its ideas in its own language.

In the late eighteenth and early nineteenth centuries, the domination of the Enlightenment over the educated public's consciousness was breached, with the shock waves also impacting the conception of military theory. The diverse currents merging into the powerful movement labelled, not entirely satisfactorily, 'Romanticism' or the 'Counter-Enlightenment' reverberated across Europe and resonated most powerfully in Germany. They emerged in Germany in two major waves. The first appeared during the 1770s, at the zenith of the German Enlightenment. It was oppositional in nature, associated with a group that initially operated outside the cultural establishment. Its most notable members included Hamann, Herder, Möser, Lavater, the young Goethe and Schiller, and the poets and dramatists of the 'Storm and Stress' movement. The second and much more sweeping wave spread throughout Europe and Germany around the turn of the nineteenth century.

We begin with the main idea of the new currents and with the question of why they became particularly powerful in Germany. Resistance and objection to the view of the thinkers of the Enlightenment that reality was subjected to uniform rules and principles emanating from universal reason was central to the Counter-Enlightenment. It was not a coincidence that this opposition grew most notably in Germany. The country, primarily a geographical, linguistic, and cultural concept, was divided into more than three hundred distinct states of various sizes – from European great powers, such as Austria and Prussia, to a multitude of tiny principalities. Each such principality had its own laws and institutions, a disorderly hotch-potch piled up over the centuries since medieval times. There was nothing more starkly at odds with the ideal of the Enlightenment of a clear unified legal code and institutional system, allegedly based on the dictates of reason and in principle applying uniformly to all places. The German scene of the eighteenth century was in any case a European backwater, parochial in all respects compared to the shining political and cultural centres such as France and Britain. Most German thinkers of the period were proponents of the Enlightenment and wished to see institutions in Germany reformed and improved accordingly. However, as early as the 1770s, stung by the condescending disdain for and mockery of native institutions and traditions expressed or implied by the celebrated *philosophes*, some German thinkers and artists championed the virtues of cultural-local diversity and historical relativity.

This early opposition became a sweeping tide in the years just before and after 1800. The French Revolution was the main impetus for this change. When the Revolution broke out, educated German public opinion was at first highly sympathetic towards it. The Revolution's principles, expressed in the slogan *Liberté, égalité, fraternité* – liberty, equality, fraternity – seemed to have embodied the best ideals of the Enlightenment. However, sublime ideals and high hopes were soon to be darkened by the reign of revolutionary terror and the guillotine in France. And to add insult to injury, the republic then gave way to a military dictatorship – Napoleon's. Moreover, defence of the Revolution and the *patrie* soon transformed into French foreign military expansion and imperialism. How was this trajectory from admirable ideals to depressing realities to be explained? The answer, first advanced by the British politician and thinker Edmund Burke in his prophetic *Reflections on the Revolution in France* (1790), was developed further by intellectuals and publicists throughout Europe, and it resonated particularly strongly in Germany. They saw the root of the problem in some of the Enlightenment's most fundamental assumptions.

It turned out, they argued, that the pretence to impose abstract principles, supposedly grounded in reason, on a very complex reality was far more problematic than the *philosophes* had ever imagined. The law of unintended consequences, as it is now known, meant that events took very unexpected turns. Whatever the shortcomings of old laws and institutions, they were deeply rooted in gradually evolving societies. There was also the often unaccounted for wisdom of tradition and the stability and sense of familiarity and happiness which constituted the particular core of each society and culture. What was now castigated as an arrogant pretension by the

21

philosophes, in their Paris salons and cafes, to preach abstract universal principles to the world was widely viewed as highly superficial and injurious. It allegedly misconceived the complex nature and true logic of reality and was oblivious to historical-cultural diversity.

These were the notions that, adapted to changing circumstances, would become the basis of modern conservatism to this day. At present, we also hear them voiced in parts of the world such as East and Southeast Asia. They are articulated against what many in these parts of the world regard as arrogant Western intellectual and political imperialism which seeks to impose its normative standards, prescribed as universal, on societies of different cultural heritages. Indeed, going back to the outset of the nineteenth century, these notions became the basis of an all-encompassing cultural outlook once they ceased to be confined to a 'philosophical' debate and to what some German thinkers and artists of the 1770s resented as French intellectual imperialism. From around 1800, this new sweeping outlook engulfed the educated public at large as it became an ideological weapon in the service of the struggle against French *political and military* imperialism.

German proponents of the Counter-Enlightenment or Romanticism challenged the Enlightenment's most fundamental conceptions of knowledge and reality, man, art, and history.

The conception of knowledge and reality

The protagonists of the Counter-Enlightenment criticised the Enlightenment for what they regarded as its misplaced attempt to force the categories which had proven successful in physics on reality as a whole. Johann Georg Hamann (1730–87), the spiritual mentor of the men of the 'Storm and Stress' movement, scorned what he saw as the Enlightenment's blindness to, and loss of touch with, a rich and vital reality which, he contended, its proponents arrogantly attempted to capture by artificial, crude, and superficial principles and conceptual frameworks. As he argued, genuine knowledge was always the knowledge of singular and unique cases.[12] Despite his admiration for the achievements of the natural sciences, Johann Gottfried Herder (1744–1803) believed that their methods, suitable for the inanimate and simple bodies of mechanics, were inappropriate for understanding other spheres of a rich and complex world, in particular for the understanding of man and society.[13] Johann Wolfgang Goethe (1749–1842), who was enthusiastically interested and actively involved in the scientific developments of his time, believed that the analytic and classifying method did not even suit the natural sciences. The discoveries in the fields of electricity and the chemistry of gases during the last third of the eighteenth century reinforced the tendency to view nature in organic and vitalist, rather than mechanical, terms. Goethe held that the long list of 'intermediate cases' and 'exceptions' created by scientific classifications imposed on a diverse reality all too clearly revealed their artificiality.[14]

In the midst of the German cultural community, Immanuel Kant's decisive role in creating the new intellectual climate was both unique and ambivalent. While he stood at the pinnacle of the German Enlightenment, he also undermined some of its more cherished assumptions. Though one of the declared aims of his *Critique of Pure Reason* (1781) was to rescue the achievements of the natural sciences from the threat of scepticism, it only achieved this by excluding whole sections of reality from the domain and capacity of reason. Moreover, the aim of his *Critique of Practical Reason* (1788) was to establish the autonomy of the human soul from the regularity which dominated nature.

These new intellectual trends found expression in the works of the early Romantics at the turn of the nineteenth century and were philosophically formulated in F. W. J. Schelling's *Naturphilosophie*. Nature embraced an endless diversity of forms, was propelled by vitalist forces, and maintained a dynamic relationship with man.[15] Fichte, Schelling, and particularly Hegel developed to the utmost the holistic and integrative notions according to which all elements of reality were but aspects and manifestations of a single whole.

Man

These new perspectives had a special bearing on the study of man. The thinkers of the Enlightenment, their critics charged, missed the essence of man as an active, creative, and imaginative unity. The deep and multifaceted human experience, as intuitively and intimately known to every individual, was diametrically opposed to the allegedly crude, mechanistic, and skeletal system portrayed both by associative psychology and by the materialists. Goethe expressed the attitude he shared with his friends when he described Holbach's man as machine, 'ghostly' and 'corpse-like'.[16]

This attitude was closely affiliated with, among others, the Pietist stream of Lutheranism whose influence from the end of the seventeenth century was considerable, particularly in East Prussia. The works of Hamann, Lavater, Herder, Jacobi, and even Kant were deeply embedded in this powerful spiritualist tradition, with its emphasis on personal experience and its suspicion of all dogma.[17] Hamann argued that only imaginative, empathic insights, rather than abstract and universal principles, could penetrate the wealth and uniqueness of human reality. Man's whole personality, rather than narrow aspects of it, were expressed in all spheres of his activity. The young Goethe and other 'Storm and Stress' writers, like Merck, Lenz, and Klinger, highlighted man's vitality, activity, and power of feelings in their plays.

Around the turn of the nineteenth century, all of these themes were highlighted in the works of the early Romantics: the brothers Schlegel, Tieck, and Novalis. Their friend, the influential preacher and religious thinker Friedrich Schleiermacher, also stressed the uniqueness and potential of feelings, sensations, and thoughts revealed in every individual. He gave these ideas systematic expression in his *Monologen* (1800). The Romantics' philosophical patron J. G. Fichte, in his *Science of Knowledge* (1794) and *Theory of Knowledge* (1797), made man the creator of reality through his free spiritual activity. The Romantics adapted this to promote the omnipotence of the creative imagination and the force of feelings in the arts.[18]

Art

The emphasis on the creative, unique, and imaginative character of the individual which could not be reduced to abstract and mechanical principles was closely associated with a growing reaction against the legacy of neo-classicism in the arts. Shaftesbury in Britain, Leibnitz in Germany, and Diderot in France celebrated the originality of genius and the force of creative imagination, weakening the conceptual rigidity of neo-classicism. In his *Critique of Judgement* (1790), Kant consolidated the transformation in the eighteenth-century outlook on artistic creation. He completely downgraded the significance and value of principles of the art, wholly subjecting artistic creation to the intrinsically irreducible quality of genius. The Romantics' celebration of creative genius gave the last great push to the decline of neo-classicism.[19]

The reaction against neo-classicism went hand in hand with a powerful wave of interest in and admiration for forms of art hitherto considered by the men of the Enlightenment to be barbarous, lacking in taste or aesthetic knowledge, and produced by primitive or semi-civilised societies. In a famous example, Herder 'revealed' to the young Goethe the beauty of Strasburg's medieval cathedral, built in the Gothic style that was despised by the men of the Enlightenment. The men of the 'Storm and Stress' movement felt an affinity to the past, and the Romantics enthusiastically embraced its diversity. All this was closely linked to a profound transformation in the understanding of history.

View of history: Historicism

By the late eighteenth century, a new historical outlook that would come to be known as historicism began to take shape. Criticism was levelled against the tendency of the men of the Enlightenment to view other societies and historical periods through the prism and values of their own time, perceived as a universal standard of measurement for the interpretation, criticism, and rejection of other historical eras.

The beginnings of this transformation can be found in the Enlightenment itself, particularly in the works of Montesquieu. His much admired *The Spirit of the Laws* introduced his contemporaries to a new depth of analysis of the relationships between the environmental, economic, religious, political, and constitutional factors which moulded the diversity of societies and cultures.[20] Herder argued in his works that every culture was a unique historical entity that stemmed from the particular circumstances and experiences of their time and place. It expressed them in the totality of its values, ways of life and thought, institutions, and creative arts. A dogmatic examination according to so-called universal standards precluded any genuine understanding of the past. This could only be achieved by sympathetic and imaginative insights into the concrete conditions of a bygone reality and consciousness, aiming to reconstruct them on their own particular terms. Rather than superficial abstractions, a close and detailed study of the diverse forms of specific historical situations was needed. As an example of such a study, the members of the 'Storm and Stress' movement were delighted with Justus Möser's close, penetrating, and vivid records of the ways of life, customs, and affairs of his fellow townsmen and peasants in the small principality of Osnabrück, and with his research into their medieval past.[21]

Folksongs and folktales, regarded as vulgar by the men of the Enlightenment, were elevated by Herder to the status of creative, authentic, and revealing manifestations of past ways of life. The Romantics embraced this view not only in their literary themes but also in compiling folksongs and legends. Clemens Brentano and Achim von Arnim published an anthology of German folksongs (1805–8), and the Grimm brothers followed suit with their famous collection of folktales (1812).

These were the beginnings of historicism whose influence on the sciences of man was revolutionary and all-embracing. Human reality, according to the historicist message, was moulded by history, and changed with time and place, thus undermining universal generalisations. It could genuinely be understood only in a particular historical context. Directed against French Revolutionary ideas, this message, bolstered by Burke's highly influential tract, was widely voiced by political theorists and publicists. Adam Müller in *Die Elemente der Staatskunst* (1809) laid the foundation of the historical school of economics. The principles that the political economists of the eighteenth century, headed by Adam Smith, had formulated and regarded as the universal rules of economics were considered by this school to be no more than a reflection of the particular conditions and interests prevailing in the capitalist, proto-industrial Britain of the time. Marx would later develop this notion in a socialist direction. Friedrich Karl Savigny launched the historical school of jurisprudence in his *Vom Beruf unserer Zeit für Gesetzgebung und Rechtswissenschaft* (1814). Law was not, and could not be, determined according to universal and abstract principles, argued Savigny. It developed out of the particular historical conditions of every society. Schleiermacher presented the dogmas, conventions, and institutions of religion as changing throughout history. And Hegel bonded the human mind and philosophy to history, which reflected the various stages in the development of consciousness. Finally, in the more strictly historical field, there emerged the great historical school of the nineteenth century, associated with the name of Leopold Ranke. It launched modern historical scholarship, centring on the meticulous study of the documents of the past as the key for reconstructing bygone eras in their own terms.

These were some of the major themes of the reaction against the dominating ideas of the Enlightenment.[22] From being a parochial and somewhat backward culture – which Möser, to the delight of his friends, defended in his *Über die deutsche Sprache und Literatur* (1781) against the scorn of the French-speaking Frederick the Great – German culture became the centre of stimulating intellectual activity in the last decades of the eighteenth century. Its growth was therefore linked with an anti-French tendency and the awakening of German national sentiments. A German cultural self-awareness emerged as a reaction against French intellectual imperialism and developed in a strong political and nationalistic direction in response to Napoleon's political and military imperialism.

Berenhorst: The Counter-Enlightenment Reaching Military Theory

As with the Enlightenment itself, the new counter-currents that affected all spheres of thought by the turn of the nineteenth century did not fail to leave their mark on military theory as well. Georg Heinrich von Berenhorst (1733–1814) was their first major proponent in this field. Berenhorst came from the very heart of the Prussian elite. He was the illegitimate son of Prince Leopold I of Anhalt-Dessau, the *Alte Dessaur*, one of the architects of the Prussian army and young Frederick's senior general. At the age of fifteen Berenhorst joined an infantry regiment, then became a member of Prince Heinrich's staff and, from 1759, in Frederick's own headquarters, took part in the great campaigns of the Seven Years' War. He later entered the diplomatic service of his native principality, and, after retirement in 1790, embarked upon his literary career.[23]

It is, however, Berenhorst's intellectual and psychological development that is of special interest. He left an autobiographical essay entitled 'Selbstbekenntnisse', 'Confessions', in direct reference to the celebrated work of Rousseau, the hero of the new appeal to emotions and the inner world. Like many representatives of the Counter-Enlightenment, he was a child of the Enlightenment who underwent a profound intellectual and psychological transformation. Experiencing the religious-spiritualist revival and influenced by Kant's critical philosophy, he adapted the new intellectual trends to the military field in a sophisticated, sometimes sardonic, sometimes aphoristic manner.

In his youth, Berenhorst tells us, he was close to religion, but as he grew up his attitude changed. He read Helvetius's *De l'esprit*, became a materialist, and lost his faith. He accepted the view of man as a machine, and his religion was 'pantheism without morality'. He went on to read Lucretius, the exponent of atomism and materialism in antiquity, and the writings of Montaigne, Bayle, and Voltaire, who promoted scepticism, the critical spirit, and religious toleration. He was deeply influenced by the works of Nicolas Freret, the leading figure in the French Academy of Inscriptions in the first half of the eighteenth century, who laid the foundations for the historical critique of the Christian scriptures.[24]

Then, in Berenhorst's late thirties and forties, came his great spiritual transformation. He read the works of a line of authors who strove to eliminate the conflict between revealed religion and reason.[25] However, he was primarily influenced by the proponents of the great Pietist spiritualist revival, most notably Lavater, whose polemics stirred the German cultural scene in the last third of the eighteenth century. He came to reject both natural law and natural religion, and to promote inner life, intuition, emotions, and free will.[26] His literary remains include several critiques of plays of the 'Storm and Stress' dramatists, particularly the 'great Goethe'. Kant's influence was equally decisive. In her perceptive portrayal of German culture, *De l'Allemagne* (1813), iv, 112, Mme de Staël described the all-embracing effect of his work: 'the *Critique* [*of Pure Reason*] created such a sensation in Germany that almost everything achieved since then, in literature as well as philosophy, derives from the impetus given by this work.' The military field was no exception. In his 'Confessions', Berenhorst wrote that he laboured much to understand Kant's works and succeeded in gaining access to his philosophy. Kant claimed to have saved free will and set the boundaries of human knowledge. Berenhorst regarded his own work to be, to some extent, a Kantian critique of military theory.[27]

The first volume of Berenhorst's *Reflections on the Art of War: Its Progress, Contradictions, and Certainty* appeared in 1796 while the second, together with a revised edition of the first, appeared in 1798, and the third in 1799. According to a contemporary, at that time 'no book was as widely read as Reflections'.[28] In a note entitled 'The Main Idea of the Whole Work', written when he was composing the *Reflections*, Berenhorst stated that the art of war, like the rest of the sciences and arts, advanced knowledge and supported innate talent. However, it was not based on immutable laws but was rather associated with the unknown and uncontrollable modifications of the human spirit and operated in an environment saturated with willpower and emotions.[29]

Thus, according to Berenhorst, the moral forces that animate the troops are a major factor in the conduct of war. Far from being automata, the troops should be inspired with a fierce fighting spirit bolstered by patriotic enthusiasm. Indeed, Berenhorst was the most respected critic of the Frederician system in the debate in Germany over the successes of French Revolutionary warfare. His criticism derived, however, from much deeper roots, reflecting an older and more comprehensive opposition. It was typical of the men of the Counter-Enlightenment who detested the 'King of Prussia' with his bureaucratic, lifeless, 'machine-like' state and French rationalistic orientation. Frederick was severely criticised by Berenhorst for lacking national consciousness and assimilation into a foreign culture.[30] The king, who preferred French to German and whose people were but subjects to him, regarded his troops as no more than soulless materiel for his war machine. According to the critics, all the interrelated elements of the Prussian military system – its mercenary troops, ruthless discipline, mechanical drill, and linear tactics – suppressed rather than enhanced moral forces.

A critique of Berenhorst's views on military theory and a defence of the Frederician system was written by the military scholar and exponent of the military theory of the Enlightenment, Colonel Massenbach, whose career would be ruined by the defeat of 1806.[31] Berenhorst replied in the same year with his own polemic, and he reasserted his ideas in his *Aphorisms* (1805). War, he wrote, unlike mathematics and astronomy, could not be formulated as an *a priori* science.[32] He emphasised his belief in the sciences but asked his critics to bear in mind the numerous examples in military history in which armies with natural courage, ignorant of the art of war, had carried the day, and the many others in which principles had been revealed as useless or inadequate. 'What then is left of the certainty, let alone usefulness, of [military] science?', he wrote.[33] Rules and principles tend to be artificial, dogmatic, and un-circumstantial; principles, abstracted from experience, are indiscriminately applied to an altered situation. 'What is the use of rules when one is covered up to one's ears with exceptions?', he asked.[34] The emphasis on the science and art of war corresponds to the old illusion of the philosophers about the intellectual essence of man.[35] In reality, the real power of armies rests in the moral and physical force of the troops rather than in all the sciences of the officers.[36] The qualities and characteristics of a general are mainly innate, which the sciences can develop only slightly, though they provide him with ideas, particularly the study of military history and the art of war, and they improve him as a human being. In the wake of Prussia's defeat by Napoleon in 1806, Berenhorst played bitterly with several variations on the ironic pun: 'the French and Prussian generals divided the art of war between them; the Prussians took the former and the French the latter.'[37]

With respect to Jomini's principles, which he regarded as fundamentally sound, Berenhorst wrote in 1809 that as long as Napoleon was the only one to exercise them, he could achieve success, but once everyone employed his system, it would cancel itself out, and numerical superiority, courage, and the general's fortunes would again reign supreme.[38] Theoretical argument aside, this was a remarkable anticipation of the campaigns of 1813–15. Responding to a letter in which Valentini told him that Clausewitz, half a century his junior, did not believe in a general art of planning operations, the old Berenhorst wrote in 1812: 'I tend to agree with him... the [plans] are rendered absurd in one way or another by unforeseen circumstances... Then should we proceed without any plan just into the blue? I wish I could reply "yes", but fear of the gentlemen who think in formulae holds me back.'[39]

All this should be enough to overcome the natural incredulity regarding the inextricable connection between the conception of the nature, scope and utility of military theory, and the dominant comprehensive outlooks or climates of ideas clashing in Europe of the late eighteenth and early nineteenth centuries. In terms of his work's remarkable career, this clash would climax with Clausewitz. Much younger than Berenhorst, he reached maturity in the early 1800s, precisely when the reaction against the worldview of the Enlightenment became a tidal wave in Germany, intertwined as it was with the great political, ideological, and military struggle against French imperialism and Napoleon. While Clausewitz's ideas differed in some of their emphases from Berenhorst's, the two shared a great deal in their general attitude. Indeed, as we move to Clausewitz, the reader will find the main themes, derived from the new climate of ideas, familiar enough.

3

Clausewitz's Reformulation
of the Notion of Military Theory

In Terms of a New Climate of Ideas

Carl Philip Gottlieb von Clausewitz was born in 1780 to a family whose claim to nobility was dubious. His father, who joined the Prussian army when it was in desperate need of men during the Seven Years' War, rose to the rank of lieutenant, only to be discharged after the war when Frederick the Great purged the Prussian officer corps of middle-class elements. After Frederick's death, he succeeded, however, in securing appointments for three of his sons as NCOs. The twelve-year-old Carl began his military service in an infantry regiment in 1792, and in 1793–1795 he took part in the campaigns of the First Coalition against Revolutionary France. The young lieutenant spent the following six years of peace in the provincial garrison town of Neuruppin. He left it only in 1801 when he was admitted to the Institute for Young Officers in Berlin, which had been revived, enlarged, and thoroughly reformed by Gerhard von Scharnhorst, the would-be leader of the Reform Movement of the Prussian army after Prussia's crushing defeat at the hands of Napoleon in 1806. This was a turning point in Clausewitz's life. During his three years of study at the Institute, he became Scharnhorst's closest protege. His education was broadened dramatically, and new intellectual horizons were opened to him. After finishing first in his class, he was on the road leading to the centre of political and military events in the Prussia of the Napoleonic Wars, the Reform Era, and the Restoration.

In 1804, Clausewitz was appointed adjutant to Prince August, cousin of Frederick Wilhelm III King of Prussia. In this capacity and as a brevet captain, he took part in the Battle of Auerstadt (1806), and after Prussia's catastrophic defeat, he and the prince fell into French captivity. At the end of 1807, the two returned from their imprisonment in France, and at the beginning of 1809, Clausewitz was co-opted by Scharnhorst as his assistant in the *Allgemeine Kriegsdepartement*, the nucleus of a newly founded ministry of war. As head of the department, Scharnhorst orchestrated the military reforms of Prussia, assisted by a group of young officers. Among the reformers, Clausewitz made the acquaintance of Gneisenau, Scharnhorst's major ally, who became an intimate friend. During this period, he married the aristocratic and cultured Countess Marie von Brühl, who had been his fiancée for five years. Their uniquely close attachment is revealed in their correspondence, which constitutes the principal source for Clausewitz's biography.

In 1810, Clausewitz was appointed major in the General Staff, instructor in the new Staff Academy, and military tutor to the Prussian crown prince. His work during the reform era, motivated by the desire to see Prussia liberated from the French yoke and its status as a great power restored, reached a crossroads in 1812. With Prussia forced by Napoleon to join his invasion of Russia, Clausewitz, like some of his comrades, resigned from the Prussian service and joined the Russian army, acting against the instructions and policy of his king. In Russia, he was promoted to colonel, served in various staff posts, and took part in the Battle of Borodino. During Napoleon's disastrous retreat, Clausewitz played a role in persuading the Prussian corps in the *Grande Armée* to switch sides. By stirring an uprising against Napoleon in East Prussia, the Prussians in the advancing Russian army forced their hesitant king to join the war against Napoleon. Under these circumstances, Frederick William III declined to accept Clausewitz back into the Prussian service. His friends, however, arranged for him to be attached to Blücher's headquarters as a Russian liaison officer. Again, working together with Scharnhorst, Clausewitz took part in the battles of Lützen and Bautzen (Scharnhorst was mortally wounded in the former). Since the efforts to obtain the king's pardon failed, Clausewitz was compelled to serve in the German Legion of Volunteers and in secondary theatres of operations for the duration of the campaigns of autumn 1813 and 1814. Only then was he accepted back into the Prussian service. In the Campaign of 1815, he served as the chief of staff to the corps which held back Grouchy at Wavre, while the main body of the Prussian army marched to join Wellington at Waterloo.

After the war, Clausewitz was appointed chief of staff to the force stationed in Prussia's newly acquired territories along the Rhine, and he remained at Koblenz in that capacity until 1818. He was then promoted to general and appointed head of the Military Academy at Berlin, largely an administrative function. The end of the era of war and the beginning of a long period of peace paralleled the triumph of the Restoration in Prussia. The disappearance of the external challenge of his youth and the king's suspicious attitude towards his reputation as a reformer, which clouded his military career, made Clausewitz concentrate on the intellectual interests which had hitherto been overshadowed by his military activities. During his time at Koblenz, Clausewitz made the first attempt to write a general theoretical work on war, and this was followed by a continuous period of work while serving in Berlin. In 1830, the course of the work was interrupted by Clausewitz's appointment as commander of one of the three artillery divisions of the Prussian army. A short time later, following the outbreak of the revolutions of 1830, he was appointed chief of staff to the army raised under Gneisenau in anticipation of a possible Prussian intervention in Poland. In 1831, both men fell victim to the great cholera epidemic which swept across the continent. Clausewitz's widow, Marie, posthumously published his works in ten volumes (1832–1837), including *On War* and his historical studies.[40]

Clausewitz's military career was continuously paralleled by intensive intellectual activity. His strong interest in military theory dates at least from his days at the Institute for Young Officers. He extensively read the works of the military thinkers of the Enlightenment and those of his own time. In a series of works written during his twenties and thirties, he formulated the theoretical concepts which were to find their final place in his major work, *On War*.

His time at the Institute, with Scharnhorst's influence, was the most crucial period for the shaping of Clausewitz's outlook. He would call Scharnhorst 'the father and friend of my spirit.'[41] Scharnhorst himself (1755–1813) was one of the most notable and best-known exponents in Germany of the Enlightenment's ideas in the military sphere. It was as a military scholar, journal editor, and educator in this domain that he had made a name for himself, and he was hired by the Prussian army primarily on this strength. Together with his contemporaries in the closing decades of the eighteenth century, he believed that war was susceptible to intellectual study, both theoretical and historical. Some branches of war, such as artillery, fortifications, and siege-craft were even susceptible to mathematical and geometrical formulations. Hence the supreme importance of the officers' military education.[42]

Scharnhorst restated the classical conceptual framework of the Enlightenment in the face of Berenhorst's undermining criticism: the art of war, like painting and the rest of the arts, has two parts; one is mechanical and susceptible to theoretical study; the other is circumstantial and dominated by creative genius and experience. He remained loyal to this conceptual framework for the rest of his life.[43] Where Berenhorst wrote that 'the Prussians won in spite of the art' (Die Preussen siegten der Kunst zum Hohn), Scharnhorst replied that 'They won to the honour of the art' (Sie siegten der Kunst zu Ehren). While admitting that theoretical considerations appeared to be against the Prussians in the situation they were in, Scharnhorst nevertheless argued that they only won because of their superior organisation, discipline, and tactics.

However, the outset of the nineteenth century was also marked by the flourishing of systems for the conduct of operations, most notably Bülow's sensational and fanciful one which claimed to have reduced the conduct of operations to a science. These were regarded by Scharnhorst as artificial and one-sided, and stood in contrast to his traditional, middle-of-the-road understanding of the theoretical ideal of the Enlightenment. Scharnhorst directed the main thrust of his criticism against them in the years during which Clausewitz became acquainted with him and absorbed the fundamentals of his theoretical approach.[44]

In his youth, Clausewitz himself was enticed by the seductive promise of Bülow's system.[45] These very early notions entirely disappeared when he entered the Berlin Institute for Young Officers. Under Scharnhorst's influence, he, like other disciples of Scharnhorst, rejected the new systems for the conduct of operations as one-sided abstractions which created an intolerable gulf between theory and reality. Instead, he learned from Scharnhorst that theory had to be concrete and circumstantial, encompass the complexity of political, human, and military conditions that formed reality, and be closely linked to historical experience.[46]

At the same time, the generation that separated Scharnhorst from his young protégé also meant that Clausewitz's formative years coincided with the great reaction against the Enlightenment which swept the German cultural scene from the turn of the nineteenth century onward. Clausewitz's intellectual environment powerfully projected the message that the worldview and precepts of the French Enlightenment, on which the old theory of war was based, were artificial, superficial, and pretentious.

A classic example of these outlooks and sentiments can be found in the comparison Clausewitz drew between the national characteristics of the French and the Germans in late 1807, upon his return from French captivity. French feelings and thinking, he wrote, were active, excited, and quick, but also shallow and always prepared to sacrifice content for form and appearance. German feelings and thinking, by contrast, were calm, deep, and penetrating; and they strove toward comprehensive expression and understanding.[47] In the spirit of our times, recent commentators on Clausewitz – despite, or indeed, because of their admiration for him – have found it necessary to criticise what they have regretted as a stereotypic, crude, and chauvinist portrayal of 'national character'. But their censure misses the point, which is the new, sweeping climate of ideas which gave rise to Clausewitz's essay. Earlier scholars of Clausewitz noted that in comparing French superficial brilliance to German profundity, he was expressing prevailing ideas propounded, for example, by Möser, Wilhelm von Humboldt, the Romantics, and Fichte (with whom Clausewitz corresponded at the time).[48] Indeed, in another, later, striking expression of contemporary attitudes in Germany, Clausewitz sarcastically criticised the views of 'philosophers, who settle everything according to universal concepts, whose minds are too distinguished to bother about local conditions and historical experience – these people were strongly taken with the philosophy and politics of Paris.'[49] There can be no more archetypal expression of the powerful reaction against the ideas of the Enlightenment sweeping Germany of his times.

Clausewitz's cultural environment was not only critical of the legacy of the Enlightenment but also provided him with an alternative conception of reality, which he used as a basis for a reformulation of military theory. This reformulation stressed the living and diverse nature of human reality and centred on the conceptions of rules and principles, genius, moral forces, elements of uncertainty, and history.

Rules and principles in the art of war

As we have seen, the military thinkers of the Enlightenment derived their conception of theory from the neo-classicist theory of art, based on the twin pillars of rules and principles and genius. The neo-classicists' rigid precepts were gradually relaxed during the eighteenth century. With Kant, the transformation in the eighteenth century's outlook on the theory of art was complete, and the emphases were reversed. According to Kant, genius did not embody the rules as the neo-classicists had believed. Nor was it an essential, creative, and imaginative force, as important as the rules themselves. Rather, genius was the exclusive source of all artistic creation which could not be adequately formalised or reduced to any set of rules. It was the measurement of all rules which were only justified as crude means for capturing, by way of concepts, something of its creative force. 'Genius', wrote Kant in his *Critique of Judgement* (1790), 'is the talent (natural endowment) which gives the rule to art... [it] is a talent for producing that for which no definite rule can be given.' The genius's example can merely provide 'a methodical instruction according to rules, collected, so far as the circumstances admit.'[50]

The fact that Clausewitz's conception of military theory was rooted in Kant's theory of art was most clearly pointed out for the first time in 1883 by Kant's student, the philosopher Hermann Cohen, and has since been repeated by all of Clausewitz's major interpreters. Clausewitz was introduced to Kant's philosophy through the lectures of Johann Gottfried Kiesewetter, one of Kant's best-known popularisers and one of the pillars of the Institute for Young Officers, where he was the instructor of mathematics and logic. And there is growing evidence that

Clausewitz also read Kant directly – no surprise, as practically every educated German of the time had at least tried.[51] Like the military thinkers of the Enlightenment, Clausewitz found in the theory of art a highly suggestive model for the theory of the 'art' of war. Both dealt with the theory of action; in both, given means were employed to achieve a required effect through a creative process which involved principles of an operational nature. From his earliest works to *On War*, Clausewitz adapted Kant's theory of art to criticise the work of the military thinkers of the Enlightenment and to develop his own conception of the theory of war.

Already in 1805, Clausewitz employed this new conceptual framework in his criticism of Bülow. He objected to Bülow's view that the general ought sometimes to follow his genius above and contrary to the rules, which implied a separation between the two: 'one never rises above the rules, and thus when one appears to go against a rule, one is either wrong, or the case does not fall under the rule any more... he who possesses genius ought to make use of it, this is completely according to the rule!'[52] Any division or conflict between genius and rules was now inadmissible. In a fragment written in 1808 or 1809, Clausewitz reasserted this: 'genius, dear sirs, never acts contrary to the rules'.[53] His miscellaneous notes, written in 1804, with additions from 1808 and 1809, were published in the twentieth century under the title 'Strategy' but deal with an assortment of military topics. As Clausewitz wrote (1809), following Kant and Scharnhorst, 'the part of strategy that deals with the combination of battles must always remain in the sphere of free (unsystematic) reasoning'.[54]

In the essay 'On Art and Theory of Art' – written as a preparatory work for the writing of *On War* – the conception of theory is elaborated upon as Clausewitz strived to clarify his ideas. Like Kant, he distinguishes between science, whose aim is knowledge through conceptualisation, and art, whose essence is the attainment of a certain aim through the creative ability of combining given means. Between the two concepts there exists, Clausewitz points out, a certain overlapping, and art is assisted by knowledge. Thus, 'the theory of art teaches this combination [of means to an end] as far as concepts can... Theory is the representation of art by way of concepts.'[55]

All these themes receive comprehensive treatment in Book II of *On War*, 'On the Theory of War'. Clausewitz again presents the distinction between a science of concepts and an art of creative capability. War fits much more into the model of art, while the title science is better kept for fields such as mathematics and astronomy. However, Clausewitz also makes it clear that the major difference between the nature of creative activity in the arts and in war is that in war the object reacts. From this point of view, as well as from that of its subject-matter, war belongs much more to the field of social intercourse, being close to commerce and, above all, to politics.[56]

The various systems for the conduct of operations are again accused of being abstracted from reality and separating genius from rules: 'Anything that could not be reached by the meagre wisdom of such one-sided points of view was held to be beyond scientific control: it lay in the realm of genius which rises above all rules. Pity the soldier who is supposed to crawl among these scraps of rules, not good enough for genius, which genius can ignore, or laugh at. No; what genius does is the best rule and theory can do no better than show how and why this should be the case.'[57] Appealing to genius which is supposed to stand above the rules 'amounts to admitting that rules are not only made for idiots, but are idiotic in themselves.'[58]

Rules and principles for action are not wholly illegitimate as long as their value and limits are understood correctly. As in Kant's theory of art, their justification is that they provide a way to give the officers some guidance for conduct in war by conceptual means. Rigorous 'laws' are inapplicable to anything in war. But progressing further down the pyramid, there are principles and rules, directions, regulations, and methods which deal with minute details.[59] At the lower levels, in the sphere of tactics, rules of action are easier to formulate because they deal with more physical, material, and technical factors. Uniform procedures, methods, and manuals are also essential at these levels to regulate and unify activity, render general training possible, and direct rapid and determined action under conditions of shortage of information and time, without the need for rethinking the situation in each individual case. By contrast, at the higher levels of war, in strategy, action is imbued with subjective factors and conscious decisions, and the issues are major and crucial. Here, the general's free considerations play a decisive role.[60]

Youri Cormier calls attention to a problem in the English translations of Clausewitz that has obscured his meaning:

the title of Clausewitz's second-most widely read book [is] *The Principles of War*, which is a rendition of a textbook he had written while serving as the crown prince's tutor. The original German title of Clausewitz's book is *Die Wichtigsten Grundsätze des Kriegführens*. This title literally means 'main grounding,' and would be more properly translated as *The Fundamentals of War* because foundations are ground up, whereas principles are top down. The problem also appears in the Howard/Paret translation of *On War*, where they make absolutely no distinction between Grundsatz and Prinzip.... In reality, Clausewitz saw an important difference between the two terms and he never used them interchangeably: Grundsatz is what a soldier may use to frame his decisions on the battlefield; Prinzip is for the higher conceptual sphere. The former has many examples, the latter is rarely used, and neither implies certainty in the link between the conceptual and the practical.[61]

Clausewitz clearly expresses the relationship between rules and genius in terms of the new paradigm in the theory of art: 'It is simply not possible to construct a model for the art of war that can serve as a scaffolding on which the commander can rely for support at any time... no matter how versatile the code, the situation will always lead to the consequences we have already alluded to: *talent and genius operate outside the rules, and theory conflicts with practice.*'[62]

The nature of military genius
Clausewitz's emphasis thus shifts from the rules to the freely operating genius. Genius, however, is not a new sort of abstraction. It is a quality of living men whose activity depends on their particular psychological profile, motivations, and aims, as well as on the conditions of their environment. Rejecting 'dead' abstractions for real life and acting personalities was a dominant theme in German cultural outlook and artistic creation since the 'Storm and Stress' period. It remained at the centre of Goethe's and Schiller's outlook in their mature works. And its importance for the Romantics cannot be exaggerated. Here too, Clausewitz gave expression to a new worldview whose domination over Germany was already secure when he began his intellectual and literary activities in the opening years of the nineteenth century. An interesting fact, pointed out by Paret, is that Schiller, the author of historical dramas based on charismatic personalities – The Maiden of Orleans, William Tell, Mary Stuart, and Wallenstein – is the author most frequently mentioned in Clausewitz's letters.[63] Schiller is also known as the most philosophically inclined among the great German artists of the late eighteenth century, as Kant's disciple, and as the author of esthetical works in which he stressed the free operation of genius.[64]

It is, therefore, not surprising that Clausewitz's emphasis on the role of the creative personality constitutes, as Paret notes here too, one of the striking differences between his outlook and that of Scharnhorst.[65] The explanation for that goes, however, further than Paret's suggestion of variations in interests or aims between the two. This difference offers, in fact, a classic demonstration of the paradigmatic change between the teacher and his pupil. Scharnhorst was a typical representative of the military school of the Enlightenment, which was institutionally and structurally oriented. Characteristically, the military thinkers of the Enlightenment interpreted Frederick the Great's victories chiefly as a product of Prussian battle deployment. Neither Frederick nor Napoleon drew Clausewitz's attention to the role of the great personality. A new worldview was needed for that, and again, it may be traced to his earliest works.

In his notes on strategy of 1804, a young Clausewitz wrote that a strategic plan 'is a pure expression of [the general's] manner of thinking and feeling, and almost never a course chosen by free consideration.'[66] In this provocative argument he expanded on Machiavelli's well-known point (whom he read and admired) and also cited the example the latter used: Fabius Cunctator 'did not delay operations against the Carthaginians because this type of war so suited circumstances, but rather because it was his nature to delay.'[67] This view, which elevates the general's personality above any abstract strategic considerations, is also strikingly manifest in Clausewitz's interpretation of the operations of Gustavus Adolphus and Frederick the Great. In 'Gustavus Adolphus's Campaigns of 1630–1632', apparently written during the Napoleonic period,[68] Clausewitz presents the personality and motivations of the king and his adversaries as the key to the events of the war, a conscious antithesis to the military thinkers of the Enlightenment.[69] Schiller's famous trilogy *Wallenstein*, published in 1800, and one of Clausewitz's favourite works, may very well have influenced both Clausewitz's choice of subject and manner of treatment. Schiller's reputation and career as a historian, which culminated in his appointment as professor of history at Jena is overshadowed by his dramatic and philosophical achievements. *Wallenstein* was preceded by a widely read *History of the Thirty Years' War* (1791–1793) in which he was already attempting to uncover the proper relation between the great personality and the conditions of his time.[70]

Historical study, writes Clausewitz, dwells on 'the mathematical level of physical forces' and ignores the subjective forces in war; yet, it is precisely these forces which are the most decisive.[71] To understand the events of the war, one should understand the particular psychological profile of the operating individuals in the context of their particular milieu. 'Is it not wiser to pay less attention to what the enemy can do and pay more attention to what he will do?... here lies a more fruitful field for strategy than the degrees of angles of operations.'[72]

The idea stressed in 'Gustavus Adolphus' is sharply expressed once more in Clausewitz's notes on strategy of 1808, now directed against Jomini's analysis of the campaigns of Frederick the Great. Clausewitz rejected the substitution of abstract, lifeless principles for Frederick's complex and concrete reality and particular psychology. As he wrote: 'To appreciate the value of his [Jomini's] abstractions, one must ask if one wants to give up all of Frederick II's practical life as a general for these couple of general maxims which are so easy to grasp?... did Frederick violate these maxims out of ignorance?... It is impossible to hang [the diversity of Frederick's generalship]... on a couple of meagre ideas... What is the conclusion of all this? That the general's temper greatly influences his actions... that one must not judge generals by mere reason alone.[73]

Not only did Clausewitz deem the abstract intellectual interpretation of the activities of great generals as fundamentally artificial, but so was the excessive emphasis on their intellectual faculties and the knowledge necessary for them. In his notes on strategy of 1804, Clausewitz lists the disciplines that the military thinkers of the Enlightenment carefully compiled for their educational programmes for officers: mathematics, map drawing, geography, artillery, fortifications, siege-craft, entrenchments, tactics, and strategy. Regarding each subject, he concludes that the general only requires a broad but sound, rather than detailed, knowledge. He has no need for 'professorial' or 'pedantic' knowledge, and he can manage with a 'few abstract truths'. What he predominantly requires is sound judgement and a strong character: 'a strong, ambitious spirit.'[74]

Clausewitz's ironic attitude towards the Enlightenment's ideal of knowledge is again manifest in his booklet of guidance for the Prussian Crown Prince (1812):

Extensive knowledge and deeper learning are by no means necessary [for the general], nor are extraordinary intellectual faculties... For a long time the contrary has been maintained... because of the vanity of the authors who have written about it... As recently as the Revolutionary War we find many men who proved themselves able military leaders, yes, even military leaders of the first order, without having had any military education. In the case of Condé, Wallenstein, Suvorov, and a multitude of others it is very doubtful whether or not they had the advantage of such education.[75]

Clausewitz discusses the qualities required of a general in his treatment of military genius in *On War*. Again, the important point is that character and spirit are more essential than cognitive faculties; fundamentally, war is an activity more than an intellectual discipline. Even the required cognitive qualities are of the empirical and applied sort.[76] Clausewitz twice repeats Napoleon's dictum that the complexity of the problems involved in war is on the order of mathematical problems that would require a Newton. However, what distinguishes military knowledge is its relation to life: 'Experience, with its wealth of lessons, will never produce a Newton or an Euler, but it may well bring forth the higher calculations of a Condé or a Frederick.'[77]

Moral forces in war

Clausewitz's emphasis on the general's personality, emotions, and motivations went hand in hand with his emphasis on the decisive role of the moral forces that animate armies. Here too, an understanding of the shift in the intellectual paradigm is essential. The military thinkers of the Enlightenment far from ignored the importance of moral forces in war. Lloyd even offered an extensive study of the subject, applying to it the notions of the contemporary psychology of desires. As Napoleon, a faithful disciple of the Enlightenment, famously put it: 'In war, moral power is to physical as three parts out of four.' However, on the whole, the military thinkers of the Enlightenment regarded moral forces as too elusive and belonging to the 'sublime', undefinable part of war. And since they were interested in intellectual control, they saw no point in discussing moral forces at length. The intellectual transformation generated by the men of the 'Storm and Stress' period and the Romantics, which placed man's inner world at the centre of human experience, involved a radical change in the interpretation of, and regard for, the ideal of knowledge. The new perspective was largely rooted in anti-rationalistic trends, and thus the focus on uncontrollable elements was, for many of its exponents, a special point to be made rather than a sacrifice. The Enlightenment's ideal of understanding and control was substituted with a vitalist one and a quest for embracing reality in its totality. Consequently, the standards for what was considered significant and worth discussing also changed.

Without attempting a full summary of this powerful trend and its influences on Clausewitz, it is worth noting the following points: that Clausewitz shared with his wife the universal admiration for Goethe and Schiller and, in fact, as was probably common with courting couples, Werther was a subject of conversation during one of their first meetings;[78] that upon their return from captivity in 1807, Clausewitz and Prince August were the guests of Madame de Staël in her place of exile at Coppet in Switzerland for two months, where Clausewitz made the acquaintance of August Wilhelm Schlegel, with whom he was impressed despite the fact that he was far from accepting his outlook as a whole;[79] and that prominent Romantic poets, dramatists and thinkers, such as Achim von Arnim, Clemens Brentano, Heinrich von Kleist, Friedrich Baron de la Motte Fouque, Adam Müller, Savigny, Clemens Brentano, Fichte and Schleiermacher often met in the same social circle in Berlin with the Clausewitzes.[80]

If the roots of Clausewitz's conception of moral forces are wide and varied, its nature is easier to define. First, he clearly rejected both idealism and mysticism. 'I recognize', he wrote, 'no pure spiritual thing apart from thoughts; all notions, even all sensations with no exceptions, are a mixture of spiritual and material nature.'[81] Clausewitz's relation to the various themes of Romanticism has been well summarized by Peter Paret:

He benefited enormously from the liberating emphasis that the early Romantics placed on the psychological qualities of the individual; but he did not follow such writers as Novalis or the Schlegel brothers in their surrender to emotion. The religious wave of Romanticism did not touch him; nor did its mysticism, nostalgia, and its sham-medieval, patriarchal view of the state. In feeling and manner he was far closer to the men who had passed through the anti-rationalist revolt of the 'Sturm und Drang' to seek internal and external harmony, and who gave expression to their belief in the unity of all phenomena.[82]

The emphasis on moral elements is already very distinct in Clausewitz's notes on strategy of 1804, and it is given systematic expression in his criticism of Bülow and the legacy of the Enlightenment. According to Clausewitz, emotional forces are indeed difficult to determine and control, but they are essential not only for a true, comprehensive, and living conception of war but also for understanding the nature and boundaries of its theory. In his quest for precision, he argued, Bülow concentrates on the material elements which are susceptible to mathematical calculations and ignores the moral forces that animate war. He thus misrepresents the real nature of war and creates a mechanistic and one-sided theory.[83]

During the Reform Era, following Prussia's defeat in 1806, the emphasis on the moral forces which animate the troops merges with the military reformers' platform for reviving their country. For the circle around Scharnhorst in the new war ministry and general staff, including the young Clausewitz, the only way to confront the fighting energies of the French mass armies of citizens was to transform the old Prussian army of mercenaries. Mass popular armies motivated by patriotic spirit were needed. Several statements that Clausewitz made during the Reform Era reflect this fusion of the new cultural paradigm and the reformers' practical vision in an especially classical manner. Immediately after rejecting the fantasies of the new mystical sects, Clausewitz went on to write that they nevertheless expressed a genuine need of the time, 'the need to return from the tendency to rationalize to the neglected wealth of feeling and fantasy'.[84] In 1809, in response to an article that Fichte wrote on Machiavelli, Clausewitz sent a letter to the famous philosopher, in which he criticised 'the tendency particularly in the eighteenth century, [to] turn the whole into an artificial machine in which psychology is subordinated to mechanical forces'. Conversely, he wrote, the 'true spirit of war seems to me to consist in mobilizing the energies of every soldier to the greatest possible extent and in infusing him with warlike feelings, so that the fire of war spreads to every component of the army'. That would be the end of the old attitudes, for 'the natural enemy of mannerism in every art is the *spirit*.'[85]

In three separate places in *On War*, Clausewitz outlines the moral forces that animate war, expanding on the ideas presented in his 1805 critique of Bülow.[86] The problem with military thinkers is that 'they direct their inquiry exclusively towards physical quantities, whereas all military action is intertwined with psychological forces and effects.' Thus, 'it is paltry philosophy if in the old fashioned way one lays down rules and principles in total disregard of moral values.[87] The one-sided nature of the old theory stems from a genuine difficulty: 'Theory becomes infinitely more difficult as soon as it touches the realm of moral values. Architects and painters know precisely what they are about as long as they deal with material phenomena... but when they come to the aesthetics of their work... the rules dissolve into nothing but vague ideas.'[88]

Moral forces do not evade theoretical treatment altogether. A series of patterns 'in the sphere of mind and spirit have been proved by experience: they recur constantly, and are therefore entitled to receive their due as objective factors.' Yet, in general, moral forces 'will not yield to academic wisdom. They cannot be classified or counted. They have to be seen or felt.'[89]

Uncertainty and 'friction' in war

The impact of moral forces and the conflictual, antagonistic nature of war are among the main factors which turn war into an activity saturated with the unknown and unforeseen and which create a gulf between planning and the actual course of war. Here too, the gap between the military thinkers of the Enlightenment and Clausewitz fits the pattern we have already met. The Enlightenment thinkers were quite aware of the factors of uncertainty but focused on what they considered to be suitable for intellectual formulation. Clausewitz regarded their attitude as dogmatic and divorced from reality and demanded an all-encompassing theory. As he wrote: 'They aim at fixed values; but in war everything is uncertain, and calculations have to be made with variable quantities.'[90]

It is illuminating to compare this with the works of the Prussian general Friedrich Constantin von Lossau (1767–1848), a participant in Scharnhorst's *Militärische Gesellschaft* (Military Society) and one of the reformers. His book *War* (1815), which Clausewitz never cites even though he was familiar with it, elaborated many of the ideas later to become famous in Clausewitz's *On War*. Because of the great progress which had been made in the arts and sciences in the previous centuries, wrote Lossau, people sought similar achievements in the study of war. They forgot, however, the decisive influence of the human personality and of chance in war, to which Berenhorst was the first to call attention. Lossau's book deals extensively with the warrior's intellectual and moral faculties, presenting war as a clash of wills motivated by patriotism and other psychological energies.[91] This close similarity with Clausewitz's well-known ideas goes to show that what we are dealing with here is a collective phenomenon, inspired by the broad intellectual trends of the time, rather than a uniquely individual and personal enterprise.

Clausewitz again expressed the attitudes of his intellectual environment, but this time there was no suitable concept ready at hand. Thus, although he had emphasised the uncertainties involved in war from his early works, he only adopted the concept of 'friction' at a later stage, initially in his booklet of instruction for the crown prince (1812). 'The conduct of war', he wrote, 'resembles the working of an intricate machine with tremendous friction, so that combinations which are easily planned on paper can be executed only with great effort.'[92] He reiterated this idea in *On War*. The gulf between planning and reality, he wrote, is mainly rooted in the enormous complexity of factors involved, whose effects are difficult to foresee. This is even more so since war is characterised by the 'uncertainty of all information', which means that 'all action takes place, so to speak, in a kind of twilight.'[93]

Most importantly, the logic of war is not linear but adversarial. An engineer building a bridge deals with fixed quantities, because the river does not attempt to undo his planning. By contrast, the object in war reacts. Each side constantly tries to outsmart and outdo the other, which continuously changes the circumstances they are facing, in an infinite series of progressions and regressions.

The role of history: historicism

Clausewitz's demand for a theory which fully expresses the diversity of reality is closely related to the emergence of a new outlook on history which he introduced into the study of war. His place in the rise of historicism, pointed out by some of his interpreters,[94] is of paramount importance to the understanding of his theoretical outlook and its inherent internal tensions. As noted by Paret, Clausewitz's early works already contain references to Machiavelli, Montaigne, Montesquieu, Robertson, the historian of the Swiss confederation Johannes von Müller, the Prussian conservative anti-Enlightenment and anti-Revolutionary historian and statesman Ancillon, and the arch-conservative and disciple of Burke, Gentz. He also read Möser and Herder. This historical reading combined with the dominant influence of Scharnhorst's concrete, particularistic, and circumstantial approach to the past.[95]

Again, one should look at the German intellectual environment in which Clausewitz operated. Adam Müller, Savigny, and Schleiermacher moved in the same social circle in Berlin as the Clausewitzes.[96] The first was the most prominent proponent of the historical approach to politics and economics;

the second, the founder of the historical school of jurisprudence; and the third, the one who offered a historically conscious explanation for the diversity of religious faiths. Rejection of the universal abstractions of the Enlightenment in favour of the belief in historical diversity and the complexity of the forms of society and politics was one of the dominant themes of the Counter-Enlightenment and characterised the disillusion with the ideas of the French Revolution. Clausewitz's criticism of the philosophers in Germany who were influenced by Parisian philosophy and politics and 'whose minds are too distinguished to bother about local conditions and historical experience', is again a classic expression of these attitudes. As he wrote: 'These philosophers were neither accustomed nor inclined to view social conditions as a product of historical forces; they proceeded from the abstract concept of a social contract and therefore found only unspeakable injustice and corruption everywhere.'[97] These lines could have been written by Möser, Burke, Adam Müller, or Gentz.

Clausewitz's historical outlook is again revealed in his early writings. As pointed out by Rothfels, it dominated his two works on the Thirty Years War: 'Gustavus Adolphus' and an apparently lost manuscript 'Views on the History of the Thirty Years War'. Clausewitz consciously chose to deal with a war whose total and devastating character had terrified the men of the eighteenth century and was regarded by them as 'inhumane and barbarous'.[98] He interpreted the events in a highly sympathetic manner, paying close attention to the particular conditions of the period and the concrete challenges that the personalities involved faced. In contrast to the universal standards employed by the thinkers of the Enlightenment, Clausewitz asserted that the nature of each war depends on the state of the countries and peoples involved, their customs, political situation, spirit, culture, and so on. Indeed, he wrote, 'The various great wars constitute many different eras in the history of the art.'[99]

Clausewitz reiterated this classic historicist statement on several later occasions. The claim to perfection, he wrote in the essay 'On the State of the Theory of the Art of War' is 'one of those boasts with which every period now and again seeks to ornament the events of its day.'[100] Against Bülow's and Jomini's universal principles, he wrote in *On War*: 'It is plain that circumstances exert an influence that cuts across all general principles... a critic has no right to rank the various styles and methods that emerge as if they were stages of excellence, subordinating one to the other. They exist side by side, and their use must be judged on its merits in each individual case.'[101]

Following in Scharnhorst's footsteps, Clausewitz emphasised the absolute dependence of theory on concrete historical experience. Historical experience is the source of all knowledge, and, in view of the artificial nature of contemporary military theory, it is by far superior to any other study. The first article of the regulations of the *Militärische Gesellschaft* that Scharnhorst founded in Berlin in 1801–1802 stated that the discussions of the society would try to avoid 'one-sidedness' and 'would put theory and practice in proper relationship.'[102]

Clausewitz's notion of the nature of historical experience and study is most fully presented in *On War*, Book II, chaps. 5 and 6. Only some of its main points can be cited here. Most historical writing, he wrote, reflected an arrogant, dogmatic, and superficial study and judgement of the past. The subjugation of the past to the rule of one-sided systems and principles entailed a disregard for the conditions and individuals peculiar to each particular case, and harnessed a wide, but tendentious, un-circumstantial, and uncritical variety of examples to support abstract conceptions. The purpose of historical study is not to provide doctrines but to train judgement through indirect experience in a profession in which direct experience of sufficient range is often unattainable. This can only be achieved through intimate familiarity with the conditions of the events studied, even at the expense of concentrating on a select few historical cases. As Clausewitz had already written in his booklet of instructions for the crown prince: 'The detailed knowledge of a few individual battles is more useful than the general knowledge of a great many campaigns.'[103]

Additionally, since the practical purpose of the study of military history is geared to the present, Clausewitz maintained that it should focus on recent history. The closer the period of study is to the present time, the more the historical conditions are likely to be similar to it. There was nothing wrong with a broad knowledge of the distant past, of course. But given the limited time of students in military academies, he believed it was by far more instructive not to go further than the wars of the recent past. As he wrote:

Wars that bear a considerable resemblance to those of the present day, especially with respect to armament, are primarily campaigns beginning with the War of the Austrian Succession [that is, from 1740 on]. Even though many major and minor circumstances have changed considerably, these are close enough to modern warfare to be instructive... The further back you go, the less useful military history becomes... The history of Antiquity is without doubt the most useless... We are in no position... to apply [it] to the wholly different means we use today.[104]

I suppose that, translated to the 2020s, Clausewitz would have recommended that the wars since, say, the First Gulf War are the most instructive for practical study, as they reflect the current era of electronic, computerised, and automated warfare.

Let us understand the general context of all this. The thinkers of the Enlightenment typically regarded history as 'philosophy by example'. From this perspective history's utility was in demonstrating universal truths and refuting universal error. The historicist view rejected this approach to the past. Applied to the military field, Clausewitz held that the study of military history across millennia to demonstrate the application of principles of war was superficial. The quality that historicists emphasised as the key to the understanding of historical situations was *Einfühlung*, empathy from within – bringing the past back to life in the mind through the faculty of imagination. These were important insights. Such notions were implemented by Scharnhorst in the Prussian *Allgemeine Kriegsschule* (established in 1810), the pioneering staff college that would become a model for all similar institutions after 1871, in the wake of Prussia's great victories in the Wars of German Unification. Studies of a select number of specific historical cases, focusing on major modern battles and campaigns, rather than broad, necessarily shallow historical surveys, became a central pillar of its educational system. Instead of searching for transhistorical principles, they were intended to train the minds of officers by recreating the particular living conditions, problems, and decisions the historical antagonists had faced.

It is therefore unsurprising that Clausewitz's historical works constitute the bulk of his literary works. Seven of the ten volumes of his *Werke* are composed of studies of the great campaigns of modern Europe, from the Thirty Years' War onward, and particularly the wars of the Revolution and Napoleon. His theoretical work is also characterized not only by many historical analyses and references, but also by a strong historical spirit. A most striking example can be found in *On War*, VIII, 6B. In the span of just a few pages, Clausewitz offers a most penetrating outline of the transformation of war throughout history as a result of the nature of states and societies as they are determined by their times and special conditions: 'The semi-barbarous Tartars, the republics of antiquity, the feudal lords and trading cities of the Middle Ages, eighteenth century kings and the rulers and peoples of the nineteenth century – all conducted war in their own particular way, using different methods and pursuing different aims.'[105]

The perceptive analysis that follows – much richer than implied in the opening passage – will not be cited here. The concept behind it, which concludes the narrative, is more important: 'Our purpose was not to assign, in passing, a handful of principles of warfare to each period. We wanted to show how every age had its own kind of war, its own limiting conditions and its own peculiar preconceptions. Each period, therefore, would have held to its own theory of war, even if the urge had always and universally existed to work things out on scientific principles.'[106]

The final sentences represent the culmination of Clausewitz's historicist outlook. Their implications for the possibility of a universal theory of war, as opposed to a theoretical formulation of the conditions peculiar to each time and place, is strikingly sceptical and destructive. They present, however, only one aspect of Clausewitz's thought. The core of his theoretical work and the major difficulties he encountered in its development revolved around formulating a universal theory of war that would be valid within the great diversity of historical experience. There is, however, one more question regarding Clausewitz's intellectual-cultural-ideological setting that needs to be clarified before turning, in the following chapter, to his attempt to formulate a positive theory of war.

Clausewitz and the Reaction against the Enlightenment
Why Have Commentators Found All This Difficult to Swallow?

I hope it is clear how closely the above fits together. And yet, commentators have recoiled from accepting Clausewitz's actual intellectual-cultural setting on one side of the tectonic clash which was rocking Europe at the start of the nineteenth century.

In my view, there have been several reasons for this avoidance. First, there has been insufficient familiarity with the history of ideas and, as a result, a reluctance to commit and become entangled in unfamiliar territory. Second, at least, if not more importantly, there has been a strong hesitation to see Clausewitz placed in the context of the 'Counter-Enlightenment'. The Enlightenment is rightly viewed as the platform of modernity, signifying the victory of rationality and science, and constituting the engine of progressive, ongoing social and political reform and steadily rising welfare. Light is at the root of the word in every European language. By contrast, the 'Counter-Enlightenment' sounds, and is associated with, the opposite of all these. Indeed, it is associated with the political Reaction imposed on Europe after 1815, and, further, with the subsequent calamitous course of German history – which drew on the intellectual-cultural-ideological tradition of the Counter-Enlightenment – in the first half of the twentieth century. Some commentators have found it necessary to suggest that Clausewitz's work expressed the ideas of both the Enlightenment and Counter-Enlightenment.[107]

Although these concerns are understandable, they involve several critical misconceptions. The Counter-Enlightenment (as mentioned, the term is not optimal) was a *dialectical* response to the Enlightenment; that is, it *incorporated* a great deal of the Enlightenment's intellectual assumptions, aims, and achievements, while, at the same time, its exponents set out to correct what they viewed as its main intellectual failings. In this sense, the Counter-Enlightenment can be seen as a further step in the dialectical advance of reason – emphasising the limitations of abstract principles and schemes to alter a complex reality; the depth of societies' historical roots; the diversity and wealth of cultural traditions; and the centrality and vividness of people's inner lives, which lie at the root of the differences between the sciences and the humanities. All these were, and remain,

59

genuine and significant contributions to our understanding of the world.

Furthermore, the Counter-Enlightenment incorporated a variety of intellectual currents and themes, some hostile to rationalism and others not. Clausewitz was emphatically on the rationalistic side.[108] Moreover, the Counter-Enlightenment's emphasis on the graduality of history – the view that historical developments did not spring out of thin air or purely from lofty abstract ideas and ideals, or from unconditioned acts of will, but evolved from earlier antecedents – could, and was, interpreted in either a conservative/reactionary or a reformist direction. On the one hand, this view allowed the ideological enemies of the French Revolution to explain its failure, caution against radicalism, or, as with the proponents of Reaction, defend the virtues and stability of traditional institutions. Yet, on the other hand, the steady flux of history meant that there was a need to advance with the times. Since I wrote my 1989 book, Frederick Beiser has forcefully made these points in a series of erudite books.[109]

It was the modernizing wing of romanticism and historicism that animated the Reform Movement in Prussia, of which Clausewitz was such an active and dedicated member. The reformers held that Prussian institutions required a far-reaching reform not because they supposedly failed the standard of abstract philosophical ideals of justice, in whose existence and applicability to a complex social reality Clausewitz and his friends did not believe. Rather, they maintained, with Scharnhorst in the lead, that the developments of modernity – such as the rise of the middle class, the spread of literacy, and much else – practically imposed the need for reform. They argued that because the French Revolution rode on these social developments to create a citizen nation-state and mass popular armies, all other powers were forced to take similar steps if they wished to survive. Napoleon's crushing defeat of Prussia made the obsolescence and weakness of its political and military institutions all too clear and prompted the reformers' work in the teeth of opposition from much of the Prussian nobility anxious about their privileges. Clausewitz offers a truly brilliant historical survey and analysis of the social, economic, and political transformation of European society since the Middle Ages – from feudalism, through absolutism, to the French Revolution – which explained the need for political, social and military reform of Prussia.[110]

This survey and analysis appear in his essay 'Agitation' which puzzled many commentators because of its ostensible support for the post-1815 Reaction. It raised the question of 'Which Side was Clausewitz On?'[111] For, once renewed popular protests and student demonstrations, propounding revolutionary slogans, broke out in Germany in 1817–1819, Clausewitz came out staunchly against them. He remained loyal to his historicist-reformist views in his harsh criticism of 'philosophers, who settle everything according to universal concepts, whose minds are too distinguished to bother about local conditions and historical experience – these people were strongly taken with the philosophy and politics of Paris'. He was not that different in this respect from Burke, a life-long Whig advocate of reform in Britain who became the foremost critic of French Revolutionary radical abstract principles. As Clausewitz wrote in 'Agitation':

Consider the changes that occurred in Prussia and the south German states after 1805. The way was opened for the great majority of the people, the peasantry, to own land; the noble was deprived of his exemption from taxes and personal service; monopolies and guild restrictions were abolished; the middle class was given access to all offices in the state; taxes paid in kind, which had been carried on the shoulders of particular groups, were lifted, and the burden was divided among the population as a whole. All these had been objectives of the French Revolution; all were now achieved in Germany without violence.[112]

Deeply concerned about the new 'political fanaticism', Clausewitz expresses open skepticism of the public demand for both a constitution and parliament. He regards parliament as a vehicle of petty interests, populist agitators, and ill-informed and irresponsible talk, which he contrasted with what he saw as the calm deliberations of the state's council and the overriding interests of the state.

Indeed, hostility towards the ideas of the Enlightenment, proclaimed superficial and pretentious, would become central to the German cultural tradition from the beginning of the nineteenth century. Among other things, this tradition became very sceptical of both democracy and the abstract notion of universal human rights. German interpreters of Clausewitz during the nineteenth century and up until 1945 well recognised and celebrated his place within this tradition, regarding it as a badge of honour. And it did not matter that within the ultra-radical twentieth century offshoot of this tradition, General Eric Ludendorff regarded Clausewitz as not radical enough, whereas the Nazi Professor and Clausewitz scholar Walter Malmsten Schering made him a precursor of the Nazi philosophy of the will. By contrast, Clausewitz's current interpreters have found it necessary to distance him as far as possible from the subsequent course of German history all the way to its horrendous manifestations in the twentieth century, with which, indeed, he should by no means be associated. Moreover, while bearing in mind the darker sides of the cultural-historical tradition that sprang from the reaction against the Enlightenment, one should not lose sight of the great intellectual contributions outlined above. They made Germany the world's leader in historical scholarship, philosophy, the social sciences, and much else during the nineteenth century. And these contributions are still with us today. This perspective should also inform our understanding of Clausewitz's place within that tradition. Two major stories, kept apart in two separate branches of historical scholarship – intellectual-cultural and military – come together to illuminate his work and ideas.

The misconception by those who have suggested that Clausewitz should be regarded as a child of both the Enlightenment and the Counter-Enlightenment-Romanticism is starkly demonstrated by his readings and by his references to other authors. With the main exception of Montesquieu, admired by the men of the Counter-Enlightenment for his pioneering historicism and attention to historical-social diversity, Clausewitz scarcely at all cites iconic Enlightenment thinkers such as Voltaire, Rousseau (whom the men of the Counter-Enlightenment also admired), Diderot, D'Alembert, Condillac, La Mettrie, Holbach, Helvétius, Turgot or Condorcet. By contrast, his references to the writers of the reaction against the Enlightenment, and in many cases his personal acquaintance with them, in profusive, as this chapter and the following ones demonstrate.

Finally, there is yet another presumed reason why commentators have been reluctant to recognise Clausewitz's setting within the reaction against the Enlightenment. Such a recognition would make him a partisan proponent of one particular school or ideological-historical camp, rather than being the voice of timeless, independent truth. In any ideological clash, the protagonists of each side, rejecting the other side's fundamental intellectual premises, are inclined towards highly critical rhetoric of 'cancelation' in the heat of the debate. Thus, Clausewitz's scathing criticism of the military thinkers of the Enlightenment, the 'system builders', has been uncritically parroted by commentators, whose familiarity with the military thinkers of the Enlightenment has been hazy in any case. As we have seen, the latter did not believe the conduct of war could be reduced to a science, nor did they underestimate the role of chance or moral forces in war. It is only that they focused on what they believed to be the aspects of war which lent themselves to theoretical formulation and relegated all the rest to the less tangible sphere. Now, the people of the Counter-Enlightenment, in their campaign against the Enlightenment's worldview, made a point of highlighting and celebrating precisely these latter aspects. To some degree, this was a matter of cultural-ideological shifts in emphases and vocabulary, as much as of substance.

Clausewitz's biting comments on Jomini are a case in point. Jomini responded to the criticism that his approach was mechanistic and geometric with somewhat justified astonishment and bitterness. He believed that he was accused of opinions he had never held. As he wrote in his *Summary of the Art of War* (1837), after the publication of Clausewitz's *On War*:

My principles have been badly comprehended by several writers... Some... have drawn from them exaggerated consequences which have never been able to enter my head; for a general officer, after having assisted in a dozen campaigns, ought to know that war is a great drama, in which a thousand physical or moral causes operate more or less powerfully, and which cannot be reduced to mathematical calculations... I hope that after these avowals, I could not be accused of wishing to make of this art a mechanism of determined wheel-work, nor of pretending, on the contrary, that the reading of a single chapter of principles is able to give, all at once, the talent of conducting an army.[113]

Jomini always stressed that he did not believe in a military 'system', and certainly not in a complete geometrical system such as that of Bülow. His principles of operations were simple, relatively undogmatic, and faithfully expressed the spirit of contemporary warfare. His comment on the conceptions associated chiefly with Bülow and Archduke Charles was in this respect characteristic: 'They want war too methodical, too measured', he wrote; 'I would make it brisk, bold, impetuous, perhaps sometimes even audacious... to reduce war to geometry would be to impose fetters on the genius of the greatest captains and to submit to the yoke of an exaggerated pedantry.'[114]

Jomini's theoretical outlook was based on the intellectual legacy of the military thinkers of the Enlightenment, which had been accepted as self-evident for a century. In view of this, Clausewitz's criticism of his work, which expressed a new intellectual-cultural paradigm, was unintelligible to him. Military views as such were not so much the issue but, rather, differing perspectives largely anchored in antagonistic ideological rhetoric regarding the question of which theoretical approach was legitimate at all.

Indeed, it was not that Clausewitz thought that 'Jomini said something which was utterly wrong'; compared with Bülow, 'it cannot be denied that he thinks and argues in an extremely more solid manner.'[115] Furthermore, until 1813, Clausewitz shared Jomini's belief in the primacy of the central position and interior lines. As we shall see, Clausewitz's concept of war and its conduct was not very different from Jomini's. Moreover, the latter was in some significant ways less dogmatic and more in tune with reality than the concept of war and its conduct advanced by Clausewitz, which we now turn to see.

4

The Nature/Concept of War: The Unnoticed Centrepiece of Clausewitz's Theory

The Napoleonic Model — and Its Crisis

How to Form a Universal Theory of War?

Clausewitz's reformulation of the notion of military theory, which was directed against the theoretical outlook of the Enlightenment, was closely related to his effort to devise an adequate military theory of his own. His ideas evolved from his early writings between 1804 and 1812 into an attempt to compose a comprehensive treatise on war during the period of peace after 1815.

In his early works, when he was mainly concerned with developing his attack which aimed at the destruction of the Enlightenment thinkers' strategic systems, Clausewitz's ideas regarding the possibility of formulating a positive theory of war appear primarily in a negative form. In his 1805 critique of Bülow, Clausewitz was almost unwilling to commit himself on this point. If he were to be asked, he wrote, whether a strategic theory was at all possible, his reply would be 'that we have neither committed ourselves to write one, nor to prove its possibility, and that we were less inclined to object to the confession: "I do not believe in the art [of war]"' [Berenhorst's], than to the 'Babylonic confusion of language which prevails in military ideas.'[116]

Clausewitz's notes on strategy of 1808–1809 reveal the problem that was to figure most prominently in his mind. In the note 'On Abstract Principles of Strategy' (1808), he briefly surveyed the transformations of the face of war since the Thirty Years' War. The result of these transformations was that military theories which, in actuality, merely reflected changing 'manners' of warfare, were always invalidated by new historical experience. These changes were so rapid and far-reaching that 'the books on war have always come out late and in all times they have described dead manners.'[117]

The theory of strategy, he wrote, 'allows the setting up of few or no abstract propositions.' One cannot escape the multitude of minor circumstances. 'All the authors that in modem times have sought to treat this part of theory abstractly and philosophically provide a clear indication of this; they are either simply trivial, or they get rid of triviality through one-sidedness.'[118] Contemporary military thinkers are criticised, but the theoretical problem preoccupies Clausewitz's own mind. One can either offer clearcut doctrines by ignoring all exceptional conditions or try to cover all possibilities and provide no positive advice. A priori abstractions always fall between the Scylla of partial validity and the Charybdis of the commonplace.

In the note of 1809, Clausewitz elaborated on this problem:

Formula [is] abstraction. When by the abstraction nothing which belongs to the thing gets lost – as is the case in mathematics – the abstraction fully achieves its purpose. But when it must omit the living matter in order to hold to the dead form, which is of course the easiest to abstract, it would be in the end a dry skeleton of dull truths squeezed into a doctrine. It is really astonishing to find people who waste their time on such efforts, when one bears in mind that precisely that which is the most important in war and strategy, namely the great particularity, peculiarity, and local circumstances, escape these abstractions and scientific systems.[119]

If so, is a universal theory of war possible at all? It is possible, according to Clausewitz, because beyond the diversity of historical experience and the changing 'manners' of each period there exists a universal, constant element, which is the true object of theory. Theory should aim at the 'lasting spirit of war', or the 'spirit of the art of war', a concept which already figures prominently in Clausewitz's notes on strategy of 1804. The various forms of the art of war rise and decline over time, but the spirit of war escapes change, and must not be 'lost sight of'.[120] The same conceptual framework is repeated in Clausewitz's letter to Fichte of 1809, in which Clausewitz criticizes Machiavelli and implicitly also Fichte himself for trying to revive the warfare of the ancients. Rather than outdated 'manners' and 'forms' it is the 'lasting spirit of war' that should be restored.[121] (It is worthwhile repeating the often-made point that the German *Geist* carries a less ghostly connotation than the English spirit.) This was the foundation for the intellectual structure that would guide Clausewitz's lifelong attempt to formulate a theory of war that would integrate the diversity of historical experience with a universal approach.

The quest to integrate the historical with the universal was deeply rooted in Clausewitz's intellectual environment. Paret has pointed out its clear affinity to Schleiermacher's celebrated conception of religion, which attracted much attention during Clausewitz's formative years. Positive religions and ethical systems, wrote Schleiermacher in his *Reden über die Religion* (1799) and *Monologen* (1800), appeared in history in a rich variety of forms; they rise and decline, but their spirit remains one and universal. In 1808, Schleiermacher became the professor of theology at the newly founded University of Berlin and was one of the major exponents of the awakening Prussian national spirit. Clausewitz knew him personally during that time. Schleiermacher's emphasis on emotion as the constitutive element of religion was similarly in step with Clausewitz's general affinity with the message of Romanticism.

Shortly before composing his note on strategy of 1808, Clausewitz wrote to his fiancée:

Religious feeling in its elemental purity will eternally exist in men's hearts, but no positive religion can last forever. Virtue will eternally exert its beneficial influence on society; but the universality of this global spirit cannot be expressed in the restrictive form of a code of laws, and form itself will shatter sooner or later when the stream of time has washed away or reshaped the surrounding contours.[122]

Schleiermacher's influence here is all too apparent. Clausewitz's conception of the compatibility of the historical and the universal also derived from several other sources and was quite common during the genesis of historicism. Here is what Herder wrote: 'The art of war may change with the changes in weapons, times, and state of the world; but the spirit of man – which invents, deceives, conceals its purposes, goes to the attack, defends itself or retreats, discovers the weaknesses of its enemy, and in one way or another uses or misuses them for its advantage – remains at all times the same.'[123] Whether Clausewitz was familiar with this passage is unknown. But compare his views with those of General Lossau, whose book *War* (1815) appeared some years before *On War*: a systematic theory of war is impossible, 'thus there can be no lasting textbook for war.' 'War always appears as new; only the spirit of war remains the same.'[124]

The beginning of the period of peace after 1815 was a turning point in Clausewitz's life. His intellectual activity – focusing on writing a comprehensive theoretical work on war – now became his major preoccupation. His main ideas, however, remained unchanged. During his period in Koblenz (1816–1818), Clausewitz wrote a concise theoretical treatise, the first attempt in a process which would lead to the writing of *On*

War. This early treatise has not survived,[125] but what appears to be its preface and an additional comment that Clausewitz wrote on the treatise's character and composition were included in the posthumous publication of his works. In the preface and comment Clausewitz again put forward the theoretical structure that he had developed in the previous decade.

The 'scientific character' of his work, wrote Clausewitz, 'consists in an attempt to investigate the essence of the phenomena of war and to indicate the links between these phenomena and the nature of their component part... the propositions of this book therefore base their inner necessity [*innere Notwendigkeit*] on the secure foundation either of experience or of the concept [*Begriff*] of war as such.'[126] (Whenever I deviate from the Princeton translation of *On War*, the German original is cited in square brackets. For an explanation, see chap. 9, below, 'Comments on the Recent Clausewitz literature'.) Thus, while its surface is in flux, war has an immutable core: its 'spirit' (*Geist*), 'essence' (*Wessen*), 'nature' (*Natur*) or 'concept' (*Begriff*). Clausewitz used the 'spirit of war' as standard in the 1800s and 1810s, while preferring 'the nature' or 'concept of war' thereafter and in *On War*. For Clausewitz the meaning of these terms was practically identical: they denoted the very same thing on which a universal theory of war could and ought to be built. Indeed, this was the cornerstone of his entire theoretical edifice, a point which commentators have missed entirely.

We have already seen the affinity of this conception of the lasting element of war to Schleiermacher. Its formulation in 1816–1818 also clearly reveals Clausewitz's profound debt to Scharnhorst. As Scharnhorst repeatedly put it from the 1780s onward, military theory provided 'correct concepts' (*richtige Begriffe*), grounded in 'the nature of things or in experience.' An inherent interdependence exists between theory and reality. Clear concepts and principles constitute the links between the parts of war and the whole, and there is no knowledge without them. However, as Scharnhorst stresses, reason alone is not sufficient for grasping reality. The application of the concepts and principles to reality requires judgement, which is in turn sharpened only by experience and constant exercise, the major means of which is historical study. The proper method for educating young officers is thus to provide them with 'correct theory' and encourage them to think independently and 'clarify their concepts'. This would create a sound basis for analysing experience.[127] Again, compare this with Lossau (1815), another disciple of Scharnhorst: theory aims at 'correct concepts' on the 'nature of war', which 'appear when one develops the concept of war.'[128]

Scharnhorst's insistence on the role of conceptualisation in coping with reality, on the one hand, and on the insufficiency of reason alone for this purpose, on the other, suggests that his views were most likely reinforced by Kant's theory of knowledge and emphasis on the interpretive role of concepts and interdependence of mind and experience. Although no direct evidence for his familiarity with Kant's work is known, the fact that Scharnhorst's early works appeared in 1782–7, right after the publication of Kant's highly influential *Critique of Pure Reason* (1781) makes such an influence very plausible.

Finally, from his early writings in the 1780s and throughout his life, Scharnhorst saw theory as 'necessarily' grounded not only in 'experience' but also in the 'nature of things', another characteristic notion he bequeathed to Clausewitz. Unaware of the part Scharnhorst played in its conveyance to him, Raymond Aron, in his treatment of Clausewitz, was the first to call attention to the striking affinity of this formula to that of Montesquieu.[129] It clearly resembles Montesquieu's famous conception of laws, defined at the opening of the *Spirit of the Laws*, as the 'necessary relations arising from the nature of things'. Indeed, it was revealed that Scharnhorst ordered the *Spirit of the Laws* from his bookseller in the mid-1790s, which does not exclude an earlier acquaintance with it.[130]

Clausewitz, too, appears to have drawn not solely from Scharnhorst but also from Montesquieu himself. In his comment on the treatise of 1816–1818, Clausewitz presents Montesquieu's work as the model that was in his mind when writing his own work.[131] Although this reference focused on structure, the content was no less involved. Clausewitz was familiar with and referred to, Montesquieu's work as a young man, and as he turned to write his theoretical treatise, Montesquieu's integration of the historical and empirical with the general emerged as a model.

Thus, Clausewitz approached the writing of *On War* with fairly consolidated ideas on both the nature and boundaries of military theory. Scharnhorst's influence and the legacy of Kant's theory of art had convinced him that doctrines of absolute applicability were inappropriate for the conduct of war. The historicist outlook and Schleiermacher's formulation of the traditional message of pietism, which rejected all religious dogmas, positive doctrines, and any other attempt to capture the variety of universal religious feeling in rigid intellectual structures, reinforced this conviction. No rule or principle could cover the diversity of reality or the different requirements of action. At the same time, the teachings of Scharnhorst, Kant, Schleiermacher, and Montesquieu also encouraged Clausewitz to embark on his enterprise to formulate a general theory of war. This was to be based on his view that theory was possible if grounded in the 'lasting spirit', 'essence', 'nature' or 'concept' of war, constantly tested against experience and pointed out the necessary relations between the parts and the whole.

Clausewitz was still troubled, however, with the tendency of universal propositions to lead towards empty formalism, triviality, and truisms. In the preface of 1816–1818, he quoted extensively from a work by the famous G. C. Lichtenberg

(1742–1799), the Göttingen science professor who grew highly sceptical about human knowledge and outlook on the world, and whose aphorisms, published posthumously, were widely read. According to Clausewitz, Lichtenberg's 'Extract from Fire Regulations', satirising the meticulous, dead formalism of system builders, strikingly fitted the existing military theories.[132] In fact, the whole issue reflects a recurring theme, and lingering doubt, in Clausewitz's own mind which also reappears in his Comment on the work of 1816–1818 and is stated in more personal terms: 'I wanted at all costs to avoid every commonplace, everything obvious.'[133]

Again, if one shrinks from one-sided doctrines, one is in danger of falling into empty formalism. 'When we contemplate all this, we are overcome by the fear that we shall be irresistibly dragged down to a state of dreary pedantry, and grub around in the underworld of ponderous concepts.'[134] The point made in 1808 is reiterated: 'all the principles, rules, and methods will increasingly lack universality and absolute truth the closer they come to being positive doctrine.'[135] 'Theory should be study, not doctrine'; it is not a 'manual for action'.[136] At the same time, theory is far from being divorced from practice. As we shall see, commentators have failed to understand this crucial point.

This, therefore, is Clausewitz's conception of theory and his guiding ideal. Above historical study and crude rules there exists a universal theory which reflects the 'lasting spirit', 'essence', 'nature' or 'concept' of war (all synonyms), transcends the diversity and transformations of past experience, and is both generally valid and instructive in preparing the mind for action.

What then is Clausewitz's application of this notion of the nature or concept of war? In an 'Undated Note', written, as I have suggested, in early 1827 or a little earlier,[137] describing the state of his work when the majority of *On War* had already been drafted, Clausewitz argued for the feasibility of a universal theory of war, citing a long list of propositions which summarized themes from the manuscript. This list is highly significant. It is rarely referred to, one dares suggest, because commentators have been somewhat confounded by its content:

It is a very difficult task to construct a philosophical [*philosophische*] theory for the art of war, and so many attempts have failed that most people say it is impossible, since it deals with matters that no permanent law can provide for. One would agree, and abandon the attempts, were it not for the obvious fact that a whole range of propositions can be demonstrated without difficulty: that defence is the stronger form of fighting with the negative purpose, attack the weaker form with the positive purpose; that major successes help bring about minor ones, so that strategic results can be traced back to certain turning points; that a demonstration is a weaker use of force than real attack, and that it must therefore be clearly justified; that victory consists not only in the occupation of the battlefield, but in the destruction of the enemy's physical and psychological forces, which is usually not attainable until the enemy is pursued after a victorious battle; that success is always greater at the point where the victory was gained, and that consequently changing from one line of operations, one direction, to another can at best be regarded as a necessary evil; that a turning movement can only be justified by general superiority or by having better lines of communication or retreat than the enemy's; that flank positions are governed by the same consideration; that every attack loses impetus as it progresses.[138]

Are you impressed by these propositions as the ostensible kernels of a universal theory of war? How universal are they and how successfully do they escape the dilemma of one-sidedness vs triviality? Indeed, nobody has ever commented on how disappointing or even pitiful this list is. Rather than discussing the above propositions eclectically, we turn to trace the development of Clausewitz's central line of thought on the nature of war from its earliest formulation to its crisis.

The Nature of War is Fighting
And the Correct Conduct of War Flows
from this Concept

The nature of war is fighting; hence all the characteristics of its 'lasting spirit': the primacy of the clash of forces and of the major battle, served by a massive concentration of forces and aggressive conduct, and aiming at the total overthrow of the enemy. Throughout his life, this conception was the centrepiece of Clausewitz's military outlook. It reflected the overwhelming impact of the Napoleonic experience, was the source of Clausewitz's attacks on the war of manoeuvre in all periods particularly those of the eighteenth century, and formed the basis for his belief in a universal theory of war.

However, in 1827, this guiding concept fell into a deep crisis. Three-quarters through the composition of *On War*, Clausewitz's entire line of thought underwent a drastic change of direction, the only revolutionary transformation in the otherwise continuous flow of his ideas. In a note on the state of his work dated 10 July 1827, Clausewitz announced his intention to revise the manuscript on the basis of two main ideas: first, that there are two types of war: all-out war and limited war; and second, that war is nothing but the continuation of politics [*Politik*] with other means. In his efforts to resolve the deep crisis his work fell into, Clausewitz transformed but did not abandon his old concept of war and resorted to completely new theoretical devices. He was preoccupied with this process of transformation during his last three working years.

Unfortunately, because the pivotal role that the 'nature/concept of war' played in Clausewitz's theory has not been understood, the sources and exact nature of this later transformation have also remained a mystery. This explains how Clausewitz's ideas could have been interpreted differently by each successive generation. Whereas the men of the nineteenth century emphasised the place of the major battle and the destruction of the enemy's armed forces in Clausewitz's thought, modern readers after 1945, contending with the problem of limited war and seeking out the full complexity of the link between political objectives and military operations, have stressed themes in his later thought. As this has been closely linked to a strong reaction against the military and political legacy of the German Reich, a new, 'good' Clausewitz was created, set apart from his 'bad' successors. While blaming their discredited predecessors for being tendentious and one-sided, modern commentators have themselves failed to recognise that the imperative of destruction was the centrepiece of Clausewitz's conception of war. Some have even denied that he held such an idea at all. The baffling obscurity of Clausewitz's text has continually left room for conflicting and unhistorical interpretations.

Clausewitz's concept of the nature of war, which was incorporated into his definition of war, stemmed from both his military and political outlook. In the military sphere, this conception reflected the earth-shattering collapse of the warfare of the *ancien régime* when confronted with Revolutionary and Napoleonic warfare. With Napoleon's great triumphs of 1805–1807, this process was complete. For the first time in the history of modem Europe, a single state had inflicted a crushing defeat on all the other powers of the continent. Eighteenth-century warfare, which had been relatively limited in aims and scope because of the political and social structure of the *ancien régime*, was now increasingly discredited and perceived as inadequate, if not absurd. The total mobilisation of forces, initiative, aggressiveness, and rapid decision in battle now dominated warfare. Nowhere was the reaction against the past and the embracing of the new spirit of war as powerful as in the defeated and humiliated Prussia. And of all of Clausewitz's contemporaries no one gave these new trends a more far-reaching expression – a fact which, until our own times, was obvious to everyone.

Closely linked to Clausewitz's concept of war and the correct way to conduct it which flows from this concept were his political attitudes. Again, commentators have not given them sufficient attention and therefore have failed to appreciate their interrelatedness to Clausewitz's view of war. Clausewitz saw the map of Europe radically altered by determined and powerful political and military actions and witnessed his country, which dabbled in diplomatic manoeuvres and military half-measures, lose its independence and status as a great power in a single powerful blow. To these experiences were added the dynamic and vitalist effects of Romanticism and the fervent energy and feelings generated by rising nationalism. Clausewitz urged the state to pursue grand objectives, to be determined in its actions, and to put the utmost power behind them.

After Prussia's disastrous defeat, Clausewitz stood out, even in the Reform circle, for his call for a bold and determined policy, and in his relentless search for every opportunity – Spanish guerrilla warfare, the Austrian war of 1809, the French invasion of Russia – to launch a total war of independence, even if it might lead to destruction. His bitter and fierce criticism of his country during this period is clearly marked by contempt for half-measures, indecisiveness, and inactivity which, in the end, are bound to lose all worlds.[139] In his defence of Machiavelli, Clausewitz wrote: 'The twenty-first chapter of Machiavelli's *Prince* [warning against neutrality and calling for rallying with one of the sides] is the basic code for all diplomacy – and woe to those who fail to heed it!'[140] Activity, vitality, and power in the political *as well as* in the military spheres were the essence of Clausewitz's outlook.

This outlook was incorporated into Clausewitz's concept of the nature of war: 'Essentially war is fighting, for fighting is the only effective principle in the manyfold activities generally designated as war.' The developments in weapons 'brought about great changes in the forms of fighting. Still, no matter how it is constituted, the concept of fighting remains unchanged.'[141] Compare this to Schleiermacher's speeches *On Religion*: 'everything called by this name [religion] has a common content', religious feeling; 'The essential oneness of religiousness spreads itself out in a great variety.'[142]

We have finally reached the actual content of Clausewitz's theoretical conception unveiled in his letter on religion, notes on strategy, and letter to Fichte. Whereas the 'forms' of war are diverse and changing, its 'spirit', 'essence', 'nature' or 'concept' are universal. Fighting is the constitutive element of war, which allows us to regard the many different wars as part of a single phenomenon. For Clausewitz, this was not merely a formal proposition defining the common denominator of all wars. In his view, rather than formal, the definition of war as fighting pervades its conduct through and through. A theory of war and its conduct which is blind to, or evades, the imperative of fighting – as the thinkers of the eighteenth century allegedly did – creates a false picture of war, which is bound to lead to disaster. The dominance of fighting determines the whole character of war. From his earliest works, Clausewitz stressed this point.

In his notes on strategy of 1804, the full scope of Clausewitz's concept of war and its conduct, inextricably linked to his political outlook, is laid out for the first time. Clausewitz rejects the limited warfare of the eighteenth century and denounces the central role of fortresses, the over-extension of armies in the field, and Fabian strategy.[143] The correct conduct of war is diametrically opposed: 'I would not like to print this, but I cannot hide from myself that a general cannot be too bold in his plans, provided that he is in full command of his senses, and only sets himself aims that he himself is convinced he can achieve.'[144]

In a nutshell, 'the art of war tells us: go for the greatest, most decisive purpose you can achieve; choose the shortest way to it that you dare to go.'[145] 'War should be conducted with the utmost possible degree of effort.'[146] One should achieve the maximal concentration of force and strike the enemy with the greatest energy. Defence ought to be adopted only if one is too weak to attack (more about this in Chapter 6). The enveloping strategic manoeuvre against the enemy's rear, recommended by Bülow with the approval of Venturini, Dumas, and Massenbach, does have the advantage of threatening the enemy's communications; but its success is dubious, and direct action from a central position is more effective. Frederick the Great's conduct in the Seven Years' War, Napoleon's Italian campaign of 1796, and many other examples from the history of war attest to this. Clausewitz worked out a strikingly similar conception to the one that Jomini developed that very same year but had not yet published.[147]

All this is derived from the following central point: 'It can be absolutely universally said: all that demands the use of military forces has the idea of the clash of forces [Gefecht] at its base.' The clash of forces and the battle are the centre of war, toward which all efforts are directed. The belief of Bülow and his fellow-thinkers that victory could be won by means of a brilliant strategic manoeuvre, without resorting to battle, was an absurd illusion. Manoeuvres are necessary, but only to achieve favourable conditions for the battle. Even when the battle itself does not take place, its expected outcome regulates the conduct of the belligerents like the effect of 'cash on credit in commerce'. 'Strategy works with no materials other than combat [Gefecht].' Thus, whereas tactics are defined as the 'use of military forces in the battle [Gefecht]', strategy is but the 'use of individual battles [*Gefechte*] to achieve the aim of the war.'[148] This view will be carried all the way to *On War*, in which Clausewitz defined strategy as 'use of the battle/clash of forces [*Gefecht*] for the purpose of the war.'[149]

This concept of war and the correct way to conduct it which flows from this concept went hand in hand with corresponding attitudes to the political aims of war and the relationship between politics and war. War is fought for the attainment of a political purpose, 'the purpose of war'. And in 1804 this purpose was also formulated in expansive and aggressive terms: either to destroy the enemy's state or to dictate the terms of peace.[150] Among Clausewitz's interpreters who have looked upon these alternatives through the prism of the intellectual revolution of 1827, Aron was the first to point out that in 1804 the choice was not between unlimited and limited war. Dictated peace terms implied bringing the enemy to his knees.[151] Indeed, *both* options are cited explicitly in 1827 under the first kind of war which is to completely overthrow the enemy. In this unlimited type, Clausewitz wrote in the Note of July 1827: 'the objective is to overthrow the enemy – to render him politically helpless or militarily impotent, thus forcing him to sign whatever peace we please'.[152] In 1804, this crushing political purpose is matched by the objective of the military operations, 'the purpose in war', which is 'to paralyse the enemy forces'. 'The destruction of the enemy's armed forces is the immediate purpose of war, and the most direct way to it always constitutes the rule for the art. This destruction can be achieved by occupying his country or annihilating his war provisions or his army... Only I must confess this: that great commanders have always kept it to annihilate the enemy army.'[153]

In considering the 'purpose of operations' one should 'always choose the most difficult, for this is the one most closely related to the spirit of the art of war.'[154]

Greater sacrifices achieve greater purposes. Here comes a maxim that is peculiar to all great generals and must be the principle of the art, or there are none: war should be waged with the highest necessary or possible degree of effort... one will not be able to come to terms with such sentences: of all the operations that lie within the scope of our forces, one should promise the greatest successes with the least effort.... No, the most decisive operations also cost the highest effort! This principle lies in *the nature of the art of war*.[155] [Emphasis in the original.]

It is therefore misleading to assume that in 1804 Clausewitz had already been aware of the range of political aims and objectives, and that in 1827 he simply elaborated on it or became fully conscious of its implications for the conduct of war. Of course, Clausewitz was always deeply aware of the relationship between war and politics. The plans of military reformers of the Prussian army under Scharnhorst were closely linked to a comprehensive reform of Prussian society and politics, based on a clear appreciation of the social and political sources of French power. However, there was a perfect harmony in 1804 (and later) between Clausewitz's political and military convictions as *both* were formulated in radical terms. Total concentration of force and the imperative of fighting for decision constituted Clausewitz's concept of the nature of war which strongly suited his general political outlook which called for determined action and the pursuit of great objectives.

Both this concept of war and its conduct and his political outlook are fully revealed once more in Clausewitz's next significant work, the booklet of instruction for the Prussian crown prince (1812). Clausewitz sent the work to the prince when he left Prussia to join the Russian army, and he made a special effort to impress the fervour of his outlook on politics and war upon the young prince in that critical hour. In the programmatic passage that concluded the work he wrote to the prince: 'A powerful emotion must stimulate the great ability of a military leader... Open your heart to such emotion. Be audacious and cunning in your plans, firm and persevering in their execution, determined to find a glorious end.'[156]

The work itself reiterates all of the themes put forward in 1804: 'We always have the choice between the most audacious and the most careful solution. Some people think that the theory of war always advises the latter. That assumption is false. If the theory does advise anything, it is the *nature of war* to advise the most decisive, that is, the most audacious.'[157] [my emphasis]

The aims in the conduct of war are (a) to conquer and destroy the armed forces of the enemy; (b) to take possession of the resources of his army; and (c) to win public opinion.[158] These aims are not alternatives but complementary. They are intended to secure the complete defeat of the enemy. The first principle of the art of war is the concentration of force, supported by dynamic and determined conduct which avoids half-measures.[159] A defensive posture should only be adopted as a means for attacking the enemy from a position of advantage.[160] The clash of forces and the great battle are the focal points of war, much more important than the skilful combination of battles (which is strategy).[161] Thus, in war, direct, crushing operations from a central position are superior to concentric enveloping manoeuvres; Jomini was right about this while Bülow indulged in illusions. Clausewitz even goes so far as to make the fantastic statement (after Marengo, Ulm, and Jena, to name only the most important examples) that 'Napoleon never engaged in strategic envelopment.'[162]

All this is enough to show that Clausewitz's views on war and its conduct were clearly a particular reflection of Napoleonic warfare as perceived at its pinnacle. This was precisely how Berenhorst saw them when he read Clausewitz's work of instruction for the crown prince:

The most significant parts of his wisdom, he abstracted from the wisdom, the actions, and the maxims of Napoleon. Indeed, his relationship to Carnot's and Napoleon's method or system of war, today's art of war, is like the relationship of Reinhold, Kiesewetter, and Berg to the philosophy of Hume and Kant [that is, they interpret and popularize it]... He certainly has the merit of explaining the new art of war very well and intelligently, and he should be recognized as the first to have done so.[163]

Thus, Berenhorst regarded Clausewitz's ideas simply as a penetrating interpretation of the particular form of warfare that prevailed at the time. This, of course, ran entirely contrary to Clausewitz's own view of his ideas as universally applicable. Paret, who cites Berenhorst's assessment, seems to be oblivious to this point.[164]

Finally, the same themes and concept of war and the correct way to conduct it which flows from this concept are expressed in the early and unrevised parts of *On War*, Books II-VII. They will be briefly noted again, to establish the clear continuity in Clausewitz's outlook:

The very concept of war will permit us to make the following unequivocal statements: 1) Destruction of the enemy forces is the overriding principle of war... 2) Such destruction of forces can usually be accomplished only by fighting. 3) Only major battle involving all forces lead to major success. 4) The greatest successes are obtained where all minor battles [*Gefechte*] coalesce into one great battle.[165]

Destruction should be the aim in each individual battle.[166] Defence is indeed stronger than attack and thus it is the weapon of the weak; but once the defender gains the advantage, he must revert to the attack. Again, to stress the link between Clausewitz's military and political outlook: the 'very destruction of the enemy's forces is also part of the final purpose [of war]. That purpose itself is only a slight modification of that destructive aim.' Ignoring this point, wrote Clausewitz, was at the root of all the false military theories before the Napoleonic Wars.[167]

From this Clausewitz derived his verdict on Archduke Charles, the Habsburg Empire's leading general and military thinker who fought Napoleon: 'Firstly, he lacks an enterprising spirit and the hunger for victory. Secondly... while his judgement is generally good, he has fundamentally a completely erroneous view of strategy. In war, all should be done in order to destroy the enemy's forces, but this destruction does not exist as a separate aim in his conceptual outlook'.[168]

Back to *On War*: Even when the battle does not take place, the very threat of it regulates the conduct of the belligerents. Any other military objective – the occupation of provinces, cities, fortresses, roads, and bridges, the seizure of ammunition, and so on – must be seen as merely an intermediate means intended to achieve a greater advantage for the battle.[169] The same applies to strategic manoeuvres. Interestingly, as the campaigns of 1813 and 1814 cast doubt on the doctrine of the interior lines, Clausewitz withdrew from his own unequivocal position of 1804 and 1812. In principle, he writes, no a priori advantage can be attributed to either interior or exterior lines; the choice between them is dependent upon the type of warfare and upon circumstances.[170] As before, he maintains that, in either case, the strategic manoeuvre is of secondary importance to the battle, and must be subservient to it:

Admittedly, the clash of forces [*Gefecht*] at one point may be worth more than at another. Admittedly, there is a skillful ordering of priority of battles [*Gefechte*] in strategy... We do claim, however, that direct annihilation of the enemy's forces must always be the dominant consideration. We simply want to establish this dominance of the destructive principle... one should not swing wider than latitude allows... rather than try to outbid the enemy with complicated schemes, one should, on the contrary, try to outdo him in simplicity.[171]

Ulm was an exceptional event; the decisive battle is the dominant feature of war.[172]

This concept of war and the correct way to conduct it which flows from this concept encompasses not only the manoeuvre, but also every other military means other than the clash of forces and the decisive battle. Once Clausewitz's fundamental concept is understood, the forest's outline emerges, embracing each and every individual tree, and all his military ideas fall into place. Thus, for all the significance of surprise, Clausewitz maintains that 'by its very nature [it] can rarely be *outstandingly successful.*' It would be a mistake, therefore, to regard surprise as a key element of success in war.'[173] The same applies to cunning. Consider Clausewitz's quite amazing statement regarding its place in history, and note his reason for it: For all its importance and 'however much one longs to see opposing generals vie with one another in craft, cleverness, and cunning, the fact remains that these qualities do not figure prominently in the history of war... The reason for this is obvious... strategy is exclusively concerned with battles [*Gefechte*].'[174] The truly important factors are the superiority of numbers and concentration of force at the decisive point.[175]

Hence Clausewitz's exclusion of all preparatory activities, as well as the supporting services such as maintenance, administration, and supply – logistics – from the theory of war proper, which has puzzled commentators. Theory only takes these activities into account as influencing conditions, because, strictly, it 'deals with the clash of forces [*Gefecht*], with fighting itself.' Marches, camps, and billets only narrowly escape the same fate, because 'in one respect [they] are still part of combat.'[176] All these notions lead to Clausewitz's surprisingly dull description of battle. No manoeuvres or stratagems are portrayed. The only image conveyed is of a direct, grey clash of physical and moral masses.[177]

'Did Clausewitz's Antidogmatism Degenerate into a New Dogmatism?'

The men of the nineteenth century, the heyday of the idea of all-out war, elevated Clausewitz to the pantheon of classics for his outlook on war described above. But for the present-day reader, after the collapse of the dogma of annihilation in the First World War and the renaissance of limited war in the nuclear age, this outlook should have raised serious questions and reservations had its real nature not been obscured by Clausewitz's later development and the difficulties of interpreting it.

Already at the beginning of the twentieth century, when the conception of all-out war still reigned supreme, Camon, one of the most important interpreters of the Napoleonic art of war, argued that Clausewitz misunderstood the essence of Napoleonic strategy, particularly the key manoeuvre against the enemy's rear, *la manœuvre sur les derrières*, and, indeed, the subtlety of his manoeuvre in general.[178] Jomini's analysis of the Napoleonic art of operations was far more concrete and realistic. In terms of their actual view of the objective of military operations, there was, as already noted, very little difference between Jomini and Clausewitz. They both expressed the rationale of Napoleon's decisive art of operations. 'The art of war', wrote Jomini, rejecting the views of Lloyd and Bülow, 'does not consist in running races upon the communications of our enemy, but in the securing of them, and marching thereon, for the purpose of bringing him to battle.'[179] Furthermore, 'after the victory, the vanquished should be allowed no time to rally, but should be pursued without relaxation.'[180] Jomini placed the initiative at the head of his principles.[181] Mobility and movement were other fundamental features of Napoleonic strategy: 'the system of rapid and continuous marches multiplies the effect of an army.'[182] Most important of all was the concentration of force: 'The employment of masses upon the decisive points', wrote Jomini, 'constitutes alone good combinations, and... it should be independent of all positions.'[183]

At the same time, Jomini never considered battle to be the exclusive means of war as Clausewitz did. 'Battles have been stated by some writers to be the chief and deciding features of war,' Jomini wrote in his *Summary of the Art of War* (1837), in direct reaction against Clausewitz's *On War*. 'This assertion is not strictly true, as armies have been destroyed by strategic operations without the occurrence of pitched battles.'[184]

Indeed, Clausewitz's conception of a strictly direct Napoleonic art of war, bereft of strategic envelopments and brilliant use of surprise and cunning, was largely a myth, born out of Prussia's traumatic experience and reflecting the prevailing emphasis on moral energies. It mirrored the reaction among the Reformers and other patriots against the old ways of warfare supposedly responsible for the crushing defeat of 1806. To draw an otherwise most unlikely parallel, Clausewitz was in a way the theoretical counterpart of the hungry for action but scarcely intellectual Field-Marshal Blücher, 'Feldmarschall Vorwärts' [forward].

Hans Delbrück, the well-known military historian, raised the theoretical problem in the late nineteenth and early twentieth centuries when he questioned the universal validity of all-out war, ironically relying on Clausewitz's later conceptions. He advocated the legitimacy of the strategy of attrition and started a much-cited but hardly successful debate in which he was attacked by Theodor and Friedrich von Bernhardi and by Colmar von der Goltz who represented the established strategic convictions of the time. Limited strategy, Delbrück maintained, such as that of the eighteenth century, was not an aberration from the correct conduct of war but had to be understood as the natural outgrowth of the particular conditions of the period.[185]

Commentators since 1945 have hastened to 'defend' Clausewitz from the claim that he advocated what came to be known in the twentieth century as 'total war'. True, the term was popularised by the far-right General Eric Ludendorff, who wrote in 1935 that Clausewitz was outdated and should be thrown overboard, as politics was now the continuation of war, and subservient to it, rather than the other way around. More to the point, the term total war is usually reserved for the wars of the industrial age, most notably the two world wars, characterized by harnessing a country's entire industrial infrastructure, and the civilian population which operated it, for war. All the same, Clausewitz's notion of the true nature or concept of war similarly entailed the mobilization of all of society's resources for the purpose of war. He believed that the French Revolution realised this true nature with the *levée en masse*. And being one of the most fervent members of the Reform Movement, he urged the total mobilisation of Prussia's resources and manpower for an all-out – total – war of national survival against Napoleon, even if this meant the destruction of the country and its people.[186]

Most strikingly, in 1990, the Clausewitz scholar and publisher of his surviving manuscripts Werner Hahlweg printed the original version of Book I of *On War*, from before the transformational changes that Clausewitz introduced into it after 1827. Subsequent commentators have overlooked the fact that in the pivotal Chapter 1 of this version Clausewitz consistently and repeatedly (7 times) refers to the true nature or concept of war as 'total' [*Total-Begriff des Krieges*].[187] More about this in the following chapter.

The crisis of all-out war and of the imperative of the decisive battle, and, with them, a direct attack on Clausewitz in this regard did not take place until after the traumatic experience of the First World War. Liddell Hart, the most renowned and influential leader of the reaction against the military school of the nineteenth century, rehabilitated the discredited warfare of the eighteenth century and very sharply criticised Clausewitz and his legacy.[188] Reacting against the eighteenth century's strategy of manoeuvre, Clausewitz held that the aim of strategy was merely to achieve the most favourable conditions of time and place for the battle and to make use of its results. One could argue, he wrote, that the perfection of strategy was therefore to achieve such favourable conditions as to render battle unnecessary. However, in reality, it was usually advisable to count on fighting. If a general could not rely on the determination of his troops to fight, he would find himself at a permanent disadvantage.[189] Unaware of this argument, Liddell Hart reversed the outlook on war: 'even if a decisive battle be the goal', he wrote, 'the aim of strategy must be to bring about this battle under the most advantageous circumstances... The perfection of strategy would be, therefore, to produce a decision without any serious fighting.'[190] Clausewitz and Liddell Hart each interpreted the same logic in terms of the warfare of their times and arrived at diametrically opposed conclusions. During the era of limited war in the eighteenth century, Marshal De Saxe declared that 'a capable general can make war all his life without being obliged to give battle', a view derided by the men of the nineteenth century, the era of all-out war. Military reality and theory completed a full circle between the military thinkers of the eighteenth century and Liddell Hart.

The main problem raised by Clausewitz's concept of war and its conduct has been well presented by Aron: 'Did Clausewitz's antidogmatism degenerate into a new dogmatism?'[191] Having seen Clausewitz's view of how military theory should look like and criticism of his predecessors, the full irony of Clausewitz's concept of war and the correct way to conduct it which flows from this concept should be clear. He, who passionately believed that his predecessors' theoretical approach and view of war were totally false, was convinced that he had the key to the true nature of war. The paradoxical result of this conviction was that some of his principal arguments against his predecessors boomeranged. His outlook on war was, in its own way, no less one-sided, dogmatic, prescriptive, and unhistorical. This puzzling discrepancy can only be understood against the background of the overwhelming role that Napoleon's crushing warfare, of which Prussia was a major victim, played in the period's consciousness. Clausewitz, who was one of the major advocates of the new pattern of warfare, gave it a formal form with his definition of war as fighting, interpreted in an expansive and imperative manner. In Clausewitz's eyes this was not one-sidedness and dogmatism but, at last, the true universal nature of war and consequently the key to its proper conduct.

Indeed, the Napoleonic phenomenon acquired a 'metaphysical' significance in the eyes of contemporaries. On par with Clausewitz's equation of the Napoleonic conduct of war with the true 'spirit of war', Hegel famously wrote, following Napoleon's triumphant entry into Jena (where Hegel lived at the time) after his great victory in 1806, about the 'world spirit' riding on horseback in the street under his window.

Consider the very similar views expressed by yet another pupil of Scharnhorst and fellow student of Clausewitz in the Institute for Young Officers, Rühle von Lilienstern. He was a man of vast intellectual interests, an intimate of Adam Müller and Heinrich von Kleist, and a friend of Goethe, Gentz, and the Schlegels. As Rühle wrote in 1817: 'The clash of forces is the principal element of war... war is fighting'; war consists of battles chained together or one great battle with intermissions. Rühle, whose military career paralleled that of Clausewitz, also stressed the dominance of moral forces and the need for a theory of war which is rooted in reality and the nature of war.[192]

The prescriptive aspect of theory is derived from these convictions. Much has been written to the effect that Clausewitz totally rejected prescriptive theory. It has been widely and confidently asserted that Clausewitz sought to lay bare the essence of war, rather than teach us how to wage it. Paret advanced this stark contrast, shaping Clausewitz's image as a kind of philosopher-social scientist, who looked for elevated, pure, abstract knowledge, and many have followed that line. However, this is a false dichotomy and a very misleading understanding of Clausewitz's approach as a whole. Indeed, commentators have equally stressed, without any sense of contradiction, that Clausewitz was a military man and a Prussian patriot, who was above all interested in practical results. Note that in his Undated Note, written in early 1827 or slightly before, he referred to his future book as 'The manuscript on the conduct of major operations'.[193] His Collected Works were also titled *Hinterlassene Werke über Krieg und Kriegführung*, that is, 'on war and the conduct of war'.

Clausewitz maintained that the theory of war was not prescriptive only in the sense that any doctrine derived from it would always be partial and require judgment in application. But he did believe that the true theory of war – deriving from its 'lasting spirit', 'nature' or 'concept' – provided lessons which trained the mind of the general for action. Theory was by no means divorced from praxis; on the contrary, it had to be translated into praxis. Again, as he wrote: 'Theory cannot equip the mind with formulas for solving problems... but it can give the mind insight into the great mass of phenomena and of their relationships, then leave it free to rise into the higher realms of action.'[194] Ultimately, theory is to become capability through critical analysis and practical rules and principles.[195] The last thing that Clausewitz, the military man and military thinker, was after was empty, barren, formal definitions. Indeed, he repeatedly expressed his fear of empty formalism. The core of his theory of war was that the nature of war revealed how it should be conducted.

Now we have also seen what concrete ideas he had in mind as to what a true theory of war taught: to aim for great objectives, to achieve the utmost concentration of force, to act as aggressively as possible in order to annihilate the enemy army in a major decisive battle, and to destroy the ability of the enemy state to resist. He believed that 'unnecessary' manoeuvres, preference for indirect military means, and evading decision in battle contradicted the 'lasting spirit', 'nature', 'essence' or 'concept' of war, were bound to lead to failure, and thus had to be avoided. These notions were highly prescriptive. Compare this with Lossau's *War* (1815): 'From these concepts [of the nature of war] there must emerge clearly what war is, what the warrior must want, and how one should study war in time of peace.'[196]

Clausewitz's strong convictions regarding the fundamental and universal nature of war and the implications for its conduct overshadowed his historical sensitivity. On the one hand, he stressed the diversity of historical experience and asserted that the theorist must not elevate himself above the times by proclaiming standards of conduct which he regarded as universal. Every period's particular form of warfare stemmed from its unique political, social, cultural, and personal conditions. As we have seen, Clausewitz concluded his historical description of the transformations of the art of war in the context of the particular conditions of each period as follows: 'Each period, therefore, would have held to its own theory of war.' This was both the pinnacle and the limit of Clausewitz's historicism. The following sentences show the limits of the relativism implicit in this historical view:

But the conduct of war [*Kriegführung*], though conditioned by the particular characteristics of states and their armed forces, must contain some more general – indeed, a universal – element with which every theorist ought above all to be concerned. *The age in which this postulate, this universally valid element was at its strongest was the most recent one, when war attained the absolute in violence.*[197] [my emphasis]

The wars of the French Revolution and Napoleon revealed the true nature of war as fighting and as a clash of forces and dispelled the false conceptions which had prevailed during various periods of the past.[198] Here too, as throughout his life, Clausewitz treats the warfare of the condottieri, denounced by Machiavelli, and that of the *ancien régime* not as genuine expressions of the conditions peculiar to their times, but as a grotesque distortion of the nature of war, necessarily leading to their defeat. Much the same applied to his criticism of Archduke Charles's generalship. He did not consider that Austria's fundamental weakness *vis-à-vis* Revolutionary and Napoleonic France, with their national mass armies, may virtually have dictated to it a more cautious strategy and hesitation to risk its limited forces in battle. For all his criticism of Jomini, Clausewitz himself turned Napoleonic warfare into a universal yardstick and employed it to dismiss the warfare of entire historical periods, disregarding their internal, circumstantial logic.

This explains Jomini's bitter complaint that Clausewitz's 'first volume [Books I-IV of *On War*; Jomini clearly referred mainly to Book II] is but a declamation against all theory of war, whilst the two succeeding volumes [the rest of *On War*], full of theoretic maxims, proves that the author believes in the efficacy of his own doctrines, if he does not believe in those of others.'[199] Clausewitz was convinced that in contrast to his predecessors' arbitrary and misleading systems, he himself had discerned the true nature of war, which manifested itself in the genius of Napoleon, 'the God of War'.[201]

Clausewitz's Crisis: The Concept of War versus Both Recent and Universal History

Much more significant than the comments by Berenhorst, Jomini, Aron or myself, suggesting an intrinsic tension between Clausewitz's historicism, on the one hand, and his concept of war and the practical implications he believed arising from it, on the other, is that Clausewitz himself finally became aware of this tension. In 1827, or slightly earlier, when most of *On War* – six out of its eight planned 'books' of the treatise – had already been drafted, this realisation triggered a profound crisis in his lifelong concept of war and the correct way to conduct it which flows from this concept, the centrepiece of his entire theory of war. The first realisation of a major problem emerges toward the end of Book VI, 'Defence', and continued to grow throughout the last six out of the Book's thirty chapters. This is no coincidence. Since the aim of defence is to preserve the status quo, the defender may choose to delay operations, withdraw, and avoid confrontation in the hope of wearing the enemy down. This may lead to what Clausewitz called in the vocabulary of the time a 'war of observation': a prolonged, indecisive struggle which lacks energy and involves almost no fighting. In truth, he wrote, the attacker too, sometimes appears to 'ignore the *strict logical necessity* of pressing on to the goal.'[201] (The emphasis on the prescriptive character of theory is mine.)

Up until then, Clausewitz did not regard the defender's choice to preserve the status quo, delay operations, withdraw, and avoid confrontation as a problem for his fundamental 'concept of war' as fighting, pursued with the utmost energy and centring on the decisive major battle. This is because he believed the defence was only called for and legitimate when one was weaker and had to be abandoned in favour of the attack when the balance of power changed. We shall see much more about this in Chapter 6. Furthermore, he believed that the defence, too, had to be conducted with the utmost energy. However, reaching the last chapters of Book VI, Clausewitz began to doubt that these provisos were enough to explain some central forms of the defence which eschewed confrontation with the enemy and battle.

Chapter 25 of Book VI, 'Retreat to the Interior of the Country', was naturally inspired by the Russian conduct against Napoleon's invasion of 1812. The Russian deep withdrawal and avoidance of major battle (except Borodino) in this campaign, in which Clausewitz participated, resulted in the demise of the *Grande Armée*, Napoleon's greatest disaster, practically without major fighting. As Clausewitz recognised: 'the tide turned without a victorious battle to provide the decision'.[202] Furthermore, this landmark case brought to Clausewitz's mind a whole list of other cases in which the result was similar, if on a smaller scale than in the gigantic Russian campaign. Among the cases he cited was, from his time, the failed, costly offensive led by the French Marshal Masséna in Portugal in 1810–1811, which Wellington countered with a deep withdrawal and scorched-earth strategy. Indeed, as Clausewitz writes: 'there are countless other situations where the principle established here [of deep withdrawal, without giving battle] was partly, if not completely responsible for the result [the enemy's ruin].'[203]

This was not all. The following Chapter 26, 'The People in Arms', deals with the form of warfare – guerrilla – that played a cardinal role in the downfall of Napoleon, again most notably in the Iberian Peninsula and Russia. These were momentous historical experiences, no less significant than Napoleon's earlier crushing victories. They could hardly be ignored or dismissed, certainly not by a man of Clausewitz's integrity and commitment to get to the bottom of things. It has long been commented that Clausewitz was among the early theorists of the guerrilla warfare in the sense we understand it. Indeed, his writings on *petite guerre*, guerrilla, 'small war', *kleiner Krieg* – the same concept, flowing between French, Spanish, English and German – have contributed to his reputation as a classic in this field as well, as guerrilla warfare has re-emerged as a trump card in the wars of the twentieth and twenty-first centuries.[204] A number of works on Clausewitz's writings on this subject have appeared in recent years.

Two of these works, by Beatrice Heuser and Sibylle Scheipers, clearly distinguish between the old usage of the term, most popular in the second half of the eighteenth century and the new meaning it was beginning to acquire during the Revolutionary and Napoleonic period.[205] Originally, *petite guerre*, guerrilla, 'small war', *kleiner Krieg* meant the use of regular light infantry and light cavalry in battles and campaigns around the operations of the main force in activities such as skirmishing, picketing, reconnaissance, patrols, avant guard, rear guard, raids, ambushes, and the like. Clausewitz's main work on the subject: 'Lectures on Small War, held at the War College in 1810 and 1811', comprising some two-thirds of the collection *Clausewitz on Small War* (2015) edited by Christopher Daase and James Davis, is limited entirely to this traditional meaning. It relies on the great volume of earlier and contemporary works in the genre and, indeed, as both Heuser and Scheipers recognise, is unoriginal. While this routine work, like others in the genre, was obviously of practical value at the time, it is now wholly outdated, can serve only scholarly historical purposes and, because of its great detail, is quite tedious, even for those interested in military history.

Furthermore, in his 'Lectures on Small War, 1810 and 1811' Clausewitz *did not* analyse 'small-unit warfare by studying the rebellion in the Vendée (1793–8), the Tyrolean uprising of 1809, and most prominently, the then ongoing Spanish insurrection', as the editors of his writings on the subject suggest.[206] Clausewitz mentioned each of these signature insurgencies only once and in an inconsequential manner in his lectures. Only a year later, fervently preaching a national insurrection against the French, did Clausewitz begin to refer to and advocate the large-scale use of militias and irregulars alongside the regular army, as in the Vendée, Spain, and the Tyrol. Surprisingly, and contrary to Heuser's claim,[207] Clausewitz's history of *The Campaign of 1812 in Russia* scarcely addresses this major aspect of the campaign at all, possibly because this work was his eyewitness account from various army headquarters and with the main armies. However, in Chapter 26, Book VI, of *On War*, 'The People in Arms', we have guerrilla warfare in the modern sense laid out.

Returning to our main line of argument, what the works on Clausewitz and guerrilla warfare have not noticed is the crucial role that guerrilla warfare played in the erosion and subsequent collapse of Clausewitz's concept of war as a relentless effort to destroy the enemy in battle – that is, in the transformation of his *overall* concept of war and its conduct. Guerrilla warfare for Clausewitz was the most extreme case of a form of war that does not actively and energetically pursue a decision in arms – the 'problem' that he began to concern himself with from 1810–1812 onwards. The chapter on the 'People in Arms' towards the end of Book VI, 'Defence', seems to have been the last straw that brought about the crisis and 1827 transformation of his entire theory of war. As he wrote, among the conditions for the success of guerrilla warfare: 'It must not be decided by a single stroke.'[208] Furthermore: 'Militia and bands of armed civilians cannot and should not be employed against the main enemy force – or indeed against any sizable enemy force. They are not supposed to pulverize the core but to nibble at the shell and around the edges.'[209]

I am quite sure you see all this as commonsensical and unproblematic. But you are not Clausewitz, or, more precisely, you do not hold Clausewitz's 'concept of war' and its conduct as a relentless pursuit of the decisive battle to annihilate the enemy's main army and crush his power of resistance. As long as one does not comprehend what Clausewitz's fundamental concept of war and the correct way to conduct it which flows from this concept was, one is unable to grasp what Clausewitz's late, decisive transformation was all about, and thus be able not only to read but also understand *On War*.

True, Clausewitz primarily saw the 'people in arms' fighting alongside a regular army, as was the case in the Iberian Peninsula, Russia, and, indeed, in the Prussian reformers' plans for their own *Landwehr*. All the same, it now occurred to Clausewitz that Napoleon's crushing strategy, centring on the decisive battle, may not, after all, be the sole key to victory in war – the 'necessary' mode of operation flowing 'logically' out of war's 'lasting spirit', 'nature' or 'concept'. And this creeping realisation leads Clausewitz to a much broader one as he gets to the end of Book VI: 'There is no denying that a great majority of wars and campaigns are more a state of observation than a struggle for life and death – a struggle, that is, in which at least one of the parties is determined to gain a decision. A theory based on this idea could be applied only to the wars of the nineteenth century.'[210]

Hence, 'To be of any practical use', theory must take into account that, apart from 'the kind of war that is completely governed and saturated by the urge for a decision – of true war', there exists a second kind of war.[211] Moreover, 'the history of war, in every age and country, shows not only that most campaigns are of this type, but that the majority is so overwhelming as to make all other campaigns seem more like exceptions to the rule'.[212]

Having seen in the previous chapter the development of Clausewitz's notion of war and military theory, the crisis into which this notion fell at the end of Book VI is clear: theory conflicted with reality; the 'concept of war' did not withstand the 'test of experience'; the universal contradicted the historical; the unity of the phenomenon of war, based on a 'lasting spirit' that encompassed the diversity of 'forms', disintegrated; and the practical imperatives derived from this 'spirit' or 'concept' – the significant content of theory – lost their validity.

Finally, having come this far, we are now in a position to answer the question posed at the end of this chapter's first section: why are the widely ignored propositions listed in the melancholic Undated Note as evidence of the feasibility of a universal theory of war are so unimpressive, disappointing, or even pitiful? As mentioned, I have shown that the Undated Note was written in early 1827 or slightly earlier.[213] This was when Clausewitz suddenly became aware that the centrepiece of his deeply-held theory of war and its conduct, which he had zealously advanced for decades – the notion that the very concept of war as fighting dictated all-out war and an uncompromising concentration of all forces for the decisive battle – might have collapsed, threatening to pull his entire intellectual edifice down with it. The propositions cited in that note are meagre remnants which an understandably depressed Clausewitz tried to assemble in an attempt to reassure himself that a universal theory of war might still be possible after his central idea regarding war and the correct way to conduct it had dissipated. Fortunately for him, although the note's propositions are so utterly unconvincing, Clausewitz would soon be able to rise from the nadir of his work and break new ground.

A subsequent note, which Clausewitz dated 10 July 1827, heralded the crucial transformation in his thought, with which he was to struggle in the writing of Book VIII and revision of Book I of *On War*. We now proceed to understand the form and significance of this transformation more fully.

5

War and Politics

Clausewitz U-Turned against His Own Lifelong Concept of War

The relationship between politics and war dominated Clausewitz's mind during his final years. It generated a far-reaching revision in his theory of war, which resulted in the inclusion of the concept of limited war and has attracted the most attention in our time.

One cannot gain a full understanding of this transformation without viewing the changes that occurred in Clausewitz's political perspectives. We saw that he championed great and far-reaching political aims during the heroic period of the Napoleonic Wars and Prussia's struggle for survival as a great power. This was the state of mind which guided his activities and harsh criticism of his country's policies and which found clear theoretical expression in his writings in 1804, 1808–1809 and 1812. It blended harmoniously with his concept of the nature of war as a relentless pursuit of the enemy's complete overthrow. However, with the end of the heroic period and with the return of the politics of European equilibrium, the problem which now claimed Clausewitz's attention was how to secure Prussia's status, strength, and stability within the European concert of powers against the dangers posed by both external and internal forces. This perspective dominated his writings on Prussia's foreign policy and European politics from that period.[214]

While it was not the direct cause of Clausewitz's conceptual change of course in 1827, shifts in European politics provided a receptive background against which this change took root, and in the process became itself conscious and pronounced. Here too, Clausewitz's political perspectives and military conceptions were complementary. This twofold nature of the transformation in Clausewitz's thought, political and military, explains why in July 1827 he put forward two ideas as the guidelines for the revision of his work: the new idea that war can be of two types [and *not one*], aiming either at completely overthrowing the enemy or at a limited objective; and that [this is *because*] the character and scale of military operations are closely linked to the character and scope of the political objectives – '*war is nothing but the continuation of politics* [Politik] *with other means.*'[215] (In the first two square brackets I aim to clarify both the novelty of, and causal relationship between, the two propositions.) To be sure, the relationship between politics and war was integral to Clausewitz's thought throughout his life. But as long as he viewed both politics and war in expansive terms, this relationship did not have much significance.

As the depth of the crisis that Clausewitz's entire theory of war and its conduct underwent in 1827 has not been fully grasped, the exact nature of his intellectual development during his last years has similarly remained obscure. This has been particularly so since, in his attempt to resolve the crisis, Clausewitz borrowed new intellectual devices from his cultural environment, whose origins and nature have also remained a mystery. For the sake of clarity, we shall first examine the nature of the transformation in Clausewitz's thought. Thereafter we shall trace and explain the new intellectual devices he employed that made his particular solution to the problem he faced possible.

The Nature of War *versus* the Political Aim

In short, the late development of Clausewitz's thought can only be understood within the context of his attempt to bridge the gulf that had emerged in his theory of war by reconciling his lifelong concept of the nature of war and its conduct, which he did not abandon, with his new awareness of the diversity of wars in historical reality. Clausewitz's revision of *On War* took shape in the following order: beginning, as we have seen, at the end of Book VI, 'Defence', it continued in Book VIII, 'War Plans', the last book of *On War*. This, Clausewitz had foreseen in the Note of July 1827 would be the natural place for clarifying his new ideas, first and foremost to himself. Finally, the revision was further developed in Book I, 'On the Nature of War', the only one which Clausewitz succeeded in addressing in his plan to go back and revise the first six books of *On War*, prior to his death.

At the end of Book VI Clausewitz realises that, by rejecting all wars which do not conform to his concept of the nature of war as an all-out effort aiming for the total destruction of the enemy's powers of resistance in a decisive battle, theory becomes cut off from historical reality. We have seen the acute threat that this growing realisation posed to the centrepiece of his entire theory of war, moulded by the Napoleonic experience. What was now to become of his fundamental concept? As Clausewitz was unprepared to abandon it, it was necessary for him to devise an intellectual structure which could accommodate it together with his new ideas.

Clausewitz had already grappled with the problem in two earlier texts and thought he had resolved it. In 1817, during his period in Koblenz, he sent Gneisenau a manuscript entitled, 'On Progress and Stagnation [*Stillstand* – standstill] in Military Activity'. Again, the problem for Clausewitz – the 'inconsistency' or 'contradiction', as he calls it – is this: 'The armed forces for war are equipped to destroy the opposing ones, thereby gaining the freedom to dictate any conditions to the enemy's government... The essence of war, then, is rapid, unstoppable action, an unstoppable progress towards the goal; that is, *a fierce, bloody, quickly accomplished decisive battle.*' [Emphasis in the original.] It follows from this 'essence of war' that 'the movement of the whole war cannot be stopped... and it therefore remains a true contradiction with the original purpose of armaments.'[216]

However, a glance through history suggests that most wars in history do not conform to the logical necessity arising from the nature of war. Why so? First, by that time Clausewitz had recognised that the defender had legitimate reasons to postpone action on its part until the balance of power shifted in its favour. But, in addition, Clausewitz now attributes the failure to pursue war energetically and towards decisive results to a number of human shortcomings: people's failure to comprehend what the nature of war dictates; fear, lack of courage and weakness which stop them from doing what is necessary; and, finally, misinterpretation, sometimes bordering on illusions, as to the exact circumstances of the situations they are facing. Having identified the 'obstacles' for the full realisation of war's nature, he thus emphasises that 'these mere phantoms cannot find a place in the theory of war. Every stoppage which for this reason takes place in the course of the act of war is therefore completely alien to the art of war.'[217]

Clausewitz incorporated the kernel of this piece as Chapter 16, Book III, of *On War*. Note what is missing in the 1817 text: *there is no mention of politics or the political aim* as a reason for wars' frequent failure to assume their full nature as unlimited use of violence to overthrow the enemy.

Indeed, the next step in this direction comes in the old Chapter 1 of Book I of *On War*, before its revision. As mentioned in the previous chapter, the old Chapter 1 was first published in 1990 by Hahlweg from Clausewitz's literary remains. It provides us with a most valuable insight into a previously missing link in the development of Clausewitz's train of thought. I was unfamiliar with it when I published my work on Clausewitz in 1989. However, inexplicably, this key text has not been referred to by Clausewitz's later commentators during the more than three decades since its publication. As Clausewitz tells us in his

Note of July 1827, the first six books of *On War* had already been copied clean, apparently in preparation for the printer, when he decided on the revision of his entire work according to his new guiding ideas. The old, pre-revision version of Book I which has now come to light, indeed has marginal notes by Clausewitz written after he decided on the revision. These pointed the way for the major changes he would introduce into that book, most notably into the signature Chapter 1. Both the old Chapter 1 and these marginal notes are critical for the understanding of Clausewitz's transformation on the themes he regarded as most crucial.

In the old Chapter 1 of Book I Clausewitz continues to grapple with the 'problem' of which he was becoming increasingly aware: the 'contradiction' or 'inconsistency' between his lifelong, passionately preached, concept of the nature of war and the correct way to conduct it which flows from this concept on the one hand, and the actual realities of historical wars, on the other. Here, for the first time, the political element is introduced as a distinct constraint on war, but it still does not take centre-stage and is only referred to in a few sentences. Most significantly, the explicit rationale of war as a continuation of politics which governs its conduct has not yet come into its own.

The chapter is very repetitive, evidently reflecting Clausewitz's struggle with the problem which preoccupies him. The following are select quotations representing his line of argument. The chapter begins with the familiar phrases from the *On War* that we have: 'War is nothing but an extended duel... Violence... is therefore the means of submitting the enemy to our will – making him incapable of further resistance is the purpose, the goal we pursue until this purpose is achieved... For the political purpose, it [the overthrow of the enemy] is the means... it is the goal towards the goal; theory must first focus on this warlike purpose.'[218] 'Human-friendly souls could easily imagine that there exists an ingenious overthrow [of the enemy], without causing too many wounds, and that this is the true tendency of the art of war... one must destroy this error, for in such dangerous things as war is the errors which arise from good-naturedness are precisely the worst.'[219]

However, 'this philosophical view of war, which in its total concept cannot be any different, loses itself so much in the concrete form of the real phenomena that it is often difficult to find out again.' The reason for this is that 'in the forces that war sets in motion, there are counterweights that reduce the swift [materialisation] of this principle [of all-out war and relentless fighting].'[220]

Still, '...we have to return to the total concept of war, to make it stand out because it is the basic idea from which everything emanates.'[221] 'This is the basic idea of the essence and purpose of war. A thousand and a thousand times this basic concept has been completely lost sight of in the real wars; one is surprised by this, but it gradually becomes clear when one becomes aware of the myriad of alien influences due to which the warlike act drags on and in doing so one thinks that an *inconsistency* in the human spirit is the first to be forgiven when it is prompted by danger and responsibility. But also [one thinks] that... the world of [military] writers never came back to this basic idea, or rather that it never assumed it, proves how bad things still are with the theory of war.'[222]

Note this particular criticism of contemporary military theorists for failing to recognise that the concept of war dictated all-out war and relentless fighting to destroy the enemy in battle. It was indeed the main theme which had ignited Clausewitz's consuming sense of originality and mission since his youth, yet was to disappear from *On War* after his transformation.

Human fear and other limitations of man's mind are responsible for the reluctance to draw rigorous conclusions emanating from the nature of war: 'Instead of narrowing the understanding into the path of philosophical inquiry and logical inferences... he prefers to dwell with his imagination in the realm of chance and fortune.'[223]

Having thus repeated his arguments of 1817, Clausewitz introduces a new element in the old Chapter 1, Book I, to explain the failure of war to assume its true nature, other than the shortcomings of human comprehension and courage: 'Finally, the political conditions from which war emerges change its nature from time to time and soon weaken its natural force...'[224] Moreover: 'it must be admitted that the magnitude of our demand can and will have an influence on the decision of the enemy, and that the point into which he must be brought in order to accept our law is therefore based on the magnitude of this demand.'[225]

Clausewitz is torn by his growing awareness that wars in historical reality seldom conform to his concept of the nature of war and the imperatives arising from it: 'The greater these difficulties are, the more the mind feels inclined to bypass them all with the stroke of a pen and to insist with logical rigour that the political purpose and the state of the enemy have no influence on the conduct of war, that one must be prepared for the utmost exertion every time... But such a stroke of the pen through this logic of difficulty would become a law book, and not one for the real world. To be strict, even if that pushing to the utmost of efforts would be an absolute, it must be admitted that the human spirit would hardly submit to this logical tyranny.'[226]

Thus, Clausewitz reconciles himself to the following conclusion: 'War in the concrete case will be a product of many interests and circumstances which, of an unequal nature, limit each other, perhaps often thwart each other, and from which a decreasing principle emerges as a finite sum.'[227]

As Clausewitz already anticipates: 'We will consider the modifications caused by these various causes in more detail in the chapters on the defence of the attack, on the stagnation

[*Stillstand*] in the act of war, on the inertia of the forces, on the character of today's wars.'[228]

Clausewitz repeats his general argument at the beginning of the old Chapter 2 of Book I, before it, too, was revised: 'The purpose of war is the destruction of enemy forces and the defeat of the enemy state. Strictly speaking, there is only one means, namely only one in which the war serves itself, *because the political ones do not belong here* [my emphasis]. This one means is battle, or rather the sum of large and small battles, of which it consists, and consists entirely alone... This truth, which has been misunderstood too often and for too long, needs little other proof than that the substance of which war uses for every great and small act is armed force. Where armed people are sent, the idea of a battle is necessarily the basis.'[229]

Again, it is essential to grasp this cornerstone of Clausewitz's entire theory. He finds in the *formal* definition of war as fighting a *logical* justification for a *practical* – prescriptive and imperative – concept of the conduct of war as relentless, all-out fighting centring on the great battle of destruction. That a formal definition does not give rise to practical action – that this logical inference is false – never occurs to him.

So, what do we already have here, and what we do not yet have? First, the growing gap in Clausewitz's mind between his fundamental concept of the nature of war and the actual diversity of historical experience leads him, for the first time, to introduce a distinction between this concept and 'the real world'. It did not appear before. Correspondingly, a new term makes its debut even prior to the revision. As already noted, and for the attention of those who have been at pains to distance Clausewitz from the notion of total war, in the old Chapter 1 Clausewitz now repeatedly calls war conducted according to its own nature of relentless and unlimited effort – which he regards as the most desirable – as being true to its 'total concept' [*Total-Begriff*]. In the *On War* that we have, he would later opt for the term 'absolute' rather than 'total', but his meaning remained the same.

Secondly, politics makes its first appearance, if fairly briefly, as an element which modifies war's true nature, constraining its scale and the scope of the military effort. However, the rationale behind the relationship between the political goal and the military purpose – that war is but a continuation of politics with other means – does not yet become conscious, and limited war is not yet defined and recognised as truly legitimate, rather than as an unfortunate consequence. As Clausewitz would later write at the margins of the old Chapter 1 as a guideline for revision: 'There is a *new* principle [my emphasis] to align the size of the efforts according to the size of the [political] demands.'[230]

We now return to the end of Book VI, where the inherent tension in Clausewitz's theory of war erupts into a full-blown crisis, followed by his declared intention to revise and transform the whole of *On War*. Because of the intrinsic features of defence and, moreover, of guerrilla warfare, Clausewitz now becomes aware that there may be *legitimate* reasons for the fact that war often does not assume its true nature of energetic, unlimited fighting centring on the great battle. At the same time, he still claims that the war of destruction takes priority as it expresses the nature of war; against a half-hearted war effort, an all-out one would always gain the upper hand. The new term 'absolute war' is now introduced at the very end of Book VI: 'the urge for decision' is 'true war, or absolute war if we may call it that'.[231] Note, that 'absolute war' *is* 'true war', rather than a pole apart, as it would be later perceived. Limited wars are not a genuine form of war but the results of various factors which exercise counter influences on the real, 'absolute' nature of war and modify it.[232]

The transformation in Clausewitz's thought continues to evolve from here. His evolution, from his 1817 essay 'On Progress and Stagnation [*Stillstand* – standstill] in Military

Activity' in which politics does not yet figure, through the first version of Book I in which it appears for the first time, now becomes a revolution. After a period of intense reflection of unknown length, he announces his planned revision of his work in the Note of July 1827. The role of politics is now reversed: from being referred to primarily as an 'obstacle' to the realisation of war's true nature, it now becomes the rationale governing its conduct. War can be of two types [rather than one], aiming either at completely overthrowing the enemy or at a limited objective; [because] the character and scale of military operations are closely linked to the character and scope of the political objectives – 'war is nothing but the continuation of politics [*Politik*] with other means.'[233]

As he anticipated in July 1827, Clausewitz examines the problem extensively in Book VIII, 'War Plans', with a view of 'clearing my own mind'. In doing so, he again expresses his agonising doubts and dilemma as follows:

One might wonder whether there is any truth at all in our concept of the absolute character of war were it not for the fact that with our own eyes we have seen warfare achieve this state of absolute perfection. After the short prelude of the French Revolution, Bonaparte brought it swiftly and ruthlessly to that point... Surely it is both natural and inescapable that this phenomenon should cause us to turn again to the *original* [*ursprünglichen*] *concept of war with all its rigorous implications*. Are we then to take this as the standard, and judge all wars by it, however much they may diverge? Should we *deduce all the demands* [*Forderungen*] *of theory* from it?... [Then] our theory will everywhere approximate to logical necessity, and will tend to be clear and unambiguous. But in that case, what are we to say about all the wars that have been fought since the days of Alexander excepting certain Roman campaigns – down to

Bonaparte?... We would be bound to say... that our theory, though strictly logical, would not apply to reality.[234] [The emphases on the prescriptive implications of theory, flowing from its 'concept', are mine.]

This dilemma shatters Clausewitz's lifelong concept of war and its conduct: 'Is one war of the same nature as another?', he asked in a note he wrote in an attempt to clarify his thoughts.[235] '*All imperatives inherent in the concept of war* seem to dissolve, and its foundations are threatened.'[236] [The emphasis on the prescriptive implications of theory, flowing from its 'concept', is mine.]

In Book VIII, Clausewitz also proceeds to develop a solution to the problem that threatens his entire theoretical edifice, repeating but also going far beyond his arguments in the old Chapter 1 of Book I:

What exactly is this nonconducting medium, this barrier that prevents a full discharge? Why is it that the philosophical conception is not sufficient? [*der philosophischen Vorstellungs-weise nicht Genüge?*] The barrier in question is the vast array of factors, forces and conditions in national affairs that are affected by war... Logic comes to a stop in this labyrinth... This inconsistency... is the reason why war runs into something quite different from what it should be according to its concept [*Begriff*] – runs into something incoherent and incomplete.[237]

As theory cannot ignore reality, how is this 'inconsistency' explained? Again, various factors which are *alien* to the nature of war prevent it from fully realising its true character. They include the uncertainty and friction of war, as well as man's shortcomings, but also the historical conditions out of which war arises. Rather than existing in isolation, war is affected by a variety of other values, goals, and considerations which guide nations and prevent a maximalisation of the conduct of war. All these factors are alien to the nature of war, yet limit its intensity in practice. Limited wars, which include most of the wars in history, are therefore the result. 'Theory must concede all this; but it has the duty to give priority to the absolute form of war.'[238]

Increasingly, however, in the process of Clausewitz's advance through Book VIII and as he gradually develops the full implications of his new ideas, the relationship between war and politics takes precedence. The influence of the political aim on the objective of military operations, he wrote in Chapter 2, 'will set its [the war's] course, prescribe the scale of means and effort which is required, and make its influence felt throughout down to the smallest operational derail.'[239] He elaborates on this point in Chapter 3B on the 'Scale of the Military Objective and the Effort to be Made'. Both, he claims, are governed by 'the scale of political demands on either side', as well as by the characteristics of the belligerents and by their reciprocal actions which lead to the escalation of the conflict.[240] This is also the theme of Chapter 6A, 'The Effect of the Political Aim on the Military Objective'. As the transformation of emphasis is now complete, Clausewitz comes to the conclusion that 'once this influence of the political objective on war is admitted, as it must be, there is no stopping it; consequently, we must also be willing to wage such minimal wars which consist in merely threatening the enemy, with negotiations held in reserve.'[241] Finally, in the signature Chapter 6B, 'War Is an Instrument of Policy', Clausewitz fully elaborates on the idea that war cannot be understood outside its political context:

War is only a branch of political activity... it is in no sense autonomous... The main lines along which military events progress, and to which they are restricted, are political lines that continue throughout the war into the subsequent peace... All the factors that go to make up war and determine its salient features – the strength and allies of each antagonist, the character of the people and their governments, and so forth... are these not all political?[242]

Still, these widely quoted passages form only half of the picture. While all the characteristics of war are decisively influenced by politics, this influence is by no means part of the nature of war. On the contrary, the influence of politics is an external force which works *against* the true essence of war, harnesses it to its needs, and in the process modifies the imperatives which it imposes. 'In making use of war, policy evades *all rigorous conclusions proceeding from the nature of war...* [It] converts the overwhelmingly destructive element of war into a mere instrument.'[243] [The emphasis on the prescriptive implications of theory, flowing from the nature of war, is mine.]

We are now in a better position to see the actual purpose of his historical survey of the development of the art of war, to which we have already referred several times. Featuring still relatively early in Book VIII, the survey was part of the process by which Clausewitz laboured to clarify his thoughts and aimed to examine concretely (a) the array of conditions which had prevented the realisation of the true, 'absolute' nature of war in most periods of history; (b) the circumstances under which this nature had nevertheless appeared under the Romans, Alexander the Great, and finally the French Revolutionaries and Napoleon; and (c) the resulting theoretical conclusions from all the above.

Under the condottieri in Renaissance Italy, 'war lost many of its risks; its character was wholly changed, and no deduction from its proper nature was still applicable.' War was also limited during the *ancien régime*: 'All Europe rejoiced at this development. It was seen as a logical outcome of Enlightenment. This was a misconception. Enlightenment can never lead to inconsistency... [Indeed] so long as this was the general style of warfare with its violence limited in such strict and obvious ways, no one saw any inconsistency in it.' However, the French Revolution and Napoleon unleashed the forces contained in society, and war then 'took on an entirely different character, or rather closely approached its true character, its absolute perfection... untrammelled by any conventional restraints, [it] had broken loose in all its elemental fury.' What does the future hold? Will limited wars reappear? This, Clausewitz wrote, was difficult to answer, yet limited wars were not very likely in the future: 'once barriers – which in a sense consist only in man's ignorance of what is possible – are torn down, they are not so easily set up again.'[244]

Thus, the compromise that Clausewitz devised between his lifelong concept of war and the correct way to conduct it which flows from this concept on the one hand, and his new awareness that the conduct of war takes many forms and that this is so primarily because of changing political conditions, on the other, led him to revise his theory as follows. He now recognised two types of war, but regarded the first, 'absolute war' – a new term – to be the genuine expression of the nature of war, and superior to the other. Yet, as he continued to explore his new ideas, this revision and adaptation became insufficient. The chapter 'War is an Instrument of Policy' marked a further shift. If the understanding of war was dominated by its political function, then the primacy assigned to 'absolute' war lost much of its justification. In the dilemma between his lifelong concept of war and its conduct on the one hand, and the diversity of political aims and military operations in historical reality on the other, Clausewitz moved a step further towards the latter. At the same time, he did not altogether abandon the core of his old concept, that the constitutive element of war – fighting – dominated the nature of war. Nor did he relinquish his belief in the superiority of the clash of forces and the battle over all other military means. This was the basis for the amended compromise

113

of Book I, which Clausewitz revised, as he had planned in July 1827, after he had completed Book VIII, the last book of *On War*.

In the revised Book I, the essence of war is also presented as a volcanic eruption of force and violence. It is a 'pulsation of violence', 'very much like a mine that can explode only in the manner or direction predetermined by the setting.'[245] 'The impulse to destroy the enemy... is central to the very concept [*Begriff*] of war... war is an act of force, and there is no... limit to the application of that force.'[246] However, the unlimited nature of violence in war no longer relies directly on the notion that all-out war is clearly superior. Napoleonic warfare is no longer perceived as the only correct form of war. Violence in war is now presented in connection with tendencies towards escalation which are inherent in the interplay between the belligerents' aims and efforts. Further advancing the arguments he already put forward in Book VIII, Clausewitz no longer presents lulls in military activity in a negative light, and the factors which explain them no longer include man's imperfection and timidity.

It is again important to understand that the influences of politics on war do not belong to the nature of war, but, on the contrary, contradict it. The political influences 'are the forces that give rise to war; the same forces circumscribe and moderate it. They themselves, however, are not part of war... To introduce the principle of moderation into the theory of war itself would always lead to... absurdity.'[247] Politics thus places itself above war and modifies it to suit its needs.

The modifications of the nature of war by the actual context in which war takes place therefore completely change its character. At this point, Clausewitz switches to discuss the characteristics of war in reality.[248] Indeed, 'absolute war' is no longer 'real war', as it was before. Elucidating the full implications of the relationship between politics and war, the new Chapter 1 of Book I grew to double the length of the old chapter, prior to the revision. In the newly added sections of the chapter, the aims and means of war are no longer dictated by the maximalist imperative inherent in the nature of war but vary according to each particular case. The aim of war is shifted from the total overthrow of the enemy to the aim put forward by politics. Consequently, war is no longer conducted on a total scale but according to the requirements of the political aim. Clausewitz again discusses the interaction between the scope of the political aim in depth, its importance to the parties involved, and the scale of the effort necessary to achieve it.[249]

In the revised Chapter 2 of Book I, Clausewitz examines the purpose and means of the conduct of war itself even closer. His discussion is highly significant because it clearly reveals how far Clausewitz retreated from his imperative of all-out war. He now gives an equal status to a variety of war aims and operational objectives. But he still regards the clash of forces as the dominant means for the attainment of any purpose and treats any means to evade it suspiciously. Following the arguments of Chapter 1:

we can now see that in war many roads lead to success, and that they do not all involve the opponent's outright defeat. They range from *the destruction of the enemy's forces, the conquest of his territory, to a temporary occupation or invasion, to projects with an immediate political purpose, and finally to passively awaiting the enemy's attacks.*[250]

At the same time, this plurality does not extend to the military means: 'There is only one: *combat.* However many forms combat takes... it is inherent in the very concept of war.'[251] The 'destruction of the enemy forces is always the superior, more effective means, with which others cannot compete.'[252]

To conclude,

our discussion has shown that while in war many different roads can lead to the goal, to the attainment of the political object, fighting is the only possible means. Everything is governed by a supreme law, *the decision by force of arms...* A commander who prefers another strategy must first be sure that bis opponent... will not appeal to that supreme tribunal... If the political aims are small, the motives slight and tensions low, a prudent general may look for any way to avoid major crises and decisive actions... and finally reach a peaceful settlement. If his assumptions are sound and promise success, we are not entitled to criticize him. But he must never forget that he is moving on devious paths where the god of war may catch him unaware.[253]

The men of the nineteenth century, criticised for their tendentious interpretations, were therefore perfectly justified here in regarding Clausewitz's writings as the classic formulation of their belief in the dominance of the great battle. On this point, Clausewitz held essentially the same position throughout his life. Indeed, here too, it is in our time that Clausewitz's position has tended to be interpreted in terms that conveniently correspond to contemporary views of war. This endemic misinterpretation of Clausewitz's ideas has been mainly due to the failure to fully grasp the origins and nature of the transformation of his thought and particularly of the new intellectual forms in which this transformation was expressed.

What Were the Origins and Nature of Clausewitz's Dialectic?

It is hardly surprising that *On War*, ever since its publication, has had the reputation of being a very difficult and complicated, 'philosophical', work. You have probably been one of the many unsuspecting readers who have wished to read the treatise which, from the time of the German Wars of Unification and the rise to dominance of the German military school, has been considered the masterpiece of military theory. Readers have encountered in the first, signature chapter of the book a highly complex intellectual structure which scarcely reveals a 'common-sense' understanding of war. They read about 'absolute war' that is first defined in maximal and dramatic terms but is then overturned and assumes completely different expressions 'in reality' as an instrument of politics. They have been given no means of understanding the reason for and nature of this structure which is supported by equally puzzling arguments that explain why any limitation is alien to the nature of war and elaborate on the reasons for lulls in military activity and for its extension over substantial periods of time. Thus, since its appearance, *On War* has had a reputation for being much quoted but little read.

Ironically, as already noted, this situation only enhanced Clausewitz's reputation. The men of the nineteenth century emphasised most of the same points as Clausewitz in any case. The obscure reasoning of Books I and VIII added to Clausewitz's image of profundity, as it was regarded as demonstrating a 'philosophical' manner of expression that was only to be expected of a philosophical masterpiece on war. It was generally assumed that this manner of reasoning was somehow related to the highly influential German idealistic philosophy, famous, or infamous, for the difficulties in understanding it, and especially to Hegel. Shortly after the publication of *On War*, one critic, alluding precisely to this view, wrote:

The streams whose crystal floods pour over nuggets of pure gold do not flow in any flat and accessible river bed but in a narrow rocky valley surrounded by gigantic Ideas, and over its entrance the mighty Spirit stands guard like a cherub with his sword, turning back all who expect to be admitted at the usual price for a play of ideas.[254]

Camon conveyed the same impression, although from a point of view which was much less favourable than that of most of his contemporaries. In a much-quoted passage, he described Clausewitz as: 'The most German of Germans... In reading him one constantly has the feeling of being in a metaphysical fog.'[255] This was the closest one could get to admitting to having failed to understand what Clausewitz actually had in mind. Bernard Brodie, one of the chief contributors to the Clausewitz Renaissance of our times, dismissed Camon's comment with the words: 'This is simply nonsense.'[256] This remark is, however, an unfortunate reflection on Brodie's own 'high spirited' commentary to *On War*.

Indeed, Clausewitz's modern interpreters have been puzzled by his late intellectual formulations too. We now have the advantage of possessing a sequence of Clausewitz's early works which provide an almost continuous picture of the development of his thought from 1804 on. Equally helpful is the fact that Clausewitz did not live to finish the revision of *On War*, and that the book we possess is, therefore, a draft which provides a history of the work's development, almost linearly documenting the development of his thought, the problems he encountered, and his struggle to resolve them. Still, the objective difficulties of the subject and biased approaches to it have reinforced each other in obscuring the nature and development of Clausewitz's ideas. The 'Emperor's New Clothes' syndrome also played a role.

Interpretations of Chapter 1 of Book I, which constitute scarcely more than an attempt to paraphrase Clausewitz's own words, have reflected this chronic confusion. Aron, unlike other commentators, very well realised the 1827 break in, and subsequent transformation of, Clausewitz's thought. But, unfortunately, he also went astray in his attempt to place Clausewitz's formulations in Chapter 1 of Book I in some meaningful general context. According to Aron, Clausewitz first uses an 'abstract model' which exists only in 'the world of concepts and ideals', and then shows how this model operates in reality.[257] Now, firstly, Clausewitz never believed in a 'world of concepts and ideals'. But, apart from that, why did Clausewitz need this kind of 'abstract model' at all? According to Aron, Chapter 1 is simply the culmination of 'Clausewitz's system', which always first distinguished sharply between concepts by way of 'antithesis' and then examined their actual appearance in reality.[258] Following in Schering's footsteps, Aron thus interprets the whole of Clausewitz's thought on the basis of 'dialectic': between ends and means, moral and physical, defence, and attack, and even numbers and morale, boldness and caution, and ambition and risk.[259]

However, as we have seen, that the notion of fighting – the constitutive element of war – should be interpreted in expansive terms stems not from Clausewitz's 'logical method' but from his lifelong view of war and the correct way to conduct it, based on the dominating experience of his age. In his attempt to gain a coherent understanding of the mystery of Clausewitz's later formulations, Aron has created a myth of 'Clausewitz's lifelong method'. As an example of the 'system of antitheses' which is supposed to have characterized Clausewitz's writing throughout his life, Aron turns to the end of Book VI of *On War* (written in 1826–1827).[260] This is no coincidence – no earlier example exists. This should have been obvious. More importantly, if the dual nature of war was part of Clausewitz's lifelong 'method', why did it appear only from 1827 on, while never existing in all of Clausewitz's earlier writings on war over the decades? This argument does not add up. Although largely aware of the transformation of Clausewitz's military outlook, Aron failed to understand its source and exact nature. While he noted the late appearance of the concept of 'absolute war' and its close link to Clausewitz's late development, he sought to explain it by referring to an early 'method'. Instead of clarifying Clausewitz's late ideas, he obscured his earlier ones as well.

The readable Howard-Paret English translation of *On War* (relatively, compared to the German original) has added to the confusion. Like many others, Paret and Howard did not quite grasp the fundamental role of Clausewitz's notion of the 'concept of war', the centrepiece of his entire theory of war. They were therefore rather cavalier in their translation of the German *Begriff*, rendering it intermittently as 'concept', 'idea' and 'theory', or even omitting it altogether. This is why I reinstate 'concept' in all my quotations from *On War*. Now, 'idea' and 'theory' have contributed to the impression among English readers that Clausewitz believed in a 'world of ideas' and that 'theory' contrasted with 'practice'. The Howard-Paret translations of Clausewitz's *Abstraction* and *Wirklichkeit* (reality) (*On War*, I, 1, p. 6), or *wirkliche Welt* and *blosse Begriff* ('real world' and 'pure concept') (*On War*, I, 1, p. 8) as 'real world' and 'abstract world' are all similarly misleading. Clausewitz never speaks of an abstract world or a world of ideas. As he wrote (also cited by Paret himself): 'I recognize no pure spiritual thing apart from thoughts.'[261] His 'concept of war' meant the essence or nature of this phenomenon in *reality*, considered in and by itself before interacting with other forces of *reality*.

The fact that something was very wrong with Clausewitz's reasoning in Books VIII and I, and consequently also in the way it was usually interpreted, was finally noticed by philosopher W. B. Gallie. Clausewitz's interpreters, he wrote, mistakenly assumed that this structure was coherent and therefore struggled in vain to explain his intellectual structure. Not being a specialist on Clausewitz and unaware of the development of his ideas, Gallie himself failed to reveal the historical and intellectual origins of Clausewitz's problematic formulations. Yet Gallie at last exposed the fact that had confounded Clausewitz's interpreters: Clausewitz's enigmatic formulations, he maintained, were the result of an unreconcilable tension between his definition of war itself and his notion that war was a political means.[262]

A full understanding of the theoretical formulations that have created so much confusion can only be achieved by comprehending the interaction between the theoretical crisis in which Clausewitz found himself in 1827 and the intellectual devices that his cultural environment offered him at that same time. The preservation of the core of his old concept of the nature of war and its conduct within his new understanding of the diversity of wars under the influence of politics, despite their contradictory nature, was made possible, and even perceived by Clausewitz as an achievement, by borrowing from the most ambitious intellectual attempt at an all-encompassing and integrative explanation of all the contrasts and contradictions of reality. This was the German idealistic philosophy which was elevated by Hegel at precisely that time to its zenith of influence, and whose influence on Clausewitz has always been the subject of wonder and speculation.

As pointed out by Paret, Clausewitz was not a professional philosopher but a typical educated representative of his period who absorbed attitudes and scraps of ideas from his cultural environment.[263] It should be added to this, however, that unlike any typically educated person of his period, Clausewitz was motivated by the desire to devise a comprehensive view of war throughout his life, and naturally he was highly sensitive to anything in his cultural environment which could have had a bearing on the realisation of this aim. This kind of involvement and interest partly explains the fact that Clausewitz drew mainly on what had already been considered classic literature: Machiavelli, Montesquieu, Goethe, Schiller, and other great figures of German *Klassizismus*, Kant, and so on. By contrast, Fichte's or Schelling's idealism was a radical trend in the first decade of the nineteenth century, albeit of wide-ranging repute. In a letter to his fiancée on 15 April 1808, Clausewitz refers to one of Fichte's political works: 'he has a manner of reasoning that pleases me very much, and I felt that all my tendency to speculative reasoning was awakened and stimulated again.'[264] Later, following Fichte's article on Machiavelli, Clausewitz wrote directly to the famous philosopher. However, there is no sign that he was substantially influenced by Fichte's philosophy or dialectic. On the contrary, while sharing Fichte's patriotic sentiments and emphases on moral forces and creativity, Clausewitz, as noted by Paret, was clearly a 'realist' and rejected purely spiritual entities, any form of 'mysticism', and teleological conceptions of history.[265] In short, he shared no affinity with idealistic metaphysics. He aimed at a realistic military theory, firmly grounded in both historical experience and the nature of war.

Furthermore, a fact that has somehow been lost sight of must again be stressed: in all of Clausewitz's extensive writings until the last stage of his life, there are no theses and antitheses, no polarity, and no dialectic (unless of course one reads them into ordinary reasoning and simple contrasts and reciprocal relations). Nor do they appear in the early or unrevised books of *On War*, which continue Clausewitz's lifelong train of thought. However, in 1827 Clausewitz's lifelong concept of war and the correct way to conduct it which flows from this concept fell into crisis, while the reputation of idealistic philosophy had reached its pinnacle – and their paths crossed. It became clear to Clausewitz that there was a serious discrepancy between his conception of the universal nature of war and the majority of historical experience. While regarding both as indispensable, he was forced to reject one of them. Fortunately, in the same years in Berlin, Clausewitz's city of residence, Hegel's idealism was reaching a climax of influence, unequalled in Germany since the days of Kant. And one of the chief lessons of this philosophy was that all the contrasts and contradictions of reality were but differing aspects of a single unity. In this, the integrative ideal of all phenomena inherent in German philosophy of the late eighteenth and early twentieth centuries reached a zenith. Thus, Clausewitz was not compelled to resolve the contradiction created in his mind by abandoning either his lifelong concept of the nature of war or his new understanding of the plurality of wars in history under the influence of politics – both of which he regarded as essential. On the contrary, resolving this contradiction, while retaining its two components by viewing them from a higher standpoint, was now perceived as an achievement and an indication that his theory of war was on the right track.

So then, was Clausewitz a disciple of Hegel, and if so, how was he influenced? This question has been the cause of much speculation ever since the publication of *On War*, and has been repeatedly expressed by as different and remote commentators as the above-cited Prussian military critic of 1832 and Lenin.[266] The first systematic attempt to address it was made in 1911 by Lieutenant-Colonel Paul Creuzinger in his *Hegel's Influence on Clausewitz*.[267] If we are to believe Creuzinger, there is not a single idea in *On War*, from tactical conceptions to strategical outlook, that is not shaped by Hegel's influence. Creuzinger knew that in all probability Clausewitz could not have been influenced by Hegel before the 1820s, since prior to then Hegel had been relatively unknown. But as Creuzinger was only familiar with *On War*, he was unaware of the fact that most of the ideas that he attributed to Hegel's influence had already been outlined by Clausewitz in his earlier works decades before.

Unfortunately, Creuzinger's work placed the whole argument on a totally misleading course. In reaction to Creuzinger, Schering laboured to show that Clausewitz's supposed dialectic was not exactly similar to Hegel's.[268] Paret followed in Schering's footsteps, adding that Clausewitz's dialectic could have been influenced by many others apart from Hegel.[269] And so did Aron, who went to great lengths to show that Clausewitz's conceptions had no affinity to Hegel's metaphysics.[270]

What, then, do we know about Clausewitz's affinity to Hegel? In contrast to Fichte's case, Hegel is not named in Clausewitz's writings. Yet this does not mean much. In Clausewitz's letters to Marie, the main source for his biography, there is a large gap in the 1820s when the couple lived together in Berlin – and these were precisely the years when Hegel served as rector of the University of Berlin and his reputation achieved unprecedented heights. Indeed, we do possess contemporary evidence, revealed by Paret, which almost certainly proves that Clausewitz was acquainted with Hegel in the salons of Berlin.[271]

As for the influence of Hegel's ideas, we do not know whether or how much Clausewitz read Hegel or indeed understood him, or, alternatively, whether he absorbed some of Hegel's ideas from the intellectual environment in Berlin. However, all that we do know of Clausewitz's intellectual interests and involvement makes it highly improbable that the philosophy which achieved such widespread influence failed to attract his attention. And, above all, we have the new and highly distinctive intellectual patterns in his late work to support this. True, this work reveals no affinity to Hegel's metaphysics, idealism, or conception of history. But it does reveal what appears to be a direct influence of Hegel's political and social ideas.[272] Furthermore, it reveals a new and vigorous use of dialectical tools, along with a much stronger comprehensive and integrative ideal. The question as to whether this new dialectic was exactly like Hegel's, or the argument that from his youth Clausewitz had come in contact with the dialectics of Fichte, Schleiermacher, and perhaps Schelling, misses the point. Clausewitz adapted scraps of ideas to his needs, and his distinctive use of dialectical tools together with a new forceful emphasis on a fully integrative nature of theory only made an appearance in the later stages of his work, during the period in which Hegel's influence surged to a peak.

The integrative quest of the time is most typically revealed in Clausewitz's 'Comment' during his early attempt to write a treatise on war in 1816–1818. In this 'Comment' he betrays a certain lack of confidence that his work, intelligent as it might be, lacks the real internal unifying logic to be the desired 'theory of war'. 'Perhaps a greater mind', he wrote, 'will soon appear to replace these individual nuggets with a single whole cast of solid metal, free from all impurity.'[273] In this respect the transition from Book VI, 'Defence', to Book VII, 'The Attack' marked a turning-point. First, there was the relationship between defence and attack, which had already appeared in Clausewitz's booklet of instruction for the crown prince (1812) and developed in Book VI (see chap. 6 below). Elaborating on this subject further, Clausewitz appears to have arrived at the conclusion that this relationship could perhaps be given a tighter theoretical expression. Precisely then, at the end of Book VI, the problem of the two types of war and the discrepancy between the nature of war and historical experience was added. Both issues now invited the employment of a new and highly acclaimed intellectual device: dialectic reconciliation.

In Book VII, 'The Attack', Clausewitz's attraction to this new device is still only alluded to, but unmistakably so. The book opens with a chapter on the relationship between attack and defence:

Where two concepts [Begriffe] form true logical contrasts [Gegensätze], each complementary to the other, then fundamentally each is implied in the other. The limitation of our mind may not allow us to comprehend both simultaneously, and to discover by contrast the totality [Totalität] of one in the totality of the other. Nevertheless each will shed enough reciprocal light to clarify many of the details. [For the problems of the Howard-Paret translation here see in the note][274]

This distinctive formulation, until then unprecedented in Clausewitz's writings, strikingly shows that the dialectical reasoning which had become dominant in his intellectual environment by the mid-1820s was beginning to influence his own thought decisively. While apart from this opening statement Clausewitz scarcely employed dialectic in Book VII, he used it with increasing skill and in a highly significant role in Book VIII and in the revision of Book I.

In the pivotal chapter 'War Is an Instrument of Policy', Clausewitz finally resolves the contradiction in his mind between war as an all-out use of force and the varying degrees of limited war revealed in historical experience without relinquishing either of these ideas. War as a political and multi-faceted phenomenon is the unity that fuses the pure nature of war, which constitutes merely a partial understanding of reality, with the political conditions and requirements:

Up to now, we have considered the difference that distinguishes the nature of war [*Natur des Krieges*] from every other human interest, individual or social... We have examined this incompatibility from various angles so that none of its conflicting elements should be missed. Now we must seek out the unity into which these contradictory elements combine in real life, which they do by partly neutralizing one another... Being incomplete and self-contradictory it [war] cannot follow its own laws, but has to be treated as a part of some other whole; the name of which is politics [*Politik*] Thus the contradictions in which war involves... man, are resolved... Only if war is looked at in this way does its unity reappear; only then can we see that all wars are things of the same nature.[275]

Thus, the unity of the phenomenon of war, that is, the constitutive element common to all wars, is salvaged. The 'primordial violence, hatred, and enmity' of the nature of war are directed by the 'commander's creative spirit' through the 'play of chance and probability' to achieve the political aim. This is the 'wonderous trinity' which is presented by Clausewitz at the end of the revised Chapter 1 of Book I, and which makes war 'more than a true chameleon that slightly adapts its characteristics to the given case.'[276]

Indeed, in the opening chapters of the revised Book I, Clausewitz's dialectic reaches its peak, and his conception of the nature of war finds its place in the actual diversity of war which previously threatened to invalidate it. Clausewitz did not become an idealist, nor did he believe in a 'world of concepts and ideals'. He considered the concept of absolute war as an analysis of the *real* forces which in his view comprise the nature of war. It was possible for him to maintain this fundamental concept of war by claiming that this nature never existed in isolation, but always interacted with the other forces and influences of reality, chiefly politics, which modified and harnessed its original tendencies. A new intellectual tool assisted him in devising what he regarded as an adequate solution to the crisis into which his universal theory of war had fallen in 1827.

Youri Cormier has recently provided additional valuable textual evidence of traces of Hegel's vocabulary in *On War*. This includes Hegel's signature concept of 'Aufhebung', whose verb form 'aufheben' Clausewitz used a few times in a sense similar to Hegel's (but occasionally also in other senses): that of sublating contradictions in a higher synthesis.[277] Cormier is on a far less solid ground when analysing the *reasons* for Clausewitz's borrowing from Hegel's dialectic. He is well-aware that Clausewitz was above all a military man, whose focus was military affairs and military theory, and who adopted and adapted scraps of ideas from his intellectual environment to the extent that he believed they could serve his purpose. And yet, Cormier wholly ignores the development of Clausewitz's military ideas; does not notice the kernel of his entire theory of war arising from its 'lasting spirit', 'nature' or 'concept': his emphasis on all-out war and the decisive battle; and fails to recognise the crisis into which it fell in 1827. Rather than Clausewitz seeking out external help to overcome the crisis that his military theory had encountered and on which he left eloquent textual evidence, we are to believe that the military thinker's motivation for turning his life work upside down was a sudden fashionable philosophical ambition to cloth his theory of war in the mantel of Hegel's dialectic.

Indeed, readers of Clausewitz, unaware of his tortuous intellectual about-face, have not understood what his curious intellectual structure was for. We naturally posit a spectrum of wars, from the most total to the most limited. But it remained a mystery why he conceptualised 'absolute war' as distinct from, and opposed to, a variably limited 'real wars'. The default interpretation for most readers and commentators has been to attribute this reverentially to Clausewitz's profound 'philosophical' manner of theorising.

How Shall We Know Which
Interpretation Is the Right One?

Readers may query why I take such a determined, categorical stance in my explanation of Clausewitz's actual views and development. Do we not have legitimate differences of inter- pretation here, natural in such a difficult case, as we have with many classical and, indeed, non-classical, texts?

The main alternative interpretation, which most commentators have traditionally held, seems to go as follows. From the start, Clausewitz approached writing *On War* with a dialectical method and view of war. He laid it out at the beginning of Book I, and, in the following books all the way to Book VIII, developed one side of the dialectic, emphasising the clash of forces and the decisive battle – a kind of intellectual exercise which he never meant as a practical imperative. Then, in Book VIII, he picked up the other side of the dialectic which he had laid out in Book I – the supremacy of politics and the political aim – and closed the circle. No crisis, break, or transformation in his thought, and nothing unusual, let alone problematic, except for an apparently sophisticated 'philosophical' edifice. So that you do not think that this is a strawman, consider, for example, that it is essentially the view held by Clausewitz's main biographer and co-translator into English, Peter Paret. By this view, everything falls into place, and we are assured that there is nothing to be concerned about in what we have already presumed to be a 'masterpiece' by the 'great philosopher of war'.

I shall now explain why this traditional interpretation, already leaving readers bemused when they only had *On War* and very few external materials to go by, is so utterly implausible, if not practically impossible. First, there is no dialectic in Clausewitz's work until 1827, including the original unrevised Book I of *On War*. If this is disputed, despite everything we have seen, then there can be no doubt regarding what Clausewitz's theory of war was all about ever since his earlier writings in 1804 and each of his subsequent works. This was his concept of the nature of war, its 'lasting spirit', as all-out fighting aiming at the complete overthrow of the enemy in a decisive battle. He passionately preached the practical implications for the conduct of war he believed flowed from this concept for his country, as for all other countries, in all times. And he was highly indignant about the blindness of all those who failed to understand this supposedly supreme truth. It is remarkable how the centrepiece of his theory of war – indeed, his concept of war consisted of little else – has been lost by modern readers. Again, this failure can only be explained by the fact that the *On War* that we have has bemused commentators so much that, quite apart from being swayed by the political and strategic predilections of our times, they have been deeply unsure where they could tread confidently.

The same applies to Clausewitz's passionate advocacy of the pursuit of great political goals, which was the natural complement to his concept of the nature of war. Paret (but not Aron) could only deceive himself about this by misinterpreting Clausewitz's two political objectives in his Note of 1804, both of which belonged to all-out war. Furthermore, he has failed to see that nothing regarding the legitimacy of limited war under the influence of politics, or, furthermore, regarding the influence of politics itself, appeared in Clausewitz's writings after 1804 and until deep into the composition of *On War*.

Indeed, lastly, there is the well-documented path of Clausewitz's development ever since his concept of the nature of war and its conduct as an all-out effort to destroy the enemy in battle came in his own mind under increasing strain. Thus, recall that in his 1817 essay on stagnation in the activity of war, the influence of politics does not yet appear at all. It is introduced for the first time in the old Chapter 1 of Book I, but primarily as an 'obstacle' for war realising its true nature. Then there is the Undated Note, misdated by some commentators (including in the Howard-Paret English translation) to 1830, but, as I have shown, clearly written before the Note of July 1827.[278] There is no mention there of the influence of politics on war and its conduct either – no mention of politics at all. Indeed, is it possible that in 1830 Clausewitz would have neglected to mention the idea he considered the most important in his work, compiling instead a pitiful list of features as a proof of the feasibility of a theory of war? Only in the Note of July 1827 does this idea make its appearance as the solution to Clausewitz's 'problem' and the basis for his planned revision of his entire work. Rather than as an 'obstacle', he now posits politics as the very rationale regulating the conduct of war and legitimising limited war.

Shortly after writing this note, in December 1827, in two letters to his acquaintance general staff officer Major von Roeder, this theme takes centre stage. Roeder sought Clausewitz's opinion on two operational problems set by the Chief of the Prussian General Staff Lieutenant-General von Müffling relating to a war with Austria. Clausewitz took this opportunity to unload on Roeder the fullness of his new ideas on which he had laboured during the previous months, including traces of his familiar travails. He replied that the scenario presented in the exercise lacks any description of the political objectives of the two sides, and that in the absence of this guiding information no military plans could be drawn up in the abstract. Here is the select essence from these long letters:

War is not an independent phenomenon, but the continuation of politics by different means. Consequently, the main lines of every major strategic plan are political in nature, and their political character increases the more the plan encompasses the entire war and the entire state. The plan for the war results directly from the political conditions of the two belligerent states, as well as from their relations to other powers... According to this point of view, there can be no question of a purely military evaluation of a great strategic issue, nor of a purely military scheme to solve it. That it is essential to see the matter in this way, that the point of view is almost self-evident if we only keep the history of war in mind, scarcely needs proof. Nevertheless, it has not yet been fully accepted, as is shown by the fact that people still like to separate the purely military elements of a major strategic plan from its political aspects and treat the latter as if they were somehow extraneous. *War is nothing but the continuation of political efforts by other means.* In my view all of strategy rests on this idea... It is this principle that makes the entire history of war comprehensible, which in its absence remains full of the greatest absurdities.[279]

It is one thing to intend to *crush* my opponent if I have the means to do so, to make him *defenceless* and force him to accept my peace terms. It is obviously something different to be content with gaining some advantage by conquering a strip of land, occupying a fortress, etc., which I can retain or use in negotiations when the fighting stops. The exceptional circumstances in which Bonaparte and France found themselves since the Wars of the Revolution, allowed him to achieve major victories on almost every occasion, and people began to assume that the plans and actions *created* by those circumstances were *universal norms*. But such a view would summarily reject all of the earlier history of war, which is absurd... Suppose we find that out of fifty wars forty-nine have been of the second kind – that is, wars with limited objectives, not directed at the total defeat of the enemy – then we would have to believe that these limitations reside in the nature of war itself, instead of being in every case brought about by wrong ideas, lack of energy, or whatever... Instead, we must recognize that war is a political act that is not wholly autonomous; a true political instrument that does not function on its own but is controlled by something else, by the hand of policy... I have no need to prove that wars exist in which the objective is even more circumscribed – a bare threat, armed negotiations, or in the case of alliances, the mere pretext of action [by one of the allies]. It would be unreasonable to maintain that such wars are beneath the art of war. As soon as we concede that logically some wars may not call for extreme goals, the utter destruction of the enemy, we must expand the art of war to include all gradations of military means by which policy can be advanced. War in its relation to policy has above all the obligation and the right to prevent policy from making demands *that are contrary to the nature of war*, to save it from misusing the military instrument from a failure to understand what it can and cannot do.'[280]

All of this is flawless, provided that one keeps in mind that 'the point of view [which] is almost self-evident', which 'scarcely needs proof', even though it 'has not yet been fully accepted' is the one Clausewitz recognized only a few months earlier, after a lifetime of a most passionate insistence on the imperative of all-out war; indeed, that it was *above all he, more than anybody else,* who had assumed that 'the exceptional circumstances in which Bonaparte and France found themselves since the Wars of the Revolution... [and] the plans and actions *created* by those circumstances were *universal norms.'* (Emphases in the original.)

Except for scholarly quibbling, why is all this important for our understanding of *On War*? Supposing that Clausewitz finally saw truth and that this truth remains his contribution to posterity, why should his intellectual journey matter to us? One obsessive commentator has written that he does not understand my 'obsession' with Clausewitz's early development.[281] The answer to this query is that without a full comprehension of where Clausewitz came from, over what 'problem' he agonised during his last years, and of the 'solution' he came up with, it is impossible to understand not only the enigmatic structure of his arguments in *On War*, but also, as a result, what he actually stood for. Indeed, this involves the very questions which, throughout the ages, have baffled readers of Clausewitz and which confounded commentators have been divided over.

Most notably, did Clausewitz put the premium on the clash of forces and the decisive battle as the centre of war, or was this just an intellectual exercise never meant to have practical implications for the actual conduct of war? It was because of such ambivalence that the Howard-Paret translation rendered the German *Gefecht* by the feeble English 'Engagement'. This is not an illegitimate option lexically, for *Gefecht* has no one-to-one

English equivalent. But in practice, this translation was chosen as a cautious refraining from the natural meaning: clash of forces, battle or combat. In view of the intrinsic uncertainty, the 'vegetarian' option was chosen, as it sat more comfortably with the current Western attitude towards war. Paret clearly veered towards a completely wrong interpretation of this core of Clausewitz's theory of war. As he writes: 'Clausewitz's supposed preference for the major, decisive battle, in particular, is an erroneous assumption, based on the very inability to follow his dialectic that he had predicted.'[282] Clausewitz, of course, did not mention dialectic or anything to that effect when expressing apprehension that his work would be misunderstood, indeed, he did not mention dialectic anywhere. Clausewitz's apprehensive comment in the wrongly dated Undated Note, during the time of his great crisis, has all too often been regarded by commentators as a blank check for everything they wished to attribute to his work.

Similarly, it is impossible to understand Clausewitz's dismissive views of the manoeuvre, surprise, and cunning without a proper understanding of his fundamental concept of the nature of war and its conduct as a most direct clash of forces. Lastly, as we shall see in the following chapter, the same applies to Clausewitz's view of defence and attack. Without a clear understanding of Clausewitz's concept of war, and the 'problem' he encountered with it and tried to resolve, one is simply wandering in the dark, trying to make sense of each tree without a full comprehension of the forest.

Because of the Emperor's New Clothes syndrome, the reality of Clausewitz's ultimate 'synthesis' in *On War*, which set the political objective *against* the true nature of war, has not been recognised for what it is. Rather than a profound 'philosophical' edifice, whose actual purpose has remained somewhat of a mystery, it was Clausewitz's 'solution' to a 'problem' of his own making. It was a patchwork on top of the contradiction that had emerged between his old and new ideas, which by using 'dialectical reconciliation' could be regarded as an achievement rather than a fatal flaw. Clausewitz tied himself in some very strange knots, which paradoxically only contributed to his reputation, leaving perplexed readers absorbed in a mixture of incomprehension and awe.

Was Clausewitz a Pioneer in Elucidating the Relationship between Politics and War?

Perhaps all the above is still no more than a matter of antiquarian interest, unimportant for the understanding of Clausewitz's true theoretical contribution, his supposedly pioneering elucidation of the crucial relationship between politics and war.

So first, the notion of the relationship between politics and war, and, more specifically, that war was an instrument of state policy that served its objectives, was quite commonplace practically everywhere in classical tracts from the early civilisations onward. 'Realists' such as Thucydides in classical Greece, Sun Tzu in Warring States China, or Kautilya in ancient India treated this relationship as a matter of course. Even moralists such as Cicero, who advocated peace, especially at home, and insisted on justice both *ad bellum* and *in bello*, wrote that 'Policy bids you increase your wealth... advance your borders, to rule over as many as possible...'[283] His provisos, as well, show a firm conception of the political motives of war: '...those wars which have the glory of rule as their object are to be waged with less bitterness... Wars were waged with the Celtiberi... for actual existence, not for rule; with the Latin, Sabines Semnites, Carthaginians, and with Pyrrhus the struggle was for rule.'[284]

Turning to the early modern period in Europe, there is again little need to dwell on Machiavelli's 'realist' view of war as an instrument of politics and state policy. The same applied to other Renaissance scholars in the age of rising centralised states. Justus Lipsius was exceptionally influential throughout Europe in the late sixteenth and early seventeenth centuries. Inter alia, he influenced the most celebrated military theorist of the seventeenth century, Raimondo Montecuccoli. Now almost forgotten, Montecuccoli was universally admired during the eighteenth century, including, most deeply, by Scharnhorst, and, like Machiavelli, he was cited by Clausewitz.[285] In Lipsius's *Six Books of Politics* (1589), Montecuccoli found a comprehensive and systematic presentation of war within a political framework, derived from political motives and directed towards political aims. Book I of Montecuccoli's *Treatise on War* is an extensive study of the nature and political context of war, based on Books 5–6 of the *Six Books of Politics*. Montecuccoli divides wars into internal and external and elaborates on their causes under the headings of either remote or immediate. He describes the political preparations for war, particularly the forming of alliances, as well as the preparations of military means, divided into provisions, arms, and money. His Book II is devoted to the conduct of war, while the final Book III deals with the conclusion of war and the attainment of a favourable peace, which is the purpose of the war.[286]

For the military thinkers of the Enlightenment in the eighteenth century, this was all obvious. Furthermore, influenced by Montesquieu, as Clausewitz would be, they sought out the deeper connections between war and military institutions, on the one hand, and the broad array of political, social, and economic conditions, on the other. Thus, Guibert opened his highly influential *A General Essay on Tactics* (1772), with a 'A Review of Modern Politics'. He wrote:

Politics is naturally divided into two parts, interior and exterior politics. The first is the basis for the second. All which belongs to the happiness and strength of a people springs from their sources, laws, manners, customs, prejudice, national spirit, justice, police, population, agriculture, trade, revenues of the nation, expenses of government, duties [and] application of their produce.[287]

No less universally read in languages throughout Europe, the first volume of Lloyd's *The History of the Late War in Germany between the King of Prussia and the Empress of Germany and her Allies* (1766) opened with an extensive theoretical and programmatic introduction. It emphasised the significance of the 'political law' in determining the face of war. Furthermore, in the late 1760s, Lloyd wrote a substantial manuscript, 'Essai philosophique sur les gouvernements', which he apparently intended to expand into a larger work 'on the different governments established among mankind.'[288] In his 'Reflections on the Principles of the Art of War' also known as 'Political and Military Memoirs' (which was added to the second edition of his *History*, 1781), Lloyd returned to the same subject in a chapter entitled the 'Connection between the Different Species of Government and Military Operations', explicitly relying on Montesquieu.[289]

Finally, in Clausewitz's own time, Jomini incorporated two chapters, 'The Relation of Diplomacy to War' and 'Military Policy', in his *Summary of the Art of War* (1837). The former 'included those considerations from which a statesman concludes whether a war is proper, opportune, or indispensable, and determines the various operations necessary to attain the object of the war.'[290] A typology of aims in war follows (rights, economic interests, balance of power, ideology, territories, and mania for conquest), together with a classification of the various types of wars. The second chapter, 'Military Policy', 'embraces the political considerations relating to the operation of armies... the passions of the people to be fought, their military system, their immediate means and reserves, their financial resources, the attachment they bear to their government or their institutions... finally, the resources and obstacles of every kind likely to be met.'[291]

Reading this, a recent commentator has been convinced that Jomini's treatment of the relationship between politics and war in his *Summary of the Art of War* (1837) was prompted by the publication of *On War* in 1832–1835 and is evidence of Clausewitz's influence.[292] He has failed to notice that, as I showed in my 1989 book, Jomini's chapters in this regard had actually appeared for the first time in an early version of the *Summary*, the *Tableau analytique des principales combinaisons de la guerre, et de leur rapports avec la politique des états* (Analytical Table of the Main Combinations of War, *and their Relationship to State Policy*; my emphasis), published in 1830. They appeared before the publication of *On War* and, indeed, before Jomini ever heard of that obscure Prussian general, Clausewitz. Moreover, Jomini first outlined the theoretical framework he would develop in 1830 regarding the deep connections between politics and war in the third edition of his celebrated and hugely influential *Treatise on Grand Military Operation* (1818). At the end of his concluding chapter of principles, Jomini wrote:

It is not necessary to remind our readers that we have here merely treated of those principles which relate... to the purely military part of the art of war; other combinations no less important... pertain more to the government of empires than the commanding of armies. To succeed in great enterprises it is... necessary... to take into consideration the resources... internal condition... the relative situation of their neighbors... the passions of the people... their peculiar institutions and the strength of their attachment to them... In a word, it is absolutely necessary to know that science which consists of a mixture of politics, administration and war, the basis of which has been so well laid by Montesquieu.[293]

Leaving military theorists aside for a moment, can any historian seriously hold that in the wars of the early modern period, famously dominated by the declared principle of *raison d'état*, people were unaware that war was an instrument of states and of state policy which dominated their conduct? Or, indeed, that during the era of the limited 'cabinet' wars of the eighteenth century, rulers did not carefully calibrate their military efforts to their political aims? Such a proposition is so absurd as to merit little further discussion.

But if so, how do we explain the fact that Clausewitz has gained 'ownership' of this subject? Paradoxically – another paradox – this has been so precisely because he started by passionately reacting *against* the eighteenth century's standard of limited cabinet wars. He realised, rather late in the day, that politics and war were not happily tuned to advance hand in hand towards the utmost, but that politics, dominating war, actually regulated, and often limited, its scope and scale. But, indeed, this was a U-turn against his own, central and most passionately held, lifelong ideas, the alpha and the omega of his theory of war.

Moreover, the age of the French Revolution and Napoleon in which Clausewitz lived ushered in the unlimited wars of nations, followed, during the era of the world wars, by industrial age 'total war'. All-out war became the standard during the nineteenth century and first half of the twentieth century, irrespective of Clausewitz, even if, for the people of this period, his name was stamped on it, and for a very good reason. However, when the United States and the West had to rediscover limited war in the nuclear age and after the Korean War, Clausewitz's latter-day U-turn against his own vehement thrashing of this concept could again be cited as a classical source. It served the West's own U-turn away from a century-and-a-half-old, deeply ingrained, doctrine and practice of all-out war; away from the almost universally held view that crushing the enemy was not only a military imperative, but, moreover, that it was also essential for, inseparable from, and even tantamount to, the attainment of the political end of the war, which, therefore, should not interfere with it. From Moltke's dispute with Bismarck in 1871, to the generals' disdain and disregard for their governments in all countries during World War I, to MacArthur versus Truman in Korea, this was the point the generals stressed. MacArthur merely expressed the standard view of the age of all-out and total war: 'In war there is no substitute for victory.' Thus, Clausewitz's U-turn with respect to the limitation of war under the influence of political considerations at the beginning of the era of all-out war anticipated that of the West at the end of that era. Both he and the people of the post-1945 era had to return to, and rehabilitate, ideas which had been quite commonplace in the wisdom of the ages before 1800. It was in this context that the Clausewitz Renaissance of our time began, with the new works on limited war, governed by political considerations, published from the mid-1950s onward, such as Robert Osgood's *Limited War: The Challenge to American Strategy* (1957), and Bernard Brodie's *Strategy in the Missile Age* (1959). In the process, the fire-eating Clausewitz has given way to a mild version of him in the current interpretations of his obscurely understood work.

6

Yes, Clausewitz's View of Defence and Attack Is a Key to His Theory of War

And He Was *Wrong* About Them, as Have Been His Interpreters

As with most of Clausewitz's ideas, commentaries on his views of the relationship between defence and attack have been influenced by the military perspectives and doctrines of the day. The men of the nineteenth century – the heyday of the idea of the war of annihilation – were often dissatisfied with Clausewitz's position that the defence was stronger than the attack. By contrast, in today's West – politically and militarily cautious, seeking to maintain the status quo and promoting the 'moderate' aspects of Clausewitz's teaching – this position has been accepted more sympathetically. Clausewitz's wisdom has often been contrasted with his successors' mania for the attack, particularly with that of the French on the eve of World War I. In this happy framework, however, most commentators have failed to note that Clausewitz's view of attack and defence, and of the relationship between them, contains some less convenient and convincing arguments. Again, it appears that Clausewitz simply could not be wrong. Most significantly, and in line with what we have already seen, the close connection between Clausewitz's intellectual constructs in this regard and his fundamental concept of the nature of war and the correct way to conduct it – the core of his theory of war – has been missed entirely. Although one recent commentator has claimed that Clausewitz's view of defence and attack is the key to his entire theory,[294] this view has been treated out of context, leaving the gate locked.

Defence Has a Negative Purpose
Therefore, It Must Be Only a Temporary Expedient

So, in what way are Clausewitz's ideas on defence and attack grounded in his overall concept of war and its conduct? From his earliest writings, his so-called notes on strategy of 1804, the twenty-four-year-old Clausewitz forcefully presents his argument that the 'lasting spirit' or 'nature' of war consists in the boldest action possible and the mobilisation of all available resources to achieve the greatest aim attainable in the quickest and most decisive manner. Defence thus raises a difficult problem which he immediately needs to confront. 'The aim of defence', he writes, 'is to preserve the status quo and to gain time'; strictly speaking, both 'contradict the spirit of the art of war.'[295] This is why defence is only allowed when one is not strong enough to take the preferred option, that is, attack, and why even under these circumstances the defence must be conducted as offensively as possible. Mere defence is not fighting.[296]

Clausewitz became truly interested in a defensive war only during a very special period of time when he passionately preached a national insurrection of his defeated and humiliated country against Napoleon. This meant a fundamentally defensive war against a superior enemy. The problem of why the defence existed at all, as it did not involve the holding of the initiative and a relentless direct action to destroy the enemy, now moved centre-stage. In Clausewitz's mind, there could only be one answer to this supposed riddle. As he wrote in 1810–1811: 'No doubt, the defensive must have its own advantages, for otherwise the defensive would not exist; everyone would proceed offensively. Hence, whatever one has said about the superiority of the offensive, there must be some qualities of the defensive to keep it in the balance.'[297] This conceptual equilibrium is further developed in his detailed call for a national war to break the French yoke, written in 1812:

'Since it always has been the weaker who traditionally assumed the role of the defender, doesn't one have to conclude that with regard to the effectiveness of the armed forces, the defensive form is stronger than the offensive?'[298] And again, in the same year, in Clausewitz's booklet of instruction for the Prussian Crown Prince: '... it should be observed that the strategic defensive, though it is stronger than the offensive, should serve only to win the first important successes.'[299]

Thus, the internal logic of Clausewitz's concept of war as relentless aggressive fighting to destroy the enemy gave rise to this carefully balanced intellectual equation, and indeed, largely predetermined his arguments and conclusions. In *On War* Clausewitz writes: 'Defence has a negative [*negativ*] purpose: *preservation*; and attack a positive one: *conquest.*'[300] In this formula, which he already put forward in 1804, Clausewitz points to the fundamental distinction between defence and attack, rooted in their relation to the status quo. However, far from being limited to this formal distinction, his usage of 'negative' and 'positive' also carries a clearly prescriptive significance. Probably to avert this conclusion, the Howard-Paret translation chose 'passive' rather than 'negative', as the German clearly is. As Clausewitz writes: 'If defence... has a negative object, it follows that it should be used only so long as weakness compels and be abandoned as soon as we are strong enough to pursue a positive object... It would therefore contradict the very concept [*Begriff*] of war to regard defence as its final purpose.'[301] Waiting and parrying are the characteristic features of defence. 'Pure defence, however, would be completely contrary to the concept [*Begriff*] of war, since it would mean that only one side was waging it.'[302] Thus, pure defence is not viable 'even when the only point of war is to maintain the status quo.'[303]

Strictly speaking, Clausewitz is right about this, for, as he points out, the defender fights back, responds to blows with blows of his own, which are in this sense offensive actions: 'our bullets take the offensive'.[304] However, Clausewitz's argument does not stop here. He insists that only if the defender turns to the attack or at least threatens to do so, can the war be brought to an end.[305] Thus, the 'transition to the counterattack must be accepted as a tendency inherent in defence – indeed as one of its essential features... [this] flashing sword of vengeance – is the greatest moment for the defence.'[306]

While these ringing lines warmed the hearts of the men of the late nineteenth and early twentieth century, modern commentators have silently passed over the full scope and meaning of Clausewitz's theoretical imperative, only mentioning the widely accepted point that defence should always remain active. Raymond Aron has been the exception in critically analysing Clausewitz's argument. Willisen, Clausewitz's contemporary and a disciple of Jomini, already wrote in criticism of Clausewitz that if defence 'intends something else it must become offensive, and thus cease to be what it is.'[307] Aron makes a similar point. Fully sharing the West's defensive, status quo-oriented political posture of Containment during the Cold War, Aron was openly dissatisfied with Clausewitz's definitions and reasoning. He writes: 'Whoever repulses the enemy and keeps what the enemy wanted to take, imposes his will on him.' Why then should he 'give himself another goal'? Why must the defender go over to the attack? Why cannot the defence be the final aim in war?[308]

Indeed, it was in relation to this point that Clausewitz became increasingly concerned. He addressed it in his 1817 essay 'On Progress and Stagnation [*Stillstand* – standstill] in Military Activity', and ultimately fell into the crisis revealed at the end of Book VI, which led to the transformation announced in July 1827. As we have seen, in the last chapters of Book VI, he found it necessary to allow the concept of 'defence which does not seek decision' into his theory of war. Not only was the existence of such a defence vindicated by history, but its validity was also implied by Clausewitz himself. The defender, by mere endurance, may frustrate the attacker's efforts, compel him to withdraw from the war, and thus maintain the status quo.[309] Indeed, this was one of Clausewitz's own arguments in claiming that the defence is stronger than the attack.

Is Defence Intrinsically and Universally Stronger Than the Attack?

Thus, Clausewitz eventually retreated from his earlier view that the defender ultimately *had to* switch to the attack, which now brings us to the other side of his equation. To repeat: having formulated his military outlook in 1804, establishing aggressive conduct as the natural and desirable form of war, flowing from its 'lasting spirit' or 'concept', Clausewitz needed an intellectual counterbalance if defence was to make any sense at all. This was introduced in 1812 and fully developed in *On War*, with the idea that 'the defensive form of warfare is intrinsically stronger than the offensive.'[310] The chronological order in which the two ideas appeared is therefore not accidental, and the understanding of Clausewitz's intellectual problem is essential. As he writes: 'If attack were the stronger form, there would be no case for using the defensive, since its purpose is only negative [*negativ*]. No one would want to do anything but attack; defence would be pointless.'[311] As we shall see, this logic is patently invalid. And yet, all the rest of Clausewitz's arguments are intended to support, and are subordinate to, his logical premise.

His reasoning in all this is, to say the least, unsystematic. At the opening of Book VI Clausewitz puts forward three general arguments for the superior power of defence. He then proceeds to assess the advantages of defence separately in the spheres of tactics and strategy. His first general argument is that, in principle, 'preservation is easier than taking' [*Erhalten ist leichter als gewinnen*], or in another version, 'it is natural that the greater object is bought by greater sacrifice.'[312] Now, like many impressionistic dicta that claim to express universal truths, the argument here appears self-evident only at first sight. Once the psychologically appealing relationship is questioned, one can cite many cases where the opposite is true. One might equally suggest that taking is easier than preserving and that the greater object is not necessarily bought by greater sacrifice. Either way, such concepts and metaphors only impose on and obscure reality.

Clausewitz's second general argument will be discussed later. The third, which, he writes, 'arises solely from the nature of war, derives from the advantage of position, which tends to favour the defence.'[313] This advantage, combined with the factor of terrain, is the only one that appears in all of Clausewitz's separate discussions on the superior strength of defence. It was clearly one of the most decisive arguments reinforcing his conviction in this regard. It probably sounds convincing to many readers to this day. However, surprising as this may appear, the effect of position and terrain is, so to speak, contingent rather than immanent in war. This can be demonstrated, for example, by sea warfare, about which Clausewitz should have known, not to mention air or space warfare. Moreover, with nuclear weapons, for example, defence is almost impossible, and a nuclear attack can be effectively prevented only by deterrence, that is, by the threat of a similar, practically unstoppable, attack. Let the argument be clear: the point is not that Clausewitz failed to anticipate nuclear weapons; it is that he confused some historically prominent, yet contingent, factors of land warfare with what flows – can be deduced – from the 'nature of war' itself.

Peter Paret argues that the criticism often levelled at Clausewitz for being totally continental-minded is fundamentally misplaced, because his theoretical framework was concerned with the phenomenon of war in itself, abstracted from any particular type of warfare. It thus applied to all types of warfare, whether or not discussed specifically.[314] While there is much truth in this argument, it does not hold here. Clausewitz derived and conceptualised the factors of position and terrain from certain features of land warfare. But as sea warfare, for example, should have suggested to him, this factor is by no means a 'necessary part' of the concept of war 'in itself', or, for that matter, of the concept of defence.

Historically, it is true that, chiefly by hindering movement and providing cover from detection, carefully chosen ground features have indeed tended to benefit the defence on land, both at the operational and tactical levels. Moreover, with the introduction of firearms, the importance of ground features and prepared positions in providing shelter increased far more than before. People still sometimes repeat the World War I trench warfare formula that for the attacker to succeed, he needs to have a 3 to 1 numerical advantage over the defender. Yet, this is just a shibboleth, contradicted whenever initiative, mobility and surprise have the upper hand. Indeed, there is a reason why a well-known maxim proclaims that 'offence is the best defence'. Do not misunderstand me: I do not think this maxim is necessarily or universally true either; only that differing circumstances alter the balance between defence and attack. Moreover, if the effect of features such as terrain and prepared positions in land warfare changes over time and does not 'arise solely from the nature of war', or 'from experience' – Clausewitz's criteria for establishing a universal theory of war – then nothing guarantees that defence 'will always be certain of having the benefit of terrain', as Clausewitz claims to know.[315] There are logical and imaginative failures here on Clausewitz's part.

Terrain is only one factor in two separate 'laundry lists' of factors, one for tactics and the other for strategy, which, according to Clausewitz, are those most responsible for success in these domains and which he examines in their relation to defence and attack. The other factors he names are somewhat different in strategy and tactics. Furthermore, in both lists he recognises that the effect of most of the factors varies, working to the advantage of the defence to some degree, but to some degree also benefiting the attack. Still, in both lists, he concludes that the balance with respect to each individual factor, as well as the final balance, tilts in favour of the defence. Given the theoretical premise he wants to validate, this is suspicious. Clausewitz advances lopsided arguments and biased judgements, because without the assumption that defence is stronger than the attack, he cannot understand why anyone would ever choose it.

In tactics, for instance, Clausewitz writes that 'only three things seem to us to produce decisive advantages: surprise, the benefit of terrain and concentric attack... the attacker is favoured by only a small part of the first and third factors while their larger part, and the second factor exclusively, are available to the defender.'[316] The argument concerning the significance of concentric attack and that it mainly favours the defender is certainly unusual, but let us concentrate on the interesting case of surprise. According to Clausewitz, 'the one advantage the attacker possesses is that he is free to launch a surprise attack [Überfall] at any point along a whole line of defence, and in full force; the defender, on the other hand, is able to surprise his opponent constantly, throughout the battle [Gefecht], by the strength and direction of his counterattacks.'[317]

This is curious. First, as Willisen noted shortly after the publication of On War, the defender appears to get credit for the virtues of his attacks. Moreover, being in possession of the initiative, the attacker is usually not regarded as inferior to the defender in his ability to surprise. Quite the opposite. Indeed, Clausewitz himself writes that 'in strategy as well as in tactics, the defender enjoys the advantages of terrain, while the attacker has the advantage of surprise attack [Überfall].'[318] If this is the case, then should not initiative and surprise, which also promise superior concentration of force, be regarded as an advantage of the attack, counterbalancing the advantage accorded to defence by terrain and prepared positions?

Given Clausewitz's theoretical starting point, this is an argument he must repulse. We have already seen that Clausewitz belittles the significance of surprise in Book III of *On War*.[319] Now, in Book VI, he writes: strategic surprise attack 'has often brought the whole war to an end at a stroke. On the other hand, the use of this device assumes major, decisive and exceptional mistakes on the enemy's part. Consequently, it will not do much to tip the scales in favour of attack.'[320] Some might argue that Clausewitz has been validated by twentieth-century experience, when major, highly successful strategic surprises – Barbarossa, Pearl Harbor – still ended in defeats in the wars for the attackers. However, without going into the particular circumstances and intervening variables in each case, the point is that, as Clausewitz saw very well, strategic surprise, such as that which Israel achieved in the Six-Day War of June 1967, has in fact 'often brought the whole war to an end at a stroke.' His problem was that he could not leave it at that.

The whole of Clausewitz's reasoning is characterised by a similar tendency to validate his theoretical premise, biasing both his choice of factors and the way in which each of them is interpreted. What are, for example, 'the diminishing force of the attack' and 'the culminating point of attack' if not the giving of universal form to certain genuine, yet (as Clausewitz would otherwise have it) one-sided, impressions that Clausewitz derived primarily from his experience in the landmark Russian campaign of 1812.[321] Present-day commentators often repeat these metaphors as an expression of important insights. But for a more balanced picture, could one not offer, for example, a concept such as 'the breaking point of defence', after which we know empirically that the defeated suffers most of his losses? As for 'the diminishing force of the attack', it undoubtedly occurs in many cases – Clausewitz was deeply impressed by the fact that in 1812: 'Half a million men crossed the Nieman; only 120,000 fought at Borodino, and still fewer reached Moscow.'[322] The remaining French troops were stretched across and defending Napoleon's long lines of communication. However, at the same time note that Clausewitz himself argued that the attack 'increases one's own capacity to wage war' by *expanding* one's resources, whereas the defence 'does not'.[323]

So which is it? Does the strength of the attack diminish over time, or does it increase with the expansion of the resources at its disposal, which at the same time might be lost to the defender? And more broadly, is the defence stronger than the attack on each dimension and in all cases – *intrinsically* and *universally* stronger than the attack – the argument that Clausewitz strives to establish?

This is where we reach the crux of the matter. It is here that Clausewitz's fundamental mistake lies, and it does no credit to his logic. He failed to realise not only that one might choose a defensive political posture – preferring the status quo – even when one is as strong as or stronger than the adversary; but, more importantly, he also failed to comprehend that for one to choose defence – at any level, and in any particular case – it is sufficient that the defence offers advantages in *that specific case*. The defence does not have to be intrinsically and universally stronger than the attack. In some cases, under specific circumstances, the defence possesses greater advantages, while in other cases and under other circumstances, offensive action might offer greater advantages – even for the weaker side. For example, the advantages promised by terrain and fortified positions in land warfare might support a decision to opt for the defence. On the other hand, in other cases, the advantages derived from the use of initiative, mobility and surprise might serve as a force multiplier for the attacker. This is so despite the often much greater logistical problems the attacker needs to overcome – a factor, 'supply', which Clausewitz mentions here only in passing.[324] In Chapter 4 we saw that, to the puzzlement of many, he excluded logistics from the theory of war, as it does not pertain directly to the activity of fighting itself.[325] Logistics is similarly underrepresented in his discussion of attack and defence.

Clausewitz's misguided attempt to establish the superior strength of defence as *intrinsic* and *universal* was a direct product of his erroneous view that, given the inherent desirability of the attack, no one would have chosen the defence *unless* it had the advantage of being stronger than the attack. In his typical biting style, he wrote that a failure to recognise this 'proves how ideas can be confused by superficial writers.'[326] However, it was he who confusedly failed to see that the answer to the question of which form of war was stronger is circumstantial, rather than general, depending on the actual conditions in each case. His assorted, hotch-potch, lists of factors, piled over one another, and changing between tactics and strategy, yet all leaning in one direction, testify to this. Indeed, because of his fundamental view that the nature/concept of war dictates relentless effort to crush the enemy, he again tied himself in some strange knots. It is in this sense, linked to his fundamental theory of war, that Clausewitz's conceptualisation of defence and attack indeed serves as a key to understanding it.

I suspect that many readers might be weary of so much abstract reasoning at this stage, so here are a few concrete historical examples. For other works of mine, I have done extensive research on pre-state warfare, during our prehistorical past. It turns out that the most common and most effective method of fighting then was the night raid on a sleeping camp or dwellings of the other tribe, which often resulted in wholesale massacre. Thus, initiative and surprise were the keys to success in pre-state warfare, which made the offensive that much more effective and the defence so helpless and disadvantageous. Lest it be thought that for whatever reason prehistory is irrelevant, note that the same applies to any case where conditions favour pre-emptive or first-strike action.

The following is another example, regarding a different aspect, that of grand strategy. During the Second Punic War, both sides, Rome and Carthage, were most vulnerable at home and on the defence. The reason for this was that the power of both derived from their imperial domains of subject satellite peoples that provided troops and resources. In both the Roman imperial domain in Italy and that of Carthage in North Africa and Spain, many of these satellite peoples were eager to break free. A successful invader thus threatened the very foundations of the other side's power. For this reason, both Rome and Carthage sought to conduct the war in the other's territory. Hannibal succeeded in being the first to invade, and his crushing battlefield victories in Italy, again holding the initiative and using cunning and surprise, indeed led to a defection of many of Rome's subject 'allies' and put Rome in its greatest danger ever. His final defeat only came when Rome was eventually able to turn the tables and invade, first Spain and later North Africa, triggering a massive defection of Carthage's subject peoples.

Do we really need to go on with this and cite the numerous historical examples in which taking the initiative and the employment of mobility and surprise gave the advantage to the attacker, at either the tactical or strategic levels, or both, and sometimes even when he was the weaker side – indeed, made 'offence the best defence'? We have already mentioned nuclear strategy, in which offensive capabilities reign supreme, whereas the defence is practically helpless. I shall not belabour the point any further.

In a different part of his mind, Clausewitz was more aware of the circumstantial – rather than intrinsic and universal – rationale behind the choice of either defence or attack. Consider this example of Clausewitz's keen and sweeping historical analyses, in which, in quite a substantial aside, he in fact provides a penetrating description of the alternating relationship between defence and attack. His study of two centuries of military history – from the Thirty Years' War and the War of the Spanish Succession through the Seven Years' War to the Wars of the Revolution and Empire – reveals that this relationship has been continuously overturned by new developments in a periodically changing art of war. Without going into Clausewitz's account, very interesting in itself, the bottom lines are as follows. At the beginning of this period, 'an army's deployment and disposition... normally worked to the advantage of the defender... this advantage was lost, and for a time the attack gained the upper hand... [Then] the defender... recovered a distinct advantage which lasted until... the offensive gained the upper hand for the third time, and once again the defensive had to change its methods.'[327]

This is clearly an entirely different picture of the relationship between defence and attack, one that is circumstantial and alternating. Indeed, what we can again see here is the inherent tension in Clausewitz's mind between his dominating universalistic mindset and his strong historicist notions. Not only did his logic concerning what arose from the nature of war with respect to defence and attack fail him; but so did the test of historical experience, which he regarded as the second source of theory. Trying to contain the implications of his historical account, Clausewitz writes that 'defence appears to fall into disrepute whenever a particular style of it has become obsolescent.'[328] But the same can surely be argued about attack. In this spiralling development, which state in the relationship between defence and attack is to be regarded as the fundamental one? In each period, or, indeed, set of circumstances, many changing factors – some more enduring than others – shape the face of war and determine the relationship between defence and attack.

With this relationship having gone through several alternations during the past two centuries – mostly technologically induced – scholars in the fields of international relations and security, having become more relativist in their approach, now tend to view the balance between defence and attack in more circumstantial and historical terms. They tend to see it more as subject to the development of weapons systems and counter-systems than to purely abstract reasoning. Nonetheless, with the partial exception of Aron, Clausewitz's conceptualisation in this regard – a misguided derivative from his fundamental concept of the nature of war – has retained the general awe surrounding everything associated with him.

Only one of Clausewitz's arguments in favour of the defence can be regarded as truly general in form. He already raised it at the beginning of Book VI, but, as we have seen, he emphasised it more forcefully toward the end of this book, as he became increasingly aware of the defender's ability to bring the attacker to withdraw from the war by sheer endurance. The defender, he wrote, 'reaps where he did not sow... In daily life, and especially in litigation... it is summed up by the Latin proverb *beati sunt possidentes* [blessed are the possessors].'[329] 'The negative aim, which lies at the heart of pure resistance, is also the natural formula for outlasting the enemy, for wearing him down.' It is enough for the defender to counterbalance the attacker's force; 'in the end his political object will not seem worth the efforts it costs. He must then renounce his policy.'[330] Rather than the claim that defence is in general stronger than attack, this means that in the case of an equality of strength and a draw, the defender *ipso facto* still achieves his objective, as the status quo remains unchanged. Here, the advantage of defence derives, so to speak, from the concept of defence itself.

7

What Is Right, What Is Wrong, and What Is Useful for Us in *On War*?

Clausewitz as a Chameleon and Holy Trinities

This book deals with a deep, multi-layered dissonance which readers of Clausewitz have encountered over the decades and generations. Like all dissonances, this is very difficult to overcome. Its first layer is the inability of readers since the publication of *On War* to decipher what exactly the author meant. Only in the light shed by the continuous line of his earlier writings from 1804 on, mostly unpublished manuscripts that have gradually become available, is the source of the difficulty understood: late in the composition of *On War*, when its first six books were already in clean copy in preparation for the press, Clausewitz changed his mind on the most crucial point of his life-long theory of war. Throughout his life, in his writings on theory as well as in his positions in practice regarding his country's fateful struggle against Napoleon, he preached the imperative of all-out war, centring on the clash of forces and the great battle, which he insisted was grounded in the 'lasting spirit', 'nature', or 'concept' of war. Only in 1827, did he come to realize – in stark contrast to the very core of his ideas – that limited war and the avoidance of battle were legitimate options under many circumstances. He explained this largely by the influence of politics that, while leaving the 'nature of war' unchanged, subordinated it to its objectives. Thus, the conflict that the unsuspecting and confused reader finds in *On War* between Clausewitz's old and new ideas is not the result of a sophisticated and profound 'philosophical' dialectic which is difficult for lesser mortals to comprehend. Rather, it is a forced, idiosyncratic 'solution' that Clausewitz devised to a problem of his own making in a book whose author changed his mind on nothing less than the fundamentals of his theory of war and its conduct while writing it.

This intrinsic difficulty of comprehension that readers have experienced ever since *On War* was first published has naturally given rise to a range of reactions. First, there is Clausewitz as a chameleon (again borrowing a phrase from his own struggle to find an enduring element in the constantly changing face of war).[331] People of each subsequent age could find in *On War* the Clausewitz who suited their own views on war and the activity of fighting. Clausewitz thus became a man for all seasons. Between 1870 and 1914, during the heyday of the newly hegemonic Prussian-German military school, he was celebrated mainly for his insistence on the clash of forces and the decisive battle and his emphasis on moral forces. After 1945, in the nuclear age, his reputation reached a second pinnacle for his later acceptance of the primacy of politics and the concept of limited war.

Another reaction to the puzzle of *On War* has been the Emperor's New Clothes syndrome. Once people have been reassured of the sublime wisdom of the author and the book, and as successive generations celebrated the 'masterpiece' as an undisputed 'classic', the only legitimate reaction to the puzzle of what *On War* actually meant has been one of admiring awe. Recurring dissenting voices, expressing bewilderment at what on earth was going on in the book, have been dismissed, and even pitied, as expressions of narrow-mindedness. After all, 'if everybody agrees' on the status of the 'masterpiece', who are we to take issue with this verdict? Clausewitz has been set in stone and could not be wrong. Clausewitz the 'absolute' has been substituted for the real one.

I have sought to demonstrate that the evidence offered by Clausewitz's texts from 1804 onward, the clear paper trail that has gradually come to light, cannot conceivably be regarded as open to 'legitimate differences of interpretation'. Still, I assume that many will dispute this claim, as well as my general arguments regarding Clausewitz's work and significance. Only, please do not quote Clausewitz's much abused disclaimer in his Note of July 1827 for this purpose: 'If an early death should terminate my work, what I have written so far would, of course, only deserve to be called a shapeless mass of ideas. Being liable to endless misinterpretation it would be the target of much half-baked criticism'.[332] Too many have cavalierly cited the second sentence of this quote against any dissenting view regarding Clausewitz's supposed greatness. But the two sentences belong together and were written in the same specific context. Clausewitz wrote them in 1827, at the point when he discovered that the centrepiece of his lifelong theory of war and of the first six books of *On War* which he had already written – the imperative of all-out war and the decisive battle, grounded in the 'lasting spirit', 'nature', or 'concept' of war – was untenable; and that it necessitated a radical revision guided by his new ideas regarding the supremacy of politics and the legitimacy of limited war. It is hardly surprising that at this turning point in his entire work, he realized that in case of 'an early death' what he had 'written so far would, of course, only deserve to be called a shapeless mass of ideas.' And his concern at this crucial moment was only natural, as his old ideas no longer represented his transformed views – even if, in a characteristic style, he transferred the blame for potential misunderstandings onto future critics rather than attributing them to his own radical change of mind.

The plot thickens. The other, Undated Note, which Clausewitz left regarding the state of his work was erroneously dated to 1830, supposedly just before his death. The Clausewitz scholar Hans Rothfels, following a mistaken assumption by Clausewitz's wife, established this view a century ago, with Howard and

Paret even taking the liberty of formally presenting it as such in their English translation of *On War*. (Werner Hahlweg was the exception in suggesting that the Undated Note was written in 1827.) As I showed, the Undated Note could not possibly have belonged to that late date, but rather was written *before* the Note of July 1827, when Clausewitz realized the crisis in his theory of war but did not yet find the 'solution' he would later adopt.[333] Is there any wonder that at this lowest point in his work, his Undated Note was so thoroughly melancholic? As this note was wrongly dated to the end of his life, it was believed that Clausewitz left the world and his work in the same incomplete state that it had been in 1827, and that his fears of misunderstanding critics remained. Now, misunderstanding critics is a natural concern for all authors, including Clausewitz, both before and after publication. That aside, the state of Clausewitz's work before his death was not at all unfinished as it had been in 1827. On the contrary, by 1830 he had completed the writing of Books VII and VIII and went back to revise Book I, fully developing his new ideas and new 'synthesis', as he had planned in 1827. As his wife writes, just before his death he was optimistic about completing the book within a few months.[334] Commentators have been quite happy to accept my dating of the Undated Note to before the Note of 1827, rather than to the end of Clausewitz's life, because this indeed meant that the *On War* that we have is a much more finished book, at least in the eyes of its author, than it was used to be believed. Supposedly, the value of the 'masterpiece' is thereby enhanced. Yet, if so, Clausewitz's fear of misunderstanding of his work must not be cited out of the context it was made in 1827 and as a blank cheque.

Finally, given the dating of the Undated Note to early 1827 or slightly earlier, Clausewitz's statement: 'The first chapter on Book One alone I regard as finished'[335] should not be seen as expressing his view at the end of his life, as it has been widely assumed. An all too natural coincidence has led scholars astray. The Undated Note reflects the deep crisis in Clausewitz's life work and his search for a solution. Now, the old Chapter 1 of Book I, by virtue of its strategic position at the opening of *On War*, comprised what he regarded as the kernel of his ideas and, indeed, already contained the influence of politics, albeit as an obstacle to war realising its true nature, rather than as the rationale guiding its conduct. At this low point, he evidently sensed that this chapter held the key to the impending necessary revision of his theory of war. Four years later, he had already developed his new ideas and new 'synthesis' in Book VIII and the revised Book I, and expressed his optimism regarding the completion of *On War* within a few months. At this point in time, he certainly did not regard his work 'as nothing but a collection of materials from which a theory of war was to have been distilled', with only Chapter 1 on Book I being the exception.

Having demystified Clausewitz, it is now necessary to clarify what he was right about, what he was wrong about, and, indeed, what in his ideas can still be useful to us – so as not to leave the reader without a reconstructed view of the subject. While the picture suggested here is much less impressive, more chequered, and more ambivalent than the canonized version, it aims to re-establish the real Clausewitz more accurately.

The Good

The relationship between politics and war, which Clausewitz developed in his final years, is rightly regarded as a very important insight, both theoretically and practically. The reason why this insight is important is that we have two quite different notions of what victory means. The first and most intuitive one is that victory means the defeat of the enemy's armed forces, the crushing of his ability to fight. This is the notion that Clausewitz preached zealously throughout his life, up until 1827. The second, much less intuitive notion people have is that victory means the attainment of the political objectives of the war. This has often and widely been regarded, including by Clausewitz prior to 1827, as inseparable from the first. However, as Clausewitz ultimately came to realize, the two were not inseparable, and, one should add, are sometimes conflicting. Liddell Hart further elaborated on this point a century after Clausewitz. In addition, post-1827 Clausewitz saw that the political objectives permeated the conduct of war itself: the scale, scope, and aims of military operations.

It is worth pointing out, because this point is often lost, that Clausewitz understood very well that the relationship between the political objectives and military means – as with all ends and means – is a two-way street: the ends direct the choice of means, but the means chosen must be available and adequate for the attainment of the required objectives. If they are not, this might mean that the political end itself requires revision. It is indeed on this latter point that Chief of Staff Moltke based his much-cited objection to Bismarck's 'interference' in the conduct of the siege of Paris in 1871, citing Clausewitz's letter to Roeder regarding the staff exercise put forward by Chief of Staff Müffling. As Clausewitz wrote: 'War in its relation to policy has above all the obligation and the right to prevent policy from making demands *that are contrary to the nature of war*, to save it from misusing the military instrument from a failure to understand what it can and cannot do.'[336] Who was 'right' on that particular occasion between Bismarck and Moltke is not our concern here. But the idea that the military means chosen must be available and adequate if the required political objectives are to be attained necessitates a two-directional process in the harmonization of means and ends. That the two are *mutually*-affecting is embedded in the very logic of the end-means relationship.

Along this line, Hew Strachan has recently corrected a common misconception. It concerns the supposed falsification of Clausewitz's meaning by the Prussian militaristic tradition from the second German edition of *On War* (1853), ostensibly put right in Hahlweg's editions from 1952 on. As Strachan writes:

The first edition contained significant corruptions and misprints which were subsequently corrected. What irked Howard and Paret was the second edition's handling of the discussion in book 8, chapter 6 of the role of the commander in the decisions of the cabinet. Howard and Paret insisted that the wording of the first edition reflected Clausewitz's true intentions, which were to enable the cabinet to take a part in the commander's decisions, not to enable the commander to take an active part in the cabinet's.... However, it is important to remind ourselves (as the Howard and Paret edition did not) that the cabinet of which Clausewitz was speaking was not the equivalent of a modern cabinet in a democratic state, but the private office of the king.... Clausewitz saw the workings of a cabinet as too often weakening the conduct of war, not strengthening it... In book 8 he goes out of his way to address the need for policy to be shaped by what is militarily possible, recognising the danger that would arise if the statesman asked war to achieve something of which it was not capable... Howard wanted Clausewitz to be addressing the civil-military relationships of liberal democracies in the late twentieth century, when in fact he was confronting those of a weak monarch who still believed in absolutism.[337]

Except for this point, all the above regarding Clausewitz's emphasis on the relationship between politics and war is pretty much in line with the prevailing view of the enduring significance of his important insight. This, however, is provided that the following is realised: First, Clausewitz did not pioneer this insight. It had been commonplace in all civilisations from ancient times on, including, most notably, in both theory and practice, in early modern Europe, whose *modus operandi* was *raison d'état* and limited 'cabinet' wars. Second, Clausewitz's 'rediscovery' of the strategic implications of the relationship between politics and war was a U-turn against his own life-long, passionately preached theory of war, modelled on Napoleonic warfare, and his out-and-out rejection of eighteenth-century limited war. Moreover, the 'rediscovery' of limited war in the West after 1945, which sparked the Clausewitz renaissance, took place against the backdrop of a century and a half, from Napoleon on, during which all-out and total war were the norm, in both theory and practice. Third and finally, Clausewitz's distinction in this context between 'absolute' and 'real' war should be recognized for what it was: a makeshift intellectual construct which he devised in order to reconcile his old and new ideas, rather than a mark of 'philosophical' genius to be treated with awe.

Other valuable ideas from Clausewitz are also quite familiar and are significant both at the intellectual level and for the education of soldiers. His emphasis on the element of danger that permeates war and on the paramount significance of the moral (in line with the Reformers' attempt to reform the Frederician military system with respect to troops' motivation) is worthwhile even if it is quite obvious. Somewhat related and of greater significance, was Clausewitz's emphasis on the intrinsic uncertainty surrounding war and military operations. Because of war's conflictual nature, this uncertainty, 'twilight', 'fog of war' and resulting 'friction' (this term may have been overused) go far beyond the usual problems of predictability. On the practical side, such recognitions informed the nimble and highly effective *Auftragstaktik*, 'mission-oriented tactics', adopted by the Prussian-German military school and more recently embraced by other militaries. It places the emphasis on commanders of all ranks taking the initiative in the field, using their own judgement on the spot in response to ever-changing circumstances, without waiting for orders and approval from above. At the same time, it needs to be added that important as this insight is, the balance between pre-planning and central command, on the one hand, and independent action by subordinates in the field, on the other, varies with the times, inter alia under the influence of technology. Note that 'mission-oriented tactics' became a compelling precept when armies began to spread out widely across vast theatres of operations, out of sight of the commanding general, from the nineteenth century on. Also, consider, for example, the differences in command and control between land and air warfare, though the former may also be changing as the electronic revolution is making the battlefield more transparent.

This brings us to Clausewitz's historicism – an important step forward, ambivalent as it was. In line with the new climate of ideas, he stressed the diversity of historical experience and the changing character of war across the epochs. At the same time, he continuously agonised over the question of what room this left for a universal theory of war. Until 1827, his view regarding the 'lasting spirit', 'nature', or 'concept' of war and its conduct, modelled on Napoleon – the 'god of war' – had the upper hand. Thereafter, his recognition of the diversity and legitimacy of other historical forms of war prevailed.

Clausewitz insisted, following Scharnhorst, that students in military institutions should focus on a few select historical cases, instead of broad, superficial, brushstroke surveys of the past. This was another important consequence of the historicist and romantic emphasis on the richness of historical situations and the right method of penetrating them. The key concept here was and remains *Einfühlung*, rendered into English as 'empathy'. This means delving into the details of a historical situation and the thought processes of the people involved in a way that brings the event back to life in the mind of the students through the faculty of imagination and allows them to actively participate in the decision-making in a form of indirect experience. This is a major idea of enduring value.

At the same time, Clausewitz's total dismissal of the notion of abstract principles of war – learned in his youth from Kant and Kiesewetter and faithfully kept throughout his life – was probably exaggerated. As Jomini was to complain, Clausewitz's own imperatives for action, supposedly derived from the 'nature' or 'concept' of war, were not very different from the 'principles' he had disavowed. Indeed, the 'principles of war' have returned in a more abstract form, formulated since the beginning of the twentieth century by various militaries with slight differences in names and emphases. Assorted and partly conflicting principles, such as 'the objective', 'concentration of force', 'economy of force', 'initiative', 'surprise', 'cunning', and 'security', have been described by some with slight mockery as 'flashes of the self-evident'. Still, as a pedagogic tool and a guide for action, they have their value, which largely explains why they are still around. Abstraction, as well as concreteness, are tools that the human mind employs to cope with a complex reality.

The Bad

Having already discussed Clausewitz's failings at length, we shall keep this summary as succinct as possible. His universalization of Napoleonic warfare as an expression of the 'lasting spirit', 'nature' or 'concept' of war, centring on all-out – indeed, 'total' – war and a relentless action to crush the enemy in a major battle, dictated every element of his theory of war and its conduct. Much of this remained unchanged even after his historicist acceptance of the legitimate diversity of wars in history took over. A significant part of what remained was misguided and wrong.

Thus, Clausewitz defined strategy as 'use of the battle/clash of forces [Gefecht] for the purpose of the war.'[338] As Liddell Hart and others have commented, that definition placed the clash of forces alone as the sole means for the proper conduct of war. As we have seen, this was no accident, for this was indeed the centrepiece of Clausewitz's entire theory of war, forged under the overwhelming impression of Napoleon's crushing victories over the armies of the *ancien régime*, including Clausewitz's Prussia. Indeed, it is precisely for this reason that he consistently belittled the significance of such central pillars of warfare as the manoeuvre, surprise, and cunning (all placed on the list of the 'Principles of War' of most militaries). He was determined that they must not distract attention from the imperative of advancing as directly and as energetically as possible to the battle. His view went contra to the all-too-familiar precept, most notably developed in the field of theory by Sun Tzu and Liddell Hart, and, ironically, in large part, also practiced by Napoleon: that success in war entailed the prior psychological and physical dislocation and undermining of the enemy by the crafty use of manoeuvre, surprise, and cunning. Commentators have been practically oblivious to Clausewitz's position on all these and the logic underlying it. But, once recognized, can any student or practitioner of war accept this lop-sided view of war and its conduct?

The same reasoning and the same explanation apply to Clausewitz's skewed, and badly misconstrued, conception of defence and attack and the relationship between them. He cornered himself into the view that the defence *must* be the stronger form of war – universally, under all circumstances. Otherwise, given his fundamental view of the nature of war as active, relentless action to destroy the enemy, he could not understand why and when the defence should be used at all. It did not occur to him that the defence might be a legitimate aim in itself, for example, as a country's grand strategy; or that it might hold the advantage and be used opportunistically under *some* circumstances, while under other circumstances the same might be true for offensive action; that the question of which form of warfare was stronger depended on the particular conditions in every specific case. This was a major instance of faulty logic on his part.

Finally, another limitation of Clausewitz's historicism should be noted. Commentators have occasionally and forgivingly remarked that much (indeed, the bulk) of *On War* deals with the details and features of armies and war that are wholly time-bound and outdated. Clausewitz, seeking to bring out the 'lasting spirit', 'nature', or 'concept' of war while recognising the great diversity of the past, simply did not realize the huge potential for a transformation of armed forces and war, of the sort, for example, that was soon to kick in with the Industrial Revolution and the ensuing consecutive and rapid technological transformations in war. The failure here was not merely one of imagination – the change was practically impossible to predict; again, it was more a failure in the rigorous application of logic as to what was truly 'intrinsic' and 'unchanging' in the 'nature' of war. Indeed, as Clausewitz repeatedly asked himself, was there such an 'intrinsic' element, a basis for an 'enduring' theory of war?

Before coming to this question in our Conclusion, there is yet another aspect of the reverence for Clausewitz that merits attention.

The Funny

As everything that Clausewitz wrote has been elevated to a quasi-sacred status, this includes not only his failings and mistakes but also other ideas and pronouncements that have attracted praise as profound truths. And what is more befitting for such a reverential discussion than what Clausewitz called the 'wonderous trinity' of war? As he wrote at the end of Chapter 1 of Book I, revised just before his death:

As a total phenomenon its dominant tendencies always make war a wonderous [*wunderliche*] trinity – composed of primordial violence, hatred, and enmity, which are to be regarded as a blind natural force; of the play of chance and probability with which the creative spirit is free to roam; and of its element of subordination, as an instrument of policy, which makes it subject to reason alone.

The first of these aspects mainly concerns the people; the second the commander and his army; the third the government. The passions that are to be kindled in war must already be inherent in the people; the scope which the play of courage and talent will enjoy in the realm of probability and chance depends on the particular character of the commander and the army; but the political aims are the business of the government alone.[339]

Well, at best, the 'trinity' is a vivid simile of almost poetic attraction, acceptable within an early nineteenth-century frame of mind. But is there much justification for the recent fuss around it? And I do not mean the (justified) criticisms levelled at the 'trinity': that the wars that are most current in today's world, those taking place in the less developed parts of the world, are 'non-trinitian'; meaning that in them local and private forces are often the main actors, states barely exist, and no neat separation between the three elements of the 'trinity', or between the attributes that Clausewitz ascribed to each of them, prevail.[340] Indeed, rather than a novelty of a 'postmodern' age, many *premodern* wars were like that, having taken place in conditions not unsimilar to those prevailing between and within today's less developed countries. Furthermore, during the vast majority of the hundreds of thousands of years of prehistory of our species, *Homo sapiens*, states and regular armies did not exist at all. They only came into being in the last millennia or centuries, depending on the region of the globe. Still, bloody tribal warfare, far bloodier than under statehood, was rife.[341]

All this aside and returning to Clausewitz's formula, did he himself, the military man, not defy his own government on Prussia's 'political aims' repeatedly in 1812–1813? Indeed, he departed for Russia to fight Napoleon in 1812, helping negotiate the change of sides by the Prussian corps in the *Grande Armée*, and participated in igniting an uprising in East Prussia against the retreating French in 1813, thereby practically forcing his monarch into the war? More fundamentally, are we really to take the stark separation between the 'passions of the people' and the 'intelligence of the state' seriously? Or are we to regard 'primordial violence, hatred, and enmity' as 'a blind natural force', independent of the antagonistic objectives of the societies engaged in the conflict? This idealistic conceptual frame and paternalistic view of the state in relation to the people was almost certainly influenced by Hegel's view of the state as personified intelligence in his renowned and highly influential *The Philosophy of Right* (1821).[342] Yet, two centuries later, poetical wonderous trinities are better left to theology.

8

Conclusion: The Nature of War — and the Persistent Nature of Myths

What Is a Classic, and Is There a Theory of War?

At the heart of this book lies a paradox: the book argues that Clausewitz has attracted massively inflated attention and admiration, because of misconceptions regarding what he actually meant and the ensuing Emperor's New Clothes syndrome; and still this book adds yet another to the stock. The only excuse for doing this is to pop the bubble, end the mystification surrounding Clausewitz the absolute, and establish a true understanding of the real Clausewitz and the exact messages of *On War*. Indeed, I argue that the stream of books purporting to explain Clausewitz to the uninitiated mainly cloud readers' understanding, adding more obscurity to the obscure.

I have few illusions that this book will be the one to end all books. By their nature, myths are very difficult to dispel, and the trend has been too powerful and wide-ranging for it to collapse in one go. People within a trend are generally much more aware of past mistakes and biases than they are able to recognize the current ones. Things are already neatly set in people's minds, and scepticism with respect to such a sweeping rejection of the prevailing picture that 'everyone agrees on' is only natural. Present-day scholars are heavily invested, in more than one way, in the Clausewitz they have construed. And the situation with respect to military schools is even more problematic: they need clear content to teach in dense, practical, programmes of education, rather than a complex broken picture. The complaint, by one heretical observer, on the current atmosphere in American institutions of military education more or less applies worldwide. He encountered there a 'Clausewitz that was the answer to all questions', with his work regarded as 'a sacred text', enjoying 'the status of holy writ and the mantle of uncritical acceptance of self-evident truths.' He viewed this all-pervasive attitude as amounting to 'a fawning sycophancy'.[343] I believe the terms herd mentality and the Emperor's New Clothes syndrome are more appropriate.

In reading Clausewitz, one is advised not to be overly impressed by his typical, very incisive, and often dismissive pronouncements and verdicts on issues and fellow military thinkers. These pronouncements and verdicts were undoubtedly authentic, for he was an authentic man who passionately believed in what he believed – including, indeed, his belief in his intellectual superiority and special calling in the field of military theory. Clausewitz was not necessarily right, indeed, he was often only partly right or entirely wrong. Remember that until 1827 his deep sense of calling centred on crowning the imperative of all-out war and the decisive battle as the cornerstone of military theory and practice. And yet, his scathing rhetoric completely changed direction after 1827, reversing the signs 'superficial', 'absurd', 'obvious', 'self-evident' which 'scarcely needs proof', but 'not yet fully accepted', on the very ideas he himself had held and passionately advocated throughout his life and up until only shortly before. Indeed, the 'people [who] began to assume that the plans and actions *created* by those circumstances [of Napoleonic warfare] were *universal norms*' were above anyone else Clausewitz himself.[344]

Another major point to remember is that rather than a timeless thinker, Clausewitz was not merely a child of his times in the trivial sense but a staunch exponent of a very specific intellectual-cultural-ideological current: the reaction against the worldview of the Enlightenment that was powerfully sweeping across Europe, most notably affecting Germany at the very moment he reached maturity. This means that his scathing criticism of his predecessors, the military thinkers of the Enlightenment, was not only permeated with that current's ferocious ideological-polemical fervour; but also that the debate between the two currents of thought often centred on different perspectives and emphases on how to approach reality as much as it was about substance. Instead of parroting Clausewitz's pronouncements, this point needs to be constantly borne in mind. Once his place in the intellectual-cultural history of Europe is grasped, two major stories, hitherto kept apart in two separate compartments of historical scholarship – intellectual-cultural and military – merge to illuminate his work and ideas.

As mentioned, commentators have been confounded by the revelation of Clausewitz's actual historical place on one side of a powerful clash of ideas, because: a) his ideas were thereby 'historicised' rather than expressing timeless wisdom; and b) probably more significantly, because he was thus identified with a very particular school of thought and ideology, one of great intellectual contributions but still awkwardly associated with the often anti-liberal Counter-Enlightenment. Moreover, this was a school of thought associated with the subsequent problematic course of German history. Indeed, Clausewitz scholars and commentators in Germany during the nineteenth and early twentieth centuries recognised his prominent position within the German cultural-intellectual tradition as a matter of course and regarded it as a mark of great distinction. Furthermore, in the context of the Prussian Reform Movement, Clausewitz forcefully advocated a national insurrection against Napoleon, come what may. With the fall of Napoleon, this passionate quest was ultimately crowned with success and has enjoyed 'good press' since the days of the German Reich. However, in 1808 and 1809, and perhaps even in 1812, it may be judged to have been a reckless gamble that could have easily ended in the destruction of Prussia, as its king had every reason to fear.

Some commentators have suggested a 'compromise' according to which Clausewitz expressed the ideas of both the Enlightenment and the Counter-Enlightenment/Romanticism. However, as we have seen, with the main exception of Montesquieu, admired by the men of the Counter-Enlightenment for his pioneering historicism and attention to historical-social diversity, Clausewitz scarcely cites the leading Enlightenment luminaries such as Voltaire, Rousseau (whom the men of the Counter-Enlightenment also admired), Diderot, D'Alembert, Condillac, La Mettrie, Holbach, Helvétius, Turgot or Condorcet. By contrast, his readings of and references to, and/or personal acquaintance with, the writers associated with the reaction against the Enlightenment read like a catalogue list of this sweeping current: the Prussian conservative anti-Enlightenment and anti-Revolutionary historian and statesman, Ancillon; the arch-conservative and disciple of Burke, Gentz; Möser, Herder, Adam Müller, Savigny, Schleiermacher, Fichte, and Hegel, to name only the most famous of them. He is in a (positive) dialogue with them, and with them alone. His use of Kant also relates predominantly to Kant's criticism in the *Critique of Judgement* of the Enlightenment's neo-classicist notions of rules and principles in the arts, which Clausewitz applied to the art of war. This stark contrast speaks volumes.

Furthermore, it needs to be emphasised once again that the reaction against the worldview of the Enlightenment in which Clausewitz partook was a *dialectical* reaction. This means that it incorporated many of the achievements of the Enlightenment while sharply criticizing a great deal of its assumptions and propositions through the faculty of reason with which the Enlightenment had adorned its flag. Moreover, the reaction against the Enlightenment was as diverse as the Enlightenment itself, with Clausewitz belonging to its emphatically rationalistic wing. Finally, to remove yet another misunderstanding, the reaction against the Enlightenment, with its strong historicist notions, had both conservative, even reactionary currents, and reformist currents. While the former embraced continuity with and attachment to the past, the latter emphasised the change in historical conditions that necessitated adaptation. The reformist outlook characterised the Prussian Reform Movement to which Clausewitz belonged. Its members based their call for far-reaching reforms not on any notion of universal human rights, which they rejected as an empty, ahistorical abstraction, but on the compelling conditions and needs of the time. As they argued, Prussia could either adapt to the social, economic, and political disintegration of the absolutist-feudal state and embrace the great forces harnessed by the French Revolution – or perish.[346] Remember that the division among the disciples of the deeply historicist Hegel between conservative Right and radical Left-Hegelians similarly rested on their contrasting interpretations of historical evolution, emphasising either continuity or change, respectively.

What Is a Classic, and Is *On War* One?

There is a deeper reason for the reverence for Clausewitz. People habitually believe that every field has its classics and great philosophers/theorists. Are *On War* and Clausewitz not those in the study of war and military theory?

The notion of the 'classic' has a firm hold in our mind, and it possesses several meanings. The classic as referring to human thought is generally understood as a work that touches on deep truths about the world and us. For this reason, it remains relevant, present, and stimulating in the intellectual discourse over the ages, at least to some degree, despite often far-reaching changes in time and circumstances. Plato and Aristotle are iconic examples. A 'classic' is also perceived as a work that most strikingly and prominently represents a certain age and worldview and hence played a major role in the consciousness of that and later ages, even if that worldview is no longer deemed much more relevant today. A possible example is the works of St. Augustine or Thomas Aquinas to non-religious or even non-Catholic people at present.

So how does *On War* measure according to these criteria? As has been made clear, much of the book's reputation rests on lingering misunderstandings of what it actually means and, hence, on an Emperor's New Clothes syndrome. Its revised standing, and that of its author, must be judged far more modestly. At the same time, some ideas of *On War*, most notably regarding the relationship between politics and war, retain conceptual and educational value even if Clausewitz was far from pioneering them, but, rather, returned to these age-old notions in a U-turn against his own life-long views on the nature of war. Moreover, the role he played in the thought of subsequent generations should be considered as a fact in itself. Clausewitz, like the far more famous and influential Jomini at the time, articulated into theory the epoch-making Napoleonic form of warfare. After 1871, as the Prussian-German military school rose to dominance in the field of military theory, he reached canonical status for the first time, in Germany and beyond, as an exponent of all-out war, crushing strategy, and the major battle, pushing Jomini aside. After a century and a half during which this doctrine reigned supreme, his name was stamped on the rediscovery of limited war, governed by the political rationale, during the nuclear age after Korea.

'Influence' is an elusive concept, but Clausewitz's name and work certainly made it to the very pinnacle of military thought and education as a 'classic' in both of the above epochs, and in this respect, it matters less how accurately he was understood and how much he 'influenced' events in practice. It is the case with all 'classics' that people adopt, adapt, and cite from them whatever they find suits their own views and convictions. 'Classics' are a repository of ideas and scraps of ideas that can find their place in the construction of subsequent intellectual edifices. From this perspective, given his place in history, Clausewitz can be said to have won the status of 'classic'. This framing of his status is more complex, nuanced, and ambivalent than the existing one, and it is more difficult to digest because of our quest for a clear-cut verdict and bottom-line. However, while far from the current framing, it is closer to reality. An early reviewer of this book expressed concern that 'many a young student of military academies would find this a welcome excuse for not reading any Clausewitz.' However, as noted here, the pedagogical use of 'classical' texts is inherently adaptive, and all the more so in busy, practically-oriented military schools. Clausewitz's later-day teaching regarding the relationship between state policy and war will likely continue to be taught, and for a good reason, notwithstanding the torturous development and subsequent contrived formulation of his concepts in this regard. However, by the same token, there is no reason students in military schools, and students of war and strategy in general, should torture themselves in, or waste time on, trying to decipher the incomprehensible structures they encounter in the 'classic', or react to them in bewildered awe as deep 'philosophical' ways of expression. Nor should they labour to follow, through thick and thin, Clausewitz's misconceptions regarding attack and defence, or anything else, without critical guidance. They will be better served that way.

Still, if Clausewitz is not the classic of military theory at the same level that we thought him to be, then who is? It is natural that this question will occur to people. Again, does not every field have its classics? We could say that Sun Tzu, with his traditional aphorismic and metaphorical Chinese style, has won such a status – indeed, somewhat amusingly, also in current business guidebooks. In addition, quite a few military authors were significant and relevant in their own and in later times, though much less so eventually: Xenophon, Caesar, Vegetius, Machiavelli, Jomini, and others mentioned in this book. Closer to the present, Mahan and Corbett, Fuller and Liddell Hart may also fit the list in one form or another. Yet the point is different. The notion of the 'classic' is often perceived too simplistically and naively. Does psychology, for example, dealing with human nature itself, have its classics in the sense we are looking for? The layperson may name Freud, but despite his huge cultural impact during the twentieth century, his ideas have been largely discredited and are cited today mainly as intellectual history or in the 'cultural studies'. Economics has a better claim for a living 'classic', Adam Smith and his *Wealth of Nations* (1776), and to a lesser degree perhaps also David Ricardo, John Maynard Keynes, Friedrich Hayek, and Milton Friedman. But are all fields of knowledge similar in this regard? Is there a universal theory of war, the question that preoccupied Clausewitz himself throughout his life?

Is There a Universal Theory of War?

Clausewitz's doubts regarding the possibility of a general theory of war were a deeply embedded and recurring theme in his mind. Of all the quotations from his work in this regard included in this book we shall re-cite here only a couple, from 1808–1809: The theory of strategy, he wrote, 'allows the setting up of few or no abstract propositions.' One cannot escape the multitude of minor circumstances.[346]

Formula [is] abstraction. When by the abstraction nothing which belongs to the thing gets lost – as is the case in mathematics – the abstraction fully achieves its purpose. But when it must omit the living matter in order to hold to the dead form, which is of course the easiest to abstract, it would be in the end a dry skeleton of dull truths squeezed into a doctrine… precisely that which is the most important in war and strategy, namely the great particularity, peculiarity, and local circumstances, escape these abstractions and scientific systems.[347]

Despite his doubts, Clausewitz believed that he had found a sound foundation for a universal theory of war and strategy in his concept of the 'lasting spirit', 'nature' or 'concept' of war as all-out fighting and energetic conduct leading to the great battle. Yet, he was later forced to recognise that this concept, and its supposed emanating guidance for action in the field, were not universal and did not even apply to the Napoleonic wars, the supreme model of his theory of war. This was strikingly demonstrated by the Spanish and Russian campaigns and by guerrilla warfare. He braved through an agonising crisis and found new inspiration in his re-discovery – at the personal level – of the important insight regarding the interrelationship between politics and war. At the same time, he retained many of the erroneous ideas regarding the conduct of war mentioned earlier in this book.

Where does this leave us with respect to the feasibility of a universal theory of war and its conduct – valid across time and applying to diverse conditions and changing historical circumstances? In addressing this question, the above, doubting, quotations from Clausewitz remain very pertinent and acute. I hope it comes as no great disappointment that the scope for a 'universal theory of war' is very limited. Some features of war and human fighting are, indeed, so to speak, analytically 'implicit' in its 'concept'. They include, 'by definition', the use of force and violence against others, ultimately rooted in the quest to attain desired human objectives, which at the state level are referred to as 'political'.[348] In the end, Clausewitz saw this clearly enough. In this context, other analytical distinctions are possible and helpful, such as the distinction between defence and attack, based on their relation to the status quo, which Clausewitz addressed, though misconceived. The adversarial nature of war may make its conduct even more unpredictable than other spheres of human activity in some ways. Courage and determination in the face of mortal danger may be regarded as intrinsic to success in war. Other prevailing notions have been enshrined in 'principles of war', a concept that Clausewitz rejected while echoing some of the same notions himself. The holding of the initiative, energetic conduct, concentration of force, and focusing on the objective – all as much as possible under the circumstances – are widely regarded as helpful precepts even if they do not apply to all circumstances and partly contradict one another. Clausewitz preached all of them. Surprise and cunning, which together with the manoeuvre Clausewitz belittled, are regarded as no less compelling measures in the conduct of war. All the above is familiar enough, but is this all that the 'theory of war' has to offer?

There are other possible analytical distinctions, but mainly most of what fills military theory with flesh is time-bound, relating to broad yet particular historical conditions: technological, economic, social, and political. Clausewitz sensed this in his more historicist moods. Shifting conditions shape what is known as 'doctrines' of various time ranges – short, medium or long. Focusing on more recent examples, we have had doctrines of trench warfare, armoured warfare, air warfare, and electronic-computerised warfare. We have had distinct doctrines for naval warfare for the oar, sail, and steam ages, as well as for the dreadnought, aircraft carrier, and missile eras. All the above categories were in their times 'stable' and 'enduring' enough to serve as crucial guidance for the activity of fighting, but none of them have been a necessarily 'permanent' feature of war.

Clausewitz sensed and agonised over this ambiguity, expressing the human quest for the universal. But our comprehension of the world of experience is more nuanced than that, making use of both abstract conceptualisation and constant adaptation to particularities. All in all, we are doing quite well, indeed, remarkably so.

A Plea to Focus on the Issues Alone

I suppose it is only natural that scholars who are heavily invested in the Clausewitz created during the last decades are not going to be pleased with the arguments and criticism expressed in this book. They hold that Clausewitz's interpreters within the German tradition of the nineteenth century, who were much closer to him in every respect, distorted his ideas. There has even been some willingness to recognise that Cold War perspectives in the West have been responsible for distortions in the opposite direction. And yet, this has scarcely bred any doubt that our *current* understanding of Clausewitz may be well off the mark.

I think it is. And what I ask readers is that they strictly focus on the issues and on the evidence, and nothing else, in judging the arguments of this book. Here are the main ones:

- Clausewitz expressed in the field of military theory the main themes of the Counter-Enlightenment/Romantic reaction against the worldview of the Enlightenment. This explains the strength and value of many of his arguments derived from this great cultural movement, but also his very harsh, not always justified, rhetoric, often uncritically reproduced by his interpreters.
- Clausewitz's interpreters have failed to recognize the centrepiece of his entire theory of war, from his earliest writings in 1804 onward: his concept of the 'lasting spirit', 'nature' or 'concept' of war, the foundation of his belief in the possibility of a universal theory of war. If this key concept is not recognised, nothing about Clausewitz is understood.

- Indeed, this failure has obscured understanding of his overriding insistence that this universal element consisted of a relentless, all-out, indeed 'total', conduct of war, centring on the clash of forces and the great battle, and his suspicion of any other means, such as manoeuvre, surprise, and cunning.

- Related to this is the prevailing misconception that Clausewitz was after an abstract theory of the nature of war and rejected prescriptive guidance for its conduct. On the contrary, Clausewitz believed that the correct conduct of war *flowed from* the imperatives inherent in war's nature. See the numerous quotations cited in this book from Clausewitz which refute the above false dichotomy. Also recall that in his Undated Note he referred to his future book as 'the manuscript on the *conduct* of major operations' [my emphasis],[349] and that his posthumous collected works were also titled *Hinterlassene Werke über Krieg und Kriegführung* [*On War and the Conduct of War*].

- The intrinsic connection between Clausewitz's view of defence and attack and the very core of his theory of war as relentless, all-out fighting, seeking a crushing annihilation of the enemy in battle, has not been recognised. Nor has his proposed relationship between defence and attack – the former is *intrinsically and universally* stronger than the latter, but must be abandoned once one becomes strong enough to attack – been questioned, as it should have, since both of its interconnected parts are fundamentally invalid. His views on the subject ultimately led to the crisis of his entire theory of war, erupting in full force at the end of Book VI of *On War*, 'Defence', and eventually revolutionising his life work.

- It has not been recognised that Clausewitz's transformed views about the relationship between politics and war and the admission of limited war into his theory constituted a U-turn against his own life-long, most strongly held, fundamental view of the nature of war. Commentators have failed to note that an understanding of the relationship between politics and war was common in all the great civilizations since ancient times. Moreover, it was the standard in early modern Europe, famously dominated by the principle of *raison d'état* and the practice of limited 'cabinet' wars, against which Clausewitz reacted. From the 1950s onward, Clausewitz has gained his supposed fatherhood over the subordination of war to politics and the ensuing, revived, concept of limited war only because of the century and a half – from Napoleon to World War II – in which all-out, total war and military victory were proclaimed the only legitimate aim in the conduct of war.

• Finally, one might wonder why my explanation of Clausewitz's ideas and development should be regarded as more compelling than other possible interpretations of this famously obscure thinker. The answer to this should again be judged not in principle but by the evidence. Clausewitz's texts from 1804 onward were unpublished for a century after his death. The old Chapter 1, Book One, did not see light until 1990. Even when these texts became available – step-by-step tracing Clausewitz's views on war, its conduct, and its theory – they have not been utilised by many of his interpreters. As mentioned, the most glaring lacuna has been interpreters' failure to notice Clausewitz's most fundamental concept from 1804 onward and throughout his life: the 'lasting spirit', 'nature', or 'concept' of war. Many of these interpreters have confined themselves mainly to *On War*, a book which, given the crisis and transformation that Clausewitz experienced, is simply impossible to decipher by itself, in isolation from the whole sequence of his writings. Any attempt to have done so typically ended either in bewilderment,

181

often pronounced, about a 'metaphysical fog', or, on the opposite pole, in the Emperor's New Clothes syndrome. Only by following the evidence offered by the complete 'paper trail' does Clausewitz's train of thought and, with it, the 'real' Clausewitz emerge, freed from the myth and much more fallible.

It would be naïve of me to think that commentators with a life-time investment in Clausewitz the 'absolute' – and they are a legion – will be willing and able to accept my plea for a focus on the evidence and issues alone. This would require super-human qualities, as people who are criticised tend to fight back, with greater or lesser subtlety. Thus, one early reviewer of this book claimed that it was 'an over-the-top exercise in Clausewitz-bashing.' I leave it to the reader, and to those unencumbered by the weight of past commitments, to judge how valid her view is.

A Final Apology in the Name of My Protagonist

Intellectual history is often an ungrateful task, cruelly described as 'the study of first-rate minds by second-rate minds.' It may be appropriate to end this Conclusion with a repeated apology for my often-severe critique of current interpretations of Clausewitz's work. It has been necessary in order to dispel the myth and bring out the real Clausewitz. Indeed, perhaps I could take cover behind the protagonist of this book. Marie's relative Caroline von der Marwitz described his personality as 'unfortunate in every respect. There was something cold and negative in his demeanour, which often went so far as to imply disdain of others. He said little, usually because he seemed to feel that people and ordinary topics were not worthy of his attention.'[350] At the same time, people noted that 'among friends he could be gay, affectionate, and even exuberant. There were times when he would succumb to such violent attacks of laughter that he had to leave the company.'[351]

Other assessments of Clausewitz convey basically the same personality traits more positively. His commander in Koblenz General Hake wrote as follows in his conduct report on him in 1816: 'Is not very communicative. I consider him a decent person. He shows much feeling for truth and justice, is generous, stimulated by honour, perhaps vain, and consequently likes to insist on his point of view... He is primarily interested in ideas, nevertheless he carries out his duties with precision, and writes in a beautiful and clear style.'[352] Clausewitz's wife, Marie, naturally a prejudiced source, cited the revealing double-edged remark made to her by friends and family that he 'could be very congenial when given a chance.'[353]

Paret rejected an earlier view that Clausewitz died a disappointed man as his hope for military glory was unfulfilled. Clausewitz certainly was disappointed about that, as his wife testifies,[354] but this did not go beyond life's normal frustrations. Again, Caroline von der Marwitz's observation is more telling: 'He had few, but close and firm friends, who expected and hoped more from him than he was able to achieve – whether because of fate, circumstances, or his off-putting personality.'[355] In the end, Clausewitz's posthumous glory in the field of military theory has been unmatched. Yet, as this study argues, it has been greatly inflated and largely a result of the confusion as to what *On War* actually meant.

9

Comments on the Recent
Clausewitz Literature

Distinguishing the Forest from the Trees

This commentary intends to be more than the standard
bibliographical notes that give a short description of one
or two sentences of the various works on the subject. In the
main, it offers some extra critiques relating to major themes
in the interpretation of Clausewitz which would be much too
cumbersome to incorporate into the main text or even notes.
The focus is on some works on Clausewitz that have appeared,
overwhelmingly in English, over the last decades, after the
publication of my 1989 book. I am not going to address every
such work and only comment where I see a need to add some
significant extra reference or information that can affect our
understanding of Clausewitz.

Because of the central place they have held in the interpretation
of Clausewitz, I begin by more or less reproducing what I
already wrote in my 1989 book on two earlier works, both
appearing in 1976: Raymond Aron, *Clausewitz*, and Peter Paret,
Clausewitz and the State.

Aron's attraction to Clausewitz is especially of interest.
Already in the 1950s, he had discovered in Clausewitz a thinker
whose ideas closely corresponded to his own regarding the
nature of theory in the study of international relations – a
problem that had preoccupied him ever since the outbreak of
the great methodological debate in that field in the early 1950s.
The far-reaching affinity in their views is revealed in Aron's
fundamental political 'realism'; in his rejection of the wider
aspirations of the 'scientific school' in the study of international

relations; in his rejection of any theory based on a single isolated factor, rendering it artificial and one-sided; in his emphasis on the primacy of historical experience in shaping theory; and last but not least, in his belief that, for all that, the concept of 'theory' can still be given much meaning and possess great value.[356]

From this unique viewpoint, Aron offers a comprehensive and elaborate analysis of Clausewitz's work. Much of his interpretation is penetrating. Inter alia, he is well aware of the 1827 break in Clausewitz's theory of war. However, his special affinity towards Clausewitz is overshadowed by a serious handicap. Despite his prestigious education in philosophy and great reputation as a social thinker, Aron is scarcely conscious of the cultural context in which Clausewitz worked and of the intellectual trends to which he gave expression. Professing to a positivist method of interpretation,[357] Aron's naiveté in this regard is astonishing. This problem cannot but contribute to the fact that Aron (following in Schering's footsteps) is inclined to read into Clausewitz's work intellectual patterns and categories which are totally artificial and which further obscure a subject that is already obscure enough. Most notably, as we have seen, he is wrong on Clausewitz's 'life-long method'; finds dialectic everywhere in Clausewitz's work, before Clausewitz actually adopted it in 1827; and his comments on the influence of Kant and Hegel on Clausewitz are not up to it.

Paret's biography Clausewitz and the State (Oxford, 1976) is the most thorough so far, combining extensive research, a comprehensive reconstruction of Clausewitz's historical environment, and a sympathetic psychological portrait. Paret also devoted much attention to Clausewitz's intellectual background and brought together a great deal of important material. Nonetheless, Paret failed to identify Clausewitz's actual intellectual-cultural-ideological context: the sweeping reaction in Germany of the 1800s against the worldview of the Enlightenment – without exaggeration the most significant development that set the future course of German culture for the next century and a half. Moreover, he failed to recognize the centrepiece of Clausewitz's entire theory – the 'lasting spirit', 'nature', or 'concept of war' – as well as the crucial significance and scope of the post-1827 transformation in his thought. He thus denied the very basis of Clausewitz's life-long theory of war: the supreme emphasis on all-out war and the decisive battle. Finally, despite the title of his book, *Clausewitz and the State*, Paret missed the exact nature of Clausewitz's political views – which prompted C.B.A. Behrens's review, 'Which Side Was Clausewitz On?'[358] As all this was largely derived from a projection of post-1945 attitudes in the West on Clausewitz's thought, Paret put the most authoritative stamp on the 'vegetarian' view of Clausewitz that has taken root in this period.

There is no escaping the conclusion that, as a historian, Paret failed in his primary task of properly historicising Clausewitz; and that in terms of the theory of war, Paret missed everything that is most crucially Clausewitzian in Clausewitz. He was a learned historian, intimately familiar with the Prussian and German military and civilian milieu. However, contrary to appearances, he fell short in the sphere of the ideas of the time, both general and as concerns military theory. His erudition, together with his elegant and authoritative style and distinguished academic status, obscured these critical failures in the eyes of readers.

I wrote most of the above at the time, and, since, like Howard, Paret lived to his late nineties, he had three decades of ample opportunity to take issue with my arguments regarding his interpretation of Clausewitz. Yet he chose not to.

Inescapably, all this also left its mark on the hugely successful and influential English translation of *On War* that Paret produced with Howard. Here were two eminent names in the field of military history, whose edition of *On War* was issued, also in 1976, by the prestigious Princeton University Press. It is no wonder that the publication was received with a hail of praise. It took time before critical voices began to be heard and gain attention. Paret was the dominant partner in this project as far as the interpretation of Clausewitz's ideas was concerned. There were two main reasons for this. He had just finished his major biography on Clausewitz, published in the same year by Oxford, and his thorough familiarity with the material was something that Howard never had. In addition, as Howard notes, Paret was born in Germany and was practically bilingual, whereas Howard's command of the language was tenuous.[359] Earlier, Howard did not recoil from expressing some criticism of Clausewitz, as in his comment that 'he defined strategy badly as the use of battles to achieve the aim of the war'. But now he took a second seat and concentrated his efforts on rendering *On War* into lucid English. Indeed, it has been remarked that the English translation of *On War* is more readable than the German original – which can be, and often is, a double-edged sword.

It is only fair to add that Paret's translation into English, with Daniel Moran, of an important collection of Clausewitz's *Historical and Political Writings* (Princeton, 1992) is exceptionally lucid. Furthermore, while the fundamental deficiencies in Paret's understanding of Clausewitz needed spelling out, this edited volume is of great value. I have adapted all my relevant citations from Clausewitz in this book to this English edition. It should also be added that while Clausewitz's prose in *On War* is anything but lucid – indeed, is often convoluted – he was capable of writing beautifully, combining elegant prose with penetrating personal observations of people and events. His 'Observations on Prussia in Her Great Catastrophe' and *The Campaign of 1812 in Russia*, in particular, are great examples.

Paret's dominance in interpreting Clausewitz's theory affected the Princeton edition of *On War* in ways we have already seen. When asked why after two translations into English – by J.J. Graham (1873, 1908) and by O.J.M. Jolles (1943) – there was a need for yet another translation, Howard replied in his memorable style that the first did not know German, whereas the second did not know English. To extend this quip, the problem with the third translation was that while the dominant figure in producing it knew both German and English perfectly, he did not understand Clausewitz's theory of war – a much more crucial factor.

Before returning to discuss some of the major errors in the Howard-Paret translation, it is necessary for me to add a little more background with respect to Howard, for I was his doctoral student at Oxford in 1984–1986, writing what would become my 1989 book. Throughout this period, and later, I received from him nothing but unwavering encouragement and warm praise. When I sent him my piece on the correct dating of Clausewitz's two 'final notes', which implied that the decision he and Paret had taken on this in their translation was misguided, he responded with a note 'Eureka!' His fairness and scholarly integrity were as admirable as they always were. He never tried to influence my judgements on issues and people. This was so even when he was sorry to read what I had written on his friend Bernard Brodie's comments on *On War* in the Princeton edition. I should add that I had a distinct sense that he was not at all unhappy to read what I was writing about Paret's work. Paret's well-known snobbism and stern attitude to people did not rub off even with respect to Howard.

Having said all that, I did not want to highlight my reservations concerning the Paret-Howard translation in my dissertation and ensuing book more than was necessary. Therefore, while using this lucid translation, I chose to change what needed changing, citing the German original word or phrase in square brackets, thereby also hinting what the problems in the translation were. I have kept, and occasionally extended, this practice in this book as well. I have no doubt that Howard would have received this book with the same dignity and commitment to the truth that characterized him. His own critical appraisals of the ideas of Liddell Hart, his close friend, which he published only after the latter's death, are a testimony to both his tact and scholarly integrity.[360] This is so even if I have taken issue with some of Howard's views in this regard in my own work on Liddell Hart, including his claim, shared by others, that 'the final picture Liddell Hart painted of Clausewitz's teaching was distorted, inaccurate, and unfair.'[361] Fundamentally it was not, or at least it can be argued that it was not more so than the picture painted by Howard and the post-1945 literature. Again, Howard received what I wrote on this subject with the same warmth and spirit of scholarly objectivity.

The major biases in the Howard-Paret translation have already been pointed out throughout this book. Denying that Clausewitz preached the imperatives of all-out war and the decisive battle, they chose to translate the German *Gefecht* as 'engagement' – which while lexically not illegitimate, was an intentionally feeble rendering of the more natural uses, and of Clausewitz's intention: fighting, combat, the clash of forces, battle. Equally gravely, Howard and Paret embraced the common assertion that Clausewitz dealt with the phenomenon of war rather than giving advice as to how to conduct it, an entirely false dichotomy. Remember that in his Undated Note of early 1827 or slightly before, he referred to his future book as 'The manuscript on the conduct of major operations'.[362] His Collected Works were also titled *Hinterlassene Werke über Krieg und Kriegführung, (On War and the Conduct of War)*. Having taken this crucial interpretative misstep, the Howard-Paret translation blurs the many instances in which Clausewitz emphasised the practical imperatives for the conduct of war that Clausewitz held flowed from its 'lasting spirit', 'nature', or 'concept'. Indeed, entirely missing the significance of these central concepts as the very core of Clausewitz's theory of war, the Howard-Paret translation was not consistent enough in producing them and often omitted them altogether, simply choosing 'war', as less cumbersome English. After all, the long and complex sentences and heavy structures of the German language conflict with the temper of English. Finally, rendering the aim of the defence as 'passive' rather than 'negative', as in the original, also biases the meaning and is indefensible.

Jan Willem Honig has offered a valuable critique of the Howard-Paret translation. Among other things, he has suggested that the German *Niederwerfung* meant, for both Clausewitz and in later German military literature, the complete 'overthrow' of the enemy, rather than 'defeat' which means something potentially more momentary. Other problems with the translation Honig has specified are neither the result of a special bias nor particularly harmful. He indicates that in Chapter I of *On War*, Clausewitz consistently distinguishes between 'the political aim, or *Zweck*, and the military *Ziel*. Howard and Paret's translation does not reproduce Clausewitz's rigour: *Zweck* variously appears as aim, object, purpose, end, goal, and requirements. These translations overlap with those chosen for *Ziel*.'[363] Finally, like others, Honig points out that the German *Politik* was translated by Howard and Paret as 'policy'. Howard has explained that although *Politik* and 'politics' are roughly equivalent in both languages, they still carry some different connotations, with some negative meaning attached to the English term.[364]

As Sibylle Scheipers adds:

Politik embodies both the concept or policy and politics. Howard and Paret mostly chose to render Politik as 'policy', thereby giving the term a strongly rationalist spin. In other instances, the translation updated Clausewitz's vocabulary by substituting historical terms such as *Hof*, royal court, with 'government'. In contrast, the translation downplayed the role of passion and emotions in war. Where Clausewitz used the word *Geist*, a term that integrates both rational and sensual faculties, Howard and Paret's translation reads 'intellect', hence reinforcing a highly rationalist reading of the original text.[365]

Another recent critique of the Howard-Paret translation, underlying its biases in the spirit of their time, is Hew Strachan, 'Michael Howard and Clausewitz', *Journal of Strategic Studies*, 45:1 (2022), 143–160. That said, I must add that I do not agree with Strachan's Clausewitz, in both this article and his *Carl von Clausewitz's On War: A Biography* (London: 2007). His *On War* remains a text of sublime wisdom, and he dismisses the often-made claims by bewildered readers ever since its publication that it is contradictory and confusing, while at the same time dithering but tending to accept the major transformation of 1827. These two positions do not quite cohere.

A valuable addition to Clausewitz's biography that has appeared of late is Vanya Eftimova Bellinger, *Marie von Clausewitz: The Woman Behind the Making of On War* (Oxford, 2016). The volume's title is too modest. The book is based on, and reproduces, the full, recently rediscovered, trove of the correspondence between Carl and Marie, a very close couple. It thus greatly augments the more partial selections from the letters by Schwartz (1878) and by Linnebach (1916) that have always been the main source for Clausewitz's life. Bellinger's treatment of the correspondence and her reconstruction of the couple's relationship is very good, even if the picture of Clausewitz reflected through the eyes of his loving wife is naturally too rosy.

Donald Stoker, *Clausewitz: His Life and Work* (Oxford, 2014), is a well-informed study, based on the sources, of Clausewitz's participation in the campaigns of his time. This is an aspect that had not been covered as extensively before. Again, the title of the book is a misnomer, as the book does not cover Clausewitz's work in any meaningful or significant way. Similarly, Bruno Colson, *Clausewitz* (Perrin, 2016), is an even more extensive biography, in French, though it does not add much on Clausewitz's work and theory of war.

This takes us to works whose subject is Clausewitz's military thought.

Andreas Herberg-Rothe, *Clausewitz's Puzzle: The Political Theory of War* (Oxford, 2007; German original, 2001), has a lot of merit. The author clearly sees that Clausewitz's theory of war is squarely rooted in the warfare of his time, the Napoleonic era; fully recognises that Clausewitz underwent a profound transformation from 1827 on; and that, as a result, the *On War* we have contains conflicting if not contradictory ideas, mixing the old and the new. He also goes against the current in pointing out that Clausewitz's insistence on the imperative of mobilizing a country's entire resources for all-out war, ultimately conceptualised as 'absolute war', in fact meant pretty much 'total war'.

Unfortunately, Herberg-Rothe's core thesis, associating the various stages in Clausewitz's thought with three signature campaigns, is not borne out by the evidence – indeed, it is misdated without exception. Thus, he argues that the root of Clausewitz's admiration for Napoleon and adoption of the imperative of all-out war and the decisive battle originated with Prussia's crushing defeat before Napoleon at the Battle of Jena-Auerstedt in 1806. Yet, Clausewitz had already forcefully presented this view of war and its conduct in his so-called notes on strategy of 1804. Similarly, Herberg-Rothe claims that Clausewitz's view regarding the superior power of the defence was a lesson he drew from the Russian Campaign of 1812. However, as we have seen, Clausewitz had already developed this view in 1810–1812, in the context of his fervent advocacy of a Prussian war of independence against Napoleon, well before his experience in Russia. Finally, Herberg-Rothe believes that Clausewitz's insight regarding the primacy of politics and the legitimacy of limited war was deduced from the Waterloo Campaign of 1815. This is even more unfounded, as this insight had to wait until 1827, to say nothing of the fact that Waterloo was among the most decisive campaigns ever, leading to Napoleon's military and political destruction, rather than being an example of limited war.

There seems to be a common root to all these errors. Herberg-Rothe focuses on the text of *On War* alone, barely addressing the long line of Clausewitz's earlier writing that throw bright light on his development. An analytical philosopher by training, he also does not deal at all with Clausewitz's intellectual background (with the exception of Hegel). Nor does he mention his military predecessors and contemporaries, such as Berenhorst and Jomini. Bülow and even Scharnhorst are mentioned only once.

Antulio Echevarria II, *Clausewitz and Contemporary War* (Oxford, 2007), also focuses on *On War* and generally neglects Clausewitz's earlier writings. Unlike Herberg-Rothe, he presents a rather static picture of Clausewitz's theory of war and seems to dither on his development and trajectory. Thus, although Echevarria is well aware that Clausewitz developed his ideas on politics and war in Books VIII and I,[366] he avoids any discussion of the transformation in Clausewitz's thought that led to this novelty. Similarly, while being aware that Clausewitz's theory was combat-centric, he recoils from the conclusion that it aimed at the destruction of the enemy's army.

Echevarria adds some valuable information on the Clausewitz-Kiesewetter connection, Clausewitz's conduit to Kant's philosophy concerning the relationship between concepts and reality. At the same time, he seems to be uncertain about Clausewitz's manifest view regarding the connection between concepts and practical guidance. Indeed, Echevarria appears to be most confused about Clausewitz and the 'principles of war'.

193

Struggling to rationalize Clausewitz's categorical rejection of this concept with the clear imperatives for its practical conduct of war that Clausewitz's believed flowed from its 'lasting spirit', 'nature', or 'concept' as relentless fighting, Echevarria begins by stating, obscurely, that: 'Contrary to conventional wisdom, Clausewitz did *not* reject martial principles, only prescriptive ones.'[367] He then claims to detect a change in the only thing Clausewitz's *did not* change his mind on: 'It is clear from the above passage that Clausewitz had changed his views: he now believed that it was possible to uncover laws or principles governing strategy, and he thought he had already discovered several... the Undated Note shows that he accepted the possibility of discovering laws and principles for strategy.'[368] As this made Clausewitz's harsh criticism of his predecessors and contemporaries unintelligible, Echevarria proceeds to explain the contradiction as follows: 'Nonetheless, the application of principles required skilled judgment, the culmination of pure and practical reasoning. The absence of that ingredient, in short, had been the problem with the principles of Bülow, Lloyd, and Jomini, which had been portrayed as applicable regardless of the situation, without the need for judgment, when in fact they were not.'[369] As we have seen, there was nothing more remote from the conceptual framework of the thinkers of the Enlightenment, including the military thinkers regarding the art of war, most emphatically stated and applied by all of them, including Lloyd and Jomini, if not Bülow. Echevarria concludes as inconsistently: 'Although Clausewitz rejected prescriptive theories and doctrines, he clearly believed certain truths, in the form of laws and principles, existed for the conduct of war.'[370]

The simple reality is that throughout his life, from his twenties to the end of *On War*, Clausewitz held the same view: while rejecting the concept of principles of war, he insisted that prescriptive imperatives for the conduct of war flowed from its 'lasting spirit', 'nature', or 'concept'. As Jomini complained, there was in practice little that distinguished between the two – except, which Jomini probably did not realise, for a change in the intellectual-cultural perspective, and vocabulary, which has continued to confound readers of *On War* to this day.

Evidently both a great believer in the principles of war and taking Clausewitz's greatness for granted, Echevarria constructs his entire discussion of *On War*'s enduring relevance on the welding together of these two strange bed fellows. The most problematic point here is that in doing so he misinterprets some of Clausewitz's most fundamental views, presenting him as basically teaching the principles of war accepted by most militaries today. Thus, he ignores Clausewitz's disparaging attitude towards surprise and cunning,[371] grounded in his concept of war as direct fighting; and he stops half-way regarding the reasons behind Clausewitz's conception of the relationship between attack and defence, while failing to appreciate this conception's fatal flaws.[372]

Jon Sumida, *Decoding Clausewitz: A New Approach to On War* (Lawrence, Kansas, 2008), while learned, complicates things hugely and unnecessarily in his stated attempt to make Clausewitz comprehensible to the lay reader. Furthermore, while arguing that Clausewitz's views on defence and attack are the key to his entire theory of war, he does not quite understand its place as a major derivative of Clausewitz's central concept of the 'lasting spirit', 'nature', or 'concept' of war. Moreover, it does not ever occur to Sumida to question Clausewitz's argument that, intrinsically and universally, the defence is the stronger form of war.

I probably would not have mentioned René Girard, *Achever Clausewitz* (Paris, 2007) if it were not for the fact that the book presents the thoughts of a well-known French anthropologist and literary critic of the old school. Characteristic of the more fanciful ideas often associate with that school of the 1960s and 1970s, the book incorporates wide-ranging musing, both mystified and mystifying. Author of *Violence and the Sacred* (1972), which, building on Freud, sees the sacrifice of the scapegoat at the basis of religion, Girard regards Clausewitz as a kindred spirit of his own 'mimetic theory'. According to his view, violence's escalation to the extreme is the rule of the world and leading to an imminent apocalypse on earth, in line with Christianity's teaching and in contrast to the rationalistic perception. Girard's Clausewitz is therefore a religious thinker of war who understood that politics was actually an expression of war, rather than the other way around.

There are problems, some of them disturbing, in Lt-Col. Anders Palmgren's works: his article, 'Clausewitz's Interweaving of *Krieg* and *Politik*', in *Clausewitz: The State and War*, ed. by A. Herberg-Rothe, J.W. Honig and D. Moran (Stuttgart, 2011), 49–69, and doctoral dissertation at the Finish National Defence University, *Visions of Strategy Following Clausewitz's Train of Thought* (Helsinki, 2014). I am writing this with some unease, as these problems also involve scholarly integrity in dealing with my work. Still, there is no escaping from clarifying these major points. Palmgren accepts as a matter of course that Clausewitz represented the Romantic reaction against the ideas of the Enlightenment. He adds that 'In Consequence, some of Clausewitz's ideas are less original than is often believed.'[373] Separately, he writes that Gat's 'standpoint that military thinking depends on its particular milieu of thought is easy to accept.'[374]

At the same time, Palmgren purports to take issue with me on quite a number of points. First, he writes: 'Had Clausewitz, as suggested by Gat, the lifelong ambition to construct a "universal theory of war"? No, the present work does not perceive his intellectual development in that way. It was more fragmentary and dependent on situation; but he had a fairly consistent set of core beliefs developed and expanded over the years in different, successive contexts. It was not until after Waterloo, working in Koblenz, that he realized he could write something more theoretically pregnant about the conduct of war'.[375] Palmgren adds: 'It is obvious the young Clausewitz had a rather sceptical view of the possibility to distil an apt theory to guide the conduct of war. The present work suggests we should interpret Clausewitz more as a concerned patriotic pragmatist than as a general theorist with no immediate practical purpose.'[376]

Some false dichotomies are involved here: few would dispute that Clausewitz (like his mentor Scharnhorst) was *both* a 'concerned patriotic pragmatist' and a 'general theorist'; and he quite obviously had *both* a sceptical view of the possibility to distil an apt theory to guide the conduct of war and a life-long burning interest in what could be the basis for one. More to the point, what was Clausewitz's 'fairly consistent set of core beliefs developed and expanded over the years'? As we have seen, from his earliest works, ever since 1804, he consistently and repeatedly expressed his belief that a true theory of war should be based on the 'lasting spirit of war' which transcended war's changing forms. One cannot get more 'universal' than that. This 'lasting spirit', which he later mostly substituted with the equivalent terms, 'nature' and 'concept' of war, remained the core of his theory of war. Like others, Palmgren has missed the centrepiece of Clausewitz's entire theoretical edifice.

Second, Palmgren claims, supposedly against my argument, that Clausewitz *always* viewed the conduct of war within the context of and as serving politics. He is aware that, rather than denying this quite obvious claim, my point is that, from 1804 on, Clausewitz viewed the political aim itself in expansive terms – that political greatness was for him the natural complement of his advocacy of aggressive and decisive conduct of war.[377] Still, Palmgren writes that Clausewitz well understood that Prussia was a smaller power, inferior to Napoleonic France, and therefore had to conduct its war effort accordingly.[378] However, in 1806 Clausewitz supported an offensive strategy for isolated and much weaker Prussia against the *Grande Armée*. As we have seen, it was only in 1810–1812, advocating a defensive war for Prussia, that Clausewitz came to grips with this point. Inter alia, it led him to develop his conception of the relationship between defence and attack, stressing that the defence must be regarded as a temporary expedience, useful only when one is weaker, for example, in order to gain time for allies to join in. Thereafter, he insisted, one must switch to the attack, because, except for the above special conditions, the defence contradicts the very concept of war as a relentless effort to crush the enemy.

Indeed, third, Palmgren purports to reveal that the relationship between defence and attack was ultimately responsible for the shift in Clausewitz's theory of war in 1827. As in other instances, he does so without any reference to my tracing of Clausewitz's development on this, from 1810–1812, through his 1817 essay 'On Progress and Stagnation [*Stillstand* – standstill] in Military Activity', to Book VI of *On War*. At the same time, Palmgren downgrades the post-1827 shift to the status of 'analytical fine tuning', arguing that the more limited conduct of war, as practised in the eighteenth century, had already been present as an option for the future in Clausewitz's earlier writings from his Koblenz period (1816–1818). He fails to note that at that time, as before, Clausewitz still regarded this option as a deviation from the imperatives inherent in the true nature of war and explained it largely by the failings of human nature, rather than by overriding political conditions and aims.[379] The influence of politics is not even mentioned in Clausewitz's key document of that period 'On Progress and Stagnation [*Stillstand* – standstill] in Military Activity'. Indeed, even after 1827, when he was only beginning to develop his new ideas in the first chapters of Book VIII, Clausewitz still held that limited wars were not very likely in the future: 'once barriers – which in a sense consist only in man's ignorance of what is possible – are torn down, they are not so easily set up again.'[380] He would mellow this judgement as he advanced further through Books VIII and I.

Fourth, Palmgren claims that 'By 1827 at the latest Clausewitz concluded that understanding war required that it be deprived of any fixed logical core.'[381] As we have seen, this is quite the opposite of Clausewitz's post-1827 'synthesis'. In this 'synthesis' he sought to preserve his fundamental, life-long view of the intrinsic 'nature' or 'concept' of war as an unlimited explosion of violence while allowing that it was harnessed to serve the political objectives, with the actual conduct of war adjusted and limited accordingly.

Finally, Palmgren writes: 'Gat suggested that Clausewitz had revised his work in small portions between 1827 and 1830: "He merely rewrote, amended and added sections (some of which were quite extensive) to be incorporated into the existing text."'[382] This, again, is the opposite of what I have argued. What I showed was that, contrary to earlier scholarly interpretations based on a misdating of the Undated Note, Clausewitz actually made major advances in his work between 1827 and 1830. In accordance with the work plan he sketched in his July 1827 note, he went on to write Books VII and VIII nearly from scratch, developing his new ideas mainly in Book VIII, and then returned to revise the first six books which were already in clean draft. It was only the beginning of Book I that he revised in the manner described (rewrote, amended, and added sections to be incorporated into the existing text), before his work was interrupted by war duties and death.

Besides such failings of commission and omission, Palmgren's work demonstrates once again that a quite extensive study of Clausewitz's writings does not guarantee a true comprehension of his work – indeed, how easy it is not to see the forest for the trees. Since Palmgren's work has been cited in later works under the standard comment that it offers a more 'nuanced' picture of

Clausewitz's views and development, the above clarifications become all the more necessary.

Paul Donker is a doctoral student who has done some important work on the surviving Clausewitz manuscripts. We have corresponded for several years regarding his dissertation. The dissertation is not yet completed, but his main claims have been published: 'The Genesis of Clausewitz's *On War* Reconsidered', *British Journal for Military History*, 2:3 (July 2016), 101–117. His thesis is that a text 'Aphorismen über den Krieg und die Kriegführung' [*Aphorisms on War and Its Conduct*], consisting of 177 short aphorisms, serialised in a German journal between 1833 and 1835,[383] is actually a presumably lost manuscript from Clausewitz's Koblenz period (1816–1818) to which Clausewitz refers, probably in 1818, as follows: 'My original intention was to set down my conclusions on the principal elements of this topic in short, precise, compact statements, without concern for system or formal connection. The manner in which Montesquieu dealt with his subject was vaguely in my mind.'[384]

While Donker's archival work is worthwhile, his thesis regarding the 'aphorisms' is quite clearly mistaken. Only the aphorismic form appears to support his claim that the later text is the conjectured 1816–1818 document, and it seems this very limited point has led him astray. Indeed, his own arguments in his article refute his claim. The latter-day 'Aphorisms' he discusses, most notably #1, 2, 13, 19, 22, 24, 26, closely corresponds to the new ideas regarding the two types of war under the supremacy of politics we find in the revised Book I of *On War*. They do not appear in the older, pre-1827, unrevised manuscript of that book. Nor do they appear in the list of propositions that Clausewitz composed in the end of the melancholic Undated Note in early 1827 or slightly before. Nor, indeed, do they figure in Clausewitz's essay from his Koblenz period 'On Progress and Stagnation [*Stillstand* – standstill] in Military Activity' (1817), his early attempt to grapple with the 'problem' of war that is not waged energetically towards decision in battle. And yet, the Koblenz period is the one to which Donker attributes the 'Aphorisms'. All this goes to show that the posthumous 'Aphorisms' reflect the post-1827 revolution in Clausewitz's thought. In the same vein, we also find in them (Aphorism 19) the distance of war from the 'absolute', a term that Clausewitz introduced only in 1827.

In addition, Aphorism 145 states: 'In the last forty years, war has taken on a completely different character by the monstrous national forces that have been put into action'. As Clausewitz clearly refers to the decades since the beginning of the wars of the Revolution and Napoleon, forty years take us to the end of his life, and certainly not to 1816–1818. (Admittedly, this particular point is less compelling, as this can be claimed to be a later editorial adjustment.) Finally, Clausewitz's wife, Marie, who closely supervised the posthumous publication of his work, was not incapable of making mistakes, as in her assumption regarding the dating of the Undated Note. Still, had she thought that these latter-day 'Aphorisms' are the fruit of the work Clausewitz referred to in his 'Comment' of 1818, she would most likely have made this point in her introduction and mentioned that such a text existed.

There is no escaping the conclusion that Hahlweg was right in dating of the 'Aphorisms' to the last years of Clausewitz's life. It must have been either Clausewitz's own draft compilation of the points he intended to plant, revise and stress in his planned revision of the first books of *On War*, as he eventually did; or, perhaps, a compilation of these points intended for journal publication by Marie, by her brother, and/or by Major O'Etzel, who collaborated with her on the editorial work.

Notes

1.   Isaiah Berlin, 'The Counter-Enlightenment', in his *Against the Current: Essays in the History of Ideas* (Oxford, 1981), 1–24.

2.   Reference is made to the modern, albeit abridged, translation of de Saxe's *Mes Rêveries*, in T. Phillips (ed.), *Roots of Strategy* (Harrisburg PA, 1940), 189.

3.   For more on Guibert, see my *The Origins of Military Thought: From the Enlightenment to Clausewitz* (Oxford, 1989), 43–53; incorporated into my *A History of Military Thought from the Enlightenment to the Cold War* (Oxford, 2001), 45–55.

4.   See my 'Lloyd: His International Career, Intellectual Scope, and the Campaigns of the Seven Years War', *The Origins of Military Thought*, 67–78; *History of Military Thought*, 69–80. We now have a military and intellectual biography: Patrick Speelman, *Henry Lloyd and the Military Enlightenment of the Eighteenth Century* (Westport CT, 2002). The book is detailed, thoroughly documented, and generally very good. At the same time, while leaning on my framework of the Enlightenment as the key to understanding Lloyd's work and that of its contemporaries, some of its contextualising of Lloyd's theories and place in the development of military thought is less sound. Importantly, Speelman also brought out a new, 750-page edition of Lloyds' works, practically unavailable for centuries except in some major libraries: *War, Society and Enlightenment: The Works of General Lloyd* (Leiden, 2005).

5.   A. H. Jomini, *Treatise on Grand Military Operations* (New York, 1865), the concluding chap., 445.

6.   *Treatise*, chap. 7, 253–4. For a similar theoretical outlook see Jomini's later *Summary of the Art of War* (Philadelphia, 1862; French original 1837), 18.

7. *OEuvres de Frédéric le grand* (Berlin, 1856), vol. 29, pp. 58–59.
8. J. Colin, *L'Éducation militaire de Napoléon* (Paris, 1901).
9. Napoleon, *Military Maxims*, in Phillips, *Roots of Strategy*, maxim no. 112, my emphases; see also no. 5.
10. Ibid., no. 77.
11. Archduke Charles [Carl von Oesterreich], *Grundsätze der höheren Kriegskunst*, in his *Ausgewählte Schriften* (Vienna and Leipzig, 1893–4), vol. I, p. 50.
12. W. M. Alexander, *Johann Georg Hamann, Philosophy and Faith* (The Hague, 1966); Isaiah Berlin, 'Hume and the Sources of German Anti-Rationalism', in his *Against the Current*, 165–170; and also his 'The Counter-Enlightenment', ibid., 6–9, to which this chapter owes a great deal.
13. H. B. Nisbet, *Herder and the Philosophy and History of Science* (Cambridge, 1970); Frederick Beiser, *Enlightenment, Revolution and Romanticism: The Genesis of Modern German Political Thought, 1790–1800* (Cambridge, Mass, 1992), chap. 8; idem, *The German Historicist Tradition* (Oxford, 2011), chap. 3.
14. George A. Wells, *Goethe and the Development of Science* (The Netherlands, 1978).
15. Alexander Gode von Aesch, *Natural Science in German Romanticism* (New York, 1941); Beiser, *Enlightenment, Revolution and Romanticism*, chap. 10; idem, *The Romantic Imperative: The Concept of Early German Romanticism* (Cambridge Mass, 2003), chap. 7
16. Goethe, *Dichtung und Wahrheit*, Bk. II, in *Werke*, x. 537–9 (Zurich, 1949–52); cited by Roy Pascal, *The German Sturm und Drang* (London, 1953), 131.
17. K. S. Pinson, *Pietism as a Factor in the Rise of German Nationalism* (New York, 1968).
18. Ralph Tymms, *German Romantic Literature* (London, 1955); H. G. Schenk, *The Mind of the European Romantics* (London, 1966); Beiser, *The Romantic Imperative*.

19. James Engell, *The Creative Imagination, Enlightenment to Romanticism* (Cambridge: Mass., 1981). For a defence of neo-classicism, see E. B. O. Borgerhoff, *The Freedom of French Classicism* (Princeton, 1950). Neo-classicism as a conception of art is not to be confused with late 18th-century German *Klassizismus* as an artistic style and view of life, mainly associated with the Weimar poets.

20. Friedrich Meinecke, *Historicism, the Rise of a New Historical Outlook* (London, 1972); G. Iggers, *The German Conception of History* (Middletown Con., 1968); P. H. Reil, *The German Enlightenment and the Rise of Historicism* (Berkeley, 1975); Frederick Beiser, *The German Historicist Tradition* (Oxford, 2011).

21. Jonathan Knudsen, *Justus Möser and the German Enlightenment* (Cambridge, 1986); Beiser, *The German Historicist Tradition*, chap. 2.

22. For the social and economic aspects of the transition, see Henri Brunschwig, *Enlightenment and Romanticism in Eighteenth Century Prussia* (Chicago, 1974); Arnold Hauser, *The Social History of Art*, (London, 1951), ii. chaps. 4 and 6.

23. Edward Bülow's introduction to a collection from Berenhorst's literary remains: *Aus dem Nachlasse* (2 vols.; Dessau, 1845 and 1847). Many other items from Berenhorst's family archives are cited in Rudolf Bahn, 'Georg Heinrich von Berenhorst' (doc. diss.; Halle, 1911). Also perceptive is Eberhard Kessel, 'Georg Heinrich von Berenhorst', in *Sachsen und Anhalt*, ix (1933), 161–98.

24. Berenhorst, 'Selbstbekenntnisse', in Bülow, *Aus dem Nachlasse*, ii. 4–5.

25. Ibid., 6–7.

26. Ibid., 6–14.

27. Ibid., 14–16.

28. Cited in Max Jähns, *Geschichte der Kriegswissenschaften* (Munich and Leipzig, 1889), 2128.

29. *Aus dem Nachlasse*, i. 3.
30. See e.g. Bernhorst's *Betrachtungen über die Kriegskunst, über ihre fortschritte, ihre Widersprüche und ihre Zuverlässigkeit* (3rd edn., Leipzig, 1827), 170.
31. *Betrachtungen über einige Unrichtigkeiten in den Betrachtungen über die Kriegskunst* (1802).
32. Berenhorst, 'Randglossen', in *Betrachtungen*, 477.
33. Ibid., 472–3.
34. Ibid., 499–500.
35. Ibid., 477.
36. Ibid., 449–50.
37. *Aus dem Nachlasse*, i. 192–3.
38. Ibid., ii. 295–6.
39. Ibid., ii. 333, 353–4; also cited by Peter Paret, *Clausewitz and the State* (Princeton, 1976), 206.
40. Despite its many failings, discussed in this book, Peter Paret, *Clausewitz and the State* (Princeton, 1976), remains the most thorough biography so far. A valuable contribution is Vanya Eftimova Bellinger, *Marie von Clausewitz: The Woman Behind the Making of On War* (Oxford, 2016), based on the full, recently rediscovered, trove of the correspondence between Carl and Marie. It thus greatly augments the more partial selections from the letters that have always been the main source for Clausewitz's life: Karl Schwartz, *Das Leben des Generals Carl von Clausewitz und der Frau Marie von Clausewitz geb. Gräfin von Brühl, in Briefen, Tagebüchern, Aufsätzen und anderen Schriftstücken* (Berlin, 1878); and Karl Linnebach (ed.) *Karl und Marie von Clausewitz: Ein Lebensbild in Briefen und Tagebuchblätter* (Berlin, 1916). Donald Stoker, *Clausewitz: His Life and Work* (Oxford, 2014), focuses on Clausewitz's participation in the campaigns of his time. Bruno Colson, *Clausewitz* (Perrin, 2016), is an extensive biography in French.
41. A letter to his fiancée, 28 Jan. 1807, in Linnebach, *Briefen* 85.

42. For a fuller account of Scharnhorst's place see my *Origins of Military Thought: From the Enlightenment to Clausewitz*, 156–167; incorporated into my *History of Military Thought: From the Enlightenment to the Cold War*, 158–169. Charles White has added two extensive studies in English: a full-scale biography of Scharnhorst's youth, including his process of education and the German Enlightenment's idea of Bildung, as well as his early combat experiences, *Scharnhorst: The Formative Years, 1755–1801* (Warwick, 2020); idem, *The Enlightened Soldier: Scharnhorst and the Militärische Geselschaft in Berlin, 1801–1805* (New York, 1989). A mammoth publication of his writings has also seen light: J. Kunisch, M. Sikora, and T. Stieve, *Gerhard von Scharnhorst: Privat und dienstliche Schriften*, 8 vols. (Köln, Weimar, Wien, 2002–2015).

43. Scharnhorst in *Neues Militärisches Journal*, XII (1804), 344 ff. For Scharnhorst's reiteration of his theoretical outlook, made in the same year, see the opening chapters of his *Handbuch der Artillerie* (Hanover, 1804), reprinted in U. von Gersdoff (ed.), *Ausgewählte Schriften*, (Osnabrück, 1983), 153–62. Also, Scharnhorst, 'Nutzen der militärischen Geschichte, Ursach ihres Mangels' (1806), ibid., 199–207.

44. Scharnhorst criticized Bülow, 'H. v. Bülow nach seiner Hypergenialität und seinen Abenteurn geschildert', *Göttinger gelehrten* (Berlin, 1807); in Max Jähns, *Geschichte der Kriegswissenschaften* (Munich and Leipzig, 1889), 2142.

45. Clausewitz, 'Bülow', in W. Hahlweg (ed.), *Clausewitz: Ventreute kleine Schriften*, (Osnabrück, 1979), 87.

46. Clausewitz, 'On the Life and Character of Scharnhorst', in *Carl von Clausewitz: Historical and Political Writings*, ed. and trans. by Peter Paret and Daniel Moran. (Princeton, 1992), 85–109; the German original appeared in L. von Ranke (ed.), *Historisch-Politiscshe Zeitschrift*, I (1832), 177, 198.

47. Clausewitz, 'The Germans and the French', in *Historical and Political Writings*, 250–262; German publication in Hans Rothfels (ed.), *Carl von Clausewitz, Politische Schriften und Briefe* (Munich, 1922), esp. 37–45.
48. Hans Rothfels, *Carl von Clausewitz: Politik und Krieg* (Berlin, 1920), 113–116; Paret, *Clausewitz*, 133–134.
49. Clausewitz, 'Agitation', *Historical and Political Writings*, 335–368, quotation from 347; German publication in Rothfels, *Schriften*, 166.
50. Immanuel Kant, *The Critique of Judgement* (Oxford, 1961), esp. articles 46–50; the quotations are from pp. 168, 181.
51. Hermann Cohen, *Von Kants Einfluss auf die deutsche Kultur* (Berlin, 1883), 31–32. Some of Clausewitz's notes, taken in one of Kiesewetter's lectures on mathematics, were found by Walrer Malmsten Schering, *Die Kriegsphilosophie von Clausewitz* (Hamburg, 1935), 105ff. Advances over the past two decades, mentioned in Chap. 9, below, 'Comments on the Recent Clausewitz Literature', are: a significant contribution on Kiesewetter's work and influence in Antulio Echevarria II, *Clausewitz and Contemporary War* (Oxford, 2007); and evidence suggesting direct quotations from Kant by Clausewitz in Youri Cormier, *War as Paradox: Clausewitz and Hegel on Fighting Doctrines and Ethics* (Montreal, 2016).
52. Clausewitz 'Bülow', in *Ventreute kleine Schriften*, 80–81.
53. Cited by Rothfels, *Politik und Krieg*, 156.
54. Clausewitz, *Strategie aus dem Jahre 1804, mit Zusätzen von 1808 und 1809* (Hamburg, 1943), 1809, section 33; also in Hahlweg (ed.), *Ventreute kleine Schriften*.
55. The fragment, 'Über Kunst and Kunsttheorie', was printed in W. M. Schering (ed.), *Clausewitz: Geist und Tat* (Stuttgart, 1941), see esp. 154–5, 159. For Kant's distinction between science and art, see his *Critique of Judgement*, article 43, pp. 162–164.

56. *On War*, II, 3, pp. 148–50.
57. *On War*, II, 2, p. 136.
58. *On War*, III, 3, p. 184.
59. *On War*, II, 4, pp. 151–2.
60. *On War*, II, 2, pp. 140–1, 147; II, 4, pp. 152–3.
61. Cormier, *War as Paradox*, 94.
62. *On War*, II, 2, p. 140.
63. Paret, *Clausewitz*, 84.
64. For Schiller's aesthetic conceptions and Kant's philosophy, see e.g. R. D. Miller, *Schiller and the Ideal of Freedom: A Study of Schiller's Philosophical Works with Chapters on Kant* (Oxford, 1970).
65. Paret, *Clausewitz*, 166.
66. *Strategie* (1804), section 5.
67. Ibid.
68. Clausewitz, 'Gustav Adolphs Feldzüge von 1630–1632', in his *Hinterlassene Werke* (Berlin, 1832–7), vol. ix; for the probable date of composition see the editor's introduction, p. vi.
69. This was first pointed out by Rothfels, *Politik und Krieg*, 61–69; touched upon in Eberhard Kessel's Introduction to *Strategie*, 24; and developed in Paret, *Clausewitz*, 85–88.
70. See also: W. M. Simon, *Friedrich Schiller: The Poet as Historian* (Keele, 1966); and Lesley Sharpe, *Schiller and the Historical Character* (Oxford, 1982). For Clausewitz's reference to Yorck's inquiry of the troops' mood at the decisive meeting in Tauroggen when he made up his mind to take his corps out of the Napoleonic army as recalling Schiller's 'Wallenstein', see Clausewitz, *The Campaign of 1812 in Russia* (London, 1843), 239; Paret, *Clausewitz*, 230.
71. 'Gustav Adolph', *Hinterlassme Werke*, ix. 8.
72. Ibid., 46.
73. *Strategie* (1808), section 29.
74. *Strategie* (1804), section 3.

75. Clausewitz, *Principles of War* (Harrisburg, 1942), 26.

76. See esp. *On War*, I, 3, 'On Military Genius'.

77. *On War*, II, 2, p. 146; I, 3, p. 112; VII, 3, p. 586.

78. See Marie's description of her first meeting with her future husband in Schwartz, *Leben*, i. 185.

79. Clausewitz's letter to his fiancée: 5 Oct. 1807, in Schwartz, *Leben*, i. 299.

80. Bellinger, *Marie von Clausewitz*, 96, 112–113.

81. From a fragment written in 1807–8, 'Historisch-Politische Aufzeichnungen', in Carl von Clausewitz, *Politische Briefe und Schriften*, ed. by Hans Rothfels (Munich, 1922), 59.

82. Paret, *Clausewitz*, 149.

83. Clausewitz, 'Bülow', *Ventreute kleine Schriften*, 79, 81.

84. Rothfels, *Politische Briefe und Schriften*, 59.

85. Paret and Moran, *Historical and Political Writings*, 282, 284.

86. *On War*, I, pp. 4–5; II, 2, pp. 137–9; III, 3–7.

87. *On War*, II, 2, p. 136; Ill, 3, p. 184.

88. *On War*, II, 2, pp. 136–7.

89. *On War*, III, 3, p. 184.

90. *On War*, II, 2, p. 136.

91. F. von Lossau, *Der Krieg* (Leipzig, 1815), 284–8. On Lossau see Ernst Hagemann, *Die deutsche Lehre vom Kriege: von Berenhorst zu Clausewitz* (Berlin, 1940), 44–55.

92. Clausewitz, *Principles of War*, 26.

93. *On War*, I, 7; II, 2, p. 140.

94. This was well treated by Rothfels, *Politik und Krieg*, 61–69; noted by Kessel (following the appearance of Meinecke's *Historismus* in 1936) in his introduction to *Strategie*, 11; and was discussed at length by Paret, *Clausewitz*.

95. Paret, *Clausewitz*, 81–82; also the references in Paret and Moran, *Historical and Political Writings*.

96. See n. 40 above.

97. Clausewitz, 'Agitation', *Historical and Political Writings*, 345 and 347.

98. Rothfels, *Politik und Krieg*, 61–2.

99. Clausewitz, 'Ansichten aus der Geschichte des Dreis-sigjahrigen Krieges'; cited by Rothfels, *Politik und Krieg*, 61–2.

100. Clausewitz, 'Ueber den Zustand der Theorie der Kriegskunst', in Werner Hahlweg (ed.), *Carl von Clausewitz: Schriften, Aufsätze, Studien, Briefe*, vol. 2 (Göttingen, 1990), 23.

101. *On War*, VI, 30, p. 516.

102. The regulations are cited in G. H. Klippel, *Das Leben des Generals von Scharnhorst* (Leipzig, 1869–71), ii. 255–62; an now also in White, *The Enlightened Soldier: Scharnhorst and the* Militärische Geselschaft *in Berlin, 1801–1805*, 191–199.

103. Clausewitz, *Principles of War*, 29; see also *On War*, II, 6, p. 170.

104. *On War*, II, 6, p. 173.

105. *On War*, VIII, 6B, p. 586.

106. Ibid., 593.

107. See, for example, Hugh Smith, *On Clausewitz: A Study of Military and Political Ideas* (New York, 2004), 68. There are others too.

108. See notes 40, 42, 43 and adjacent text, above.

109. See esp. Frederick Beiser, *Enlightenment, Revolution and Romanticism: The Genesis of Modern German Political Thought, 1790–1800* (Cambridge, Mass, 1992); idem, *The German Historicist Tradition* (Oxford, 2011).

110. For Scharnhorst's early analysis of the socio-political sources of French might, see his 'Entwicklung der allgemeinen Ursachen des Glücks der Franzosen in dem Revolurionskriege', *Neues Militärisches Journal*, viii (1797); reprinted in C. von de Goltz (ed.), *Militärische Schriften von Scharnhorst* (Berlin, 1881), 192–242. For Clausewitz, see 'Agitation', *Historical and Political Writings*, 338–346.

111. C. B. A. Behrens, 'Which Side was Clausewitz On?' in *The New York Review of Books*, 14 Oct. 1976; on Clausewitz's political and ethical worldview, see my *Origins of Military Thought*, 236–250; incorporated into my *History of Military Thought*, 238–252.

112. Clausewitz, 'Agitation', *Historical and Political Writings*, 345, 347, 349.

113. Jomini, *Summary*, 17–18.

114. Ibid., 135.

115. *Strategie* (1808), section 29.

116. Clausewitz, 'Bülow', in W. Hahlweg (ed.), *Clausewitz: Ventreute kleine Schriften*, (Osnabrück, 1979), 82.

117. Clausewitz, *Strategie* (1808), section 29.

118. Ibid.

119. Ibid., (1809), section 33.

120. Ibid. (1808), section 29.

121. Clausewitz, 'Letter to Fichte', in *Carl von Clausewitz: Historical and Political Writings*, ed. and trans. by Peter Paret and Daniel Moran. (Princeton, 1992), 279–284, esp. 282–283.

122. Letter to Marie, 5 Oct. 1807, Linnebach, *Briefen*, 142–143, cited by Paret, *Clausewitz*, 167. Clausewitz's affinity to Schleiermacher's ideas was briefly pointed out by Erich Weniger, 'Philosophie und Bildung im Denken von Clausewitz', in W. Hubatsch (ed.), *Schicksalswege Deutscher Vergangenbeit* (Düsseldorf, 1950), 143. For Schleiermacher's ideas in this connection, see his speeches *On Religion* (London, 1893), esp. speeches 1, 2, 5.

123. Herder, *Ideen zur Philosophie der Geschichte der Menschheit* (1784–1791), XIII, 6; ciled by Rothfels, *Clausewitz*, 63.

124. F. von Lossau, *Der Krieg* (Leipzig, 1815), 35.

125. This is despite the claim by Paul Donker; see in chap. 9, below.

126. 'Author's Preface', *On War*, p. 61.

127. The focus on the role of conceptualization in the creation of theory, the relationship between theory and reality, and the link between the parts of war and the whole are strikingly similar to that of the leading seventeenth century general and military author Raimondo Montecuccoli in his introduction to his celebrated *War against the Turks in Hungary*. In a letter to a friend written in 1810, Scharnhorst recommended Montecuccoli's work, calling it *Lebensbuch*, and wrote that it had been his constant companion accompanying him through good and bad times: Letter of 30 Aug. 1810, in K. Linnebach (ed.), *Scharnhorsts Briefe* (Munich and Leipzig, 1914), 404–405; Rudolf Stadelmann, *Scharnhorst, Schicksal und geistige Welt, ein Fragment*, (Wiesbaden, 1952), 92–99. For Montecuccoli, see my 1989/2001 book, chap. 1.

128. Lossau, *Der Krieg*, 2 and 6.

129. Raymond Aron, *Clausewitz: den Krieg denken* (Frankfurt am Main, 1980), esp. 163, 308, 331–335. Since the English edition is substantially abridged, all references are made to the German version.

130. Stadelmann, *Scharnhorst*, 105–8.

131. 'Comment', *On War*, p. 63.

132. 'Author's Preface', *On War*, pp. 61–62. For Lichtenberg see J. P. Stern, *Lichtenberg: A Doctrine of Scattered Occasions* (Indiana, 1959).

133. 'Comment', *On War*, p. 63.

134. *On War*, VIII, 1, p. 578.

135. *On War*, II, 5, pp. 157–158; see again the section 'A Positive Doctrine is Unattainable', ibid. II, 2, p. 140.

136. *On War*, II, 2, p. 141.

137. Gat, 'Clausewitz's Final Notes Revisited', in my *Origins*, 255–263; *History of Military Thought*, 257–265.

138. 'Undated Note', *On War*, p. 71.

139. Clausewitz, 'Notes on History and Politics 1807–1809', *Historical and Political Writings*, 263–278; Clausewitz, 'Testimonial (*Bekenntnisdenkschrift*)', in *Clausewitz on Small War*, edited and translated by C. Daase and J.W. Davis (Oxford, 2015), 169–216.

140. 'Notes on History and Politics' (1807), 269. On Clausewitz's affinity to Machiavelli, see my *Origins of Military Thought*, 201–202; *History of Military Thought*, 203–204.

141. *On War*, II, 1, p. 127.

142. Schleiermacher, *On Religion*, 13 and 15.

143. *Strategie* (1804), section 9.

144. Ibid., section 12.

145. Ibid.

146. Ibid., section 13.

147. Ibid., sections 22, 13, 15 and 19, respectively.

148. Ibid., sections 20 and 21.

149. *On War*, III, 1, p. 177; also II, 1, p. 128.

150. *Strategie* (1804), section 13.

151. Aron, *Clausewitz*, 88–9. The term 'two types' (*doppelte Art*) which is repeated in 1827, added to this confusion.

152. 'Note of 10 July 1827', *On War*, p. 69.

153. *Strategie* (1804), section 13.

154. Ibid., section 12.

155. Ibid., section 12; repeated in section 13.

156. Clausewitz, *Principles of War* (Harrisburg, 1942), 69.

157. Ibid., 13–14.

158. Ibid., 45.

159. Ibid., 12, 17–19, 21, 46.

160. Ibid., 17.

161. Ibid., 15.

162. Ibid., 48–9.

163. Berenhorst to Valentini, 1 Nov. 1812, in E. Bülow (ed.), *Aus dem Nachlasse* (Dessau, 1845 and 1847), ii. p. 353.

164. Paret, *Clausewitz*, 20.
165. *On War*, IV, 11, p. 258.
166. *On War*, IV, 3, p. 229.
167. *On War*, IV, 3, esp. p. 228.
168. 'Die Feldzüge von 1799 in Italien und in der Schweiz', in Clausewitz, *Hinterlassene Werke*, (Berlin, 1832–1837), v. p. 152.
169. Ibid. III, 1, pp. 181–182.
170. *On War*, VII, 13, pp. 541–542.
171. *On War*, IV, 3, pp. 228–229.
172. *On War*, IV, 11, p. 260.
173. *On War*, III, 9, p. 198.
174. *On War*, III, 10, p. 202.
175. *On War*, III, 11, p. 204.
176. *On War*, II, 1; for the citations, see pp. 132, 129.
177. *On War*, IV, 2, p. 226.
178. H. Camon, *Clausewitz* (Paris, 1911).
179. A. H. Jomini, *Treatise on Grand Military Operations* (New York, 1865), chap. 27, p. 323.
180. Ibid., chap. 13, p. 443.
181. Ibid., chap. 5, principle 1, p. 201; the concluding chap. principle 1, pp. 448–9.
182. Jomini, *Summary of the Art of War* (Philadelphia, 1862), pp. 176, 137.
183. *Treatise*, chap. 3, p. 149; see also chap. 7, p. 252, and *Summary*, 'The Fundamental Principles of War', p. 71.
184. *Summary*, p. 178.
185. For a summary of the debate see Hans Delbrück, *History of the Art of War* (1920) (Nebraska, 1920), iv. pp. 378–82; also, my *History of Military Thought*, 373–376.
186. Clausewitz, 'Notes on History and Politics' (1809), *Historical and Political Writings*, 278.
187. Werner Hahlweg (ed.), *Carl von Clausewitz: Schriften, Aufsätze, Studien, Briefe*, vol. 2 (Göttingen, 1990), 630–644.

188. See esp. B. H. Liddell Hart, *The Ghost of Napoleon* (New Haven, 1934); my *History of Military Thought*, 671–672, 678–681, 685, 690–695.

189. Clausewitz, 'Bülow', 78–9.

190. B. H. Liddell Hart, *Strategy, the Indirect Approach* (London, 1954), 338.

191. Aron, *Clausewitz*, 85.

192. Rühle von Lilienstern, *Handbuch für den Offizier*, a rev. edn. of Scharnhorst's work (Berlin, 1817), pp. 1, 435, 438–44. For Rühle, see Hagemann, *Von Berenhorst zu Clausewitz*, 55–66; Louis Sauzin's introd. to *Rühle von Lilienstern et son apologie de la guerre* (Paris, 1937); and Peter Paret, 'A Learned Officer among Others', in his collection of articles: *Clausewitz in His Time: Essays in the Cultural and Intellectual History of Thinking about War* (New York, 2014), 18–76.

193. *On War*, p. 70.

194. *On War*, VIII, 1, p. 578; compare this with the preface to the work of 1816–1818 where Clausewitz wrote that instead of presenting ready-made doctrinal structures (*fertigen Lehrgebäudes*), his work offered material for them: 'Author's Preface', ibid., p. 61.

195. See esp. *On War*, II, 2, pp. 141 and 147; II, 5, p. 156; VIII, 1, p. 578.

196. Lossau, *Der Krieg*, 2.

197. *On War*, VIII, 3B, p. 593.

198. Ibid.

199. Jomini, *Summary*, p. 15.

200. *On War*, VIII, 3B, p. 593.

201. *On War*, VI, 30, p. 501.

202. *On War*, VI, 25, p. 478.

203. Ibid.

204. For the widely misunderstood reasons why this has been so, see: Gil Merom, *How Democracies Lose Small*

Wars (Cambridge, 2003); Azar Gat and Gil Merom, 'Why Counterinsurgency Fails', in Gat, *Victorious and Vulnerable: Why Democracy Won in the 20th Century and How it is Still Imperiled*, (Stanford, 2010), chap. 7.

205. Beatrice Heuser, 'Small Wars in the Age of Clausewitz: The Watershed between Partisan War and People's War', *Journal of Strategic Studies*, 33/1 (2010), 139–62; and Sibylle Scheipers, *On Small War: Carl von Clausewitz and People's War* (Oxford, 2018).

206. Christopher Daase and James Davis (eds.), *Clausewitz on Small War* (Oxford, 2015), 3.

207. Heuser, 'Small Wars in the Age of Clausewitz', 158.

208. *On War*, VI, 25, p. 480.

209. Ibid., 480–481.

210. *On War*, VI, 28, pp. 488.

211. *On War*, VI, 28, pp. 488–9.

212. *On War*, VI, 30, p. 501.

213. See n. 22, above.

214. Clausewitz, 'Europe since the Polish Partitions' (1831), and 'On the Basic Question of Germany's Existence', (1831), *Historical and Political Writings*, 369–384.

215. 'Note of 10 July 1827', *On War*, p. 69.

216. Clausewitz, 'Ueber das Fortschreiten und den Stillstand der kriegerischen Begebenheiten' in Werner Hahlweg (ed.), *Carl von Clausewitz: Schriften, Aufsätze, Studien, Briefe*, vol. 2 (Göttingen, 1990), 249 (emphasis in the original), 250.

217. Ibid., 254.

218. Ibid., 630.

219. Ibid., 630–631.

220. Ibid., 632.

221. Ibid., 635.

222. Ibid., 636.

223. Ibid., 634.

224. Ibid., 632.
225. Ibid., 633.
226. Ibid.
227. Ibid., 635.
228. Ibid., 632.
229. Ibid., 636–637.
230. Ibid., 632.
231. *On War*, VI, 28, pp. 488–489.
232. *On War*, VI, 30, p. 501.
233. 'Note of 10 July 1827', *On War*, p. 69.
234. *On War*, VIII, 2, p. 580.
235. W. M. Schering (ed.), *Clausewitz: Geist und Tat* (Stuttgart, 1942), p. 309; Raymond Aron, *Clausewitz: den Krieg denken* (Frankfurt am Main, 1980), 101. Again, as the English edition is substantially abridged, all references are made to the German version.
236. *On War*, VIII, 6A, p. 604.
237. *On War*, VIII, 2, pp. 579–80.
238. Ibid., pp. 580–581.
239. *On War*, VIII, 2, 579.
240. *On War*, VIII, 3B, p. 585
241. *On War*, VIII, 6A, pp. 603–604.
242. *On War*, VIII, 6B, pp. 605–606.
243. Ibid.
244. *On War*, VIII, 3B, pp. 587, 591, 593.
245. *On War*, I, 1, section 23, p. 87
246. *On War*, I, 1, section 3, pp. 76–7.
247. Ibid, p. 76.
248. *On War*, I, 1, section 6, p. 78.
249. *On War*, I, 1, section 10–1 1, pp. 80–81.
250. *On War*, I, 2, p. 94 (emphasis in the original).
251. Ibid. p. 95.
252. Ibid. p. 97.
253. Ibid. p. 99 (emphasis in the original).

254. Quoted by Howard, 'The Influence of Clausewitz', in *On War*, p. 27.

255. Camon, *Clausewitz*, p. viii.

256. Bernard Brodie, 'The Continuing Relevance of On War', and 'A Guide to the Reading of On War', in *On War*, the quotation is from p. 18.

257. Aron, *Clausewitz*, 106, 114.

258. Ibid, 104, 111.

259. Ibid., 322, 325.

260. Ibid., 79.

261. Rothfels, *Politische Briefe und Schriften*, 59.

262. W. B. Callie, 'Clausewitz On the Nature of War', *Philosophers of Peace and War, Kant, Clausewitz, Marx, Engels and Tolstoy* (Cambridge, 1978), 48–65.

263. Paret, *Clausewitz*, 151.

264. Karl Schwartz, *Das Leben des Generals Carl von Clausewitz und der Frau Marie von Clausewitz geb. Gräfin von Brühl, in Briefen, Tagebüchern, Aufsätzen und anderen Schriftstücken* (Berlin, 1878), i. 305.

265. Paret, *Clausewitz*, 151, 350; and chap. 3, p. 49 of this work.

266. V. I. Lenin, 'The Collapse of rhe Second International', *Collected Works* (Moscow, 1964), vol. 21, p. 219.

267. Paul Creuzinger, *Hegels Einfluss auf Clausewitz* (Berlin, 1911). Lenin possibly relied on this work in his explicit presentation of Clausewitz as Hegel's disciple.

268. Schering, *Kriegsphilosophie*, 111–119.

269. Paret, *Clausewitz*, 84, 150.

270. Aron, *Clausewitz*, 321–31.

271. Paret, *Clausewitz*, 316.

272. See my *Origins*, 236–250; *History of Military Thought*, 238–252.

273. 'Author's Preface', *On War*, pp 61–62.

274. *On War*, VII, 1, p. 523. The Howard-Paret translation of *Begriffe* and *Gegensätze* as 'ideas' and 'antithesis' is

misplaced and tends to assume the required. For more, see chap. 9 below, 'Comments on the Recent Clausewitz Literature'.

275. *On War*, VIII, 68, pp. 605–606.
276. *On War*, I, 1, 28, p. 89.
277. Youri Cormier, *War as Paradox: Clausewitz and Hegel on Fighting Doctrines and Ethics* (McGill, 2016).
278. Gat, 'Clausewitz's Final Notes Revisited', in my *Origins*, 255–263; *History of Military Thought*, 257–265.
279. Carl von Clausewitz, *Two Letters on Strategy*, ed. and trans. by P. Paret and D. Moran (Fort Leavenworth, Kansas, 1984), first letter from December 22, 1827, 21–22; emphasis in the original.
280. Ibid., 24–26; emphases in the original.
281. Christopher Bassford, in *Clausewitz in the Twenty-First Century*, ed. by H. Strachan and A. Herberg-Rothe (Oxford, 2007), 74.
282. Paret, *Clausewitz*, 369.
283. Cicero, *De republica*, iii. 15. 24.
284. Cicero, *De officiis*, i. 12. 38.
285. See chap. 4, n. 12, above.
286. Gat, *Origins*, esp. 16, 21; *History of Military Thought*, 18, 23.
287. J. A. H. Guibert, *A General Essay on Tactics* (London, 1781), vol. i, p. xxi; French Original 1772.
288. See my *Origins*, 69; *History of Military Thought*, 71.
289. *Origins*, 73; *History*, 75.
290. Jomini, *Summary of the Art of War*, 14.
291. Ibid., 38.
292. Youri Cormier, *War as Paradox: Clausewitz and Hegel on Fighting Doctrines and Ethics* (Montreal, 2016), chap. 4.
293. Jomini, *Treatise on Grand Military Operations* (New York, 1865), 460–1.
294. Jon Sumida, *Decoding Clausewitz: A New Approach to On War* (Lawrence, Kansas, 2008).

295. *Strategie* (1804), section 13.

296. Ibid.

297. Carl von Clausewitz, 'Lectures on Small War, given at the War College in 1810', in *Clausewitz on Small War*, ed. and trans. by C. Daase and J.W. Davis, (Oxford, 2015), 63–64.

298. Clausewitz, 'Addendum', 'On the Nature of Defence', to his 'Testimonial' of Feb. 1812, Ibid., 215.

299. Clausewitz, *The Principles of War*, 25.

300. Clausewitz, *On War*, VI, 1, 2, p. 358.

301. Ibid.

302. *On War*, VI, 1, 1, p. 357.

303. *On War*, VI, 5, p. 370.

304. *On War*, VI, 1, 1, p. 357; also see 1, 2, p. 358.

305. Ibid. VI, 1, 2, pp. 358–359.

306. See several formulations of the same ideas in *Strategie* (1804), section13; *Principles of War*, pp. 7 and 19; *On War*, VI, 1, 2, p. 358; and 5, p. 370 (citations are respectively from the last two references). See also *On War*, VI, 8, p. 380, and VII, 2, p. 524.

307. W. von Willisen, *Theorie des grossen Krieges* (Berlin, 1840), I, p. 45; quoted in R. Caemmerer, *The Development of Strategical Science during the 19th Century* (London, 1905), 136.

308. Aron, *Clausewitz, den Krieg denken* (Frankfurt am Main, 1980), 229, 244 and 248–9.

309. *On War*, VI, 30, p. 502; I, 2, p. 94.

310. *On War*, VI, 1, 2, p. 358.

311. Ibid., 359.

312. Ibid., 357 and 359.

313. Ibid., 358.

314. Peter Paret, 'Clausewitz', in Paret (ed.), *Makers of Modern Strategy from Machiavelli to the Nuclear Age* (Princeton, 1986), 208.

315. *On War*, VI. 2, p. 362.

316. *On War*, VI, 2, p. 360.
317. Ibid.
318. *On War*, VI, 3, p. 363.
319. *On War*, III, 9, p. 198.
320. *On War*, VI, 3, pp. 363–4; for a similar twofold argument, incorporating recognition and rejection, see ibid., 5, p. 371.
321. *On War*, VII, 4–5.
322. *On War*, VI, 3, p. 365.
323. *On War*, VI, 1, 2, p. 358.
324. *On War*, VI, 3, p. 365.
325. *On War*, II, 1, 129–132.
326. *On War*, VI, 1, p. 358.
327. *On War*, VI, 2, pp. 361–362.
328. *On War*, p. 361.
329. *On War*, VI, 1, 2, p. 358; for an almost identical formulation, see ibid. 30, p. 502.
330. *On War*, I, 2, p. 94.
331. *On War*, I, i. 28, p. 89.
332. 'Note of 10 July 1827', in *On War*, 70.
333. Gat, 'Clausewitz's Final Notes Revisited', in Gat, *Origins of Military Thought*, 255–263; *History of Military Thought*, 257–265.
334. 'Preface' by Marie von Clausewitz, in *On War*, 66.
335. *On War*, p. 70.
336. Clausewitz, *Two letters on Strategy*, 24–26; emphases in the original.
337. Hew Strachan, 'Michael Howard and Clausewitz', *Journal of Strategic Studies*, 45:1 (2022), 143–160, quotation form pp. 156–157.
338. *On War*, III, 1, p. 177; also II, 1, p. 128; and already in *Strategie* (1804), section 20, p. 33; section 21, p. 35.
339. *On War*, I, i. 28, p. 89.

340. I wrote that much in my 1989 book. But see mainly: Martin van Creveld, *The Transformation of War* (New York, 1991); John Keegan, *A History of Warfare* (New York, 1993); Mary Kaldor, *New and Old Wars: Organized Violence in a Global Era* (Cambridge, 2012).

341. See my *War in Human Civilization* (Oxford, 2006), *The Causes of War and the Spread of Peace* (Oxford, 2017), 'Proving Communal Warfare among Hunter-Gatherers: The Quasi-Rousseauan Error', *Evolutionary Anthropology*, 24 (2015), 111–126.

342. See my *The Origins of Military Thought*, 241–249; incorporated into to my *A History of Military Thought*, 243–251.

343. H.P. Willmott and Michael Barrett, *Clausewitz Reconsidered* (Santa Barbara, 2010), ix and 3. Similarly see Philip Meilinger, *Thoughts on War* (Lexington, Kentucky, 2020), pp. 2–3 and chap. 1.

344. See, for example, Clausewitz's Dec. 1827 letters to Roeder, cited in Chap. 5, above, emphases in the original.

345. See my *The Origins of Military Thought*, 241–249; incorporated into to my *A History of Military Thought*, 243–251.

346. *Strategie* (1808), section 29, p. 46.

347. *Strategie* (1809), section 33, pp. 60–61.

348. See my *War in Human Civilization* (Oxford, 2006), *The Causes of War and the Spread of Peace* (Oxford, 2017), 'Proving Communal Warfare among Hunter-Gatherers: The Quasi-Rousseauan Error', *Evolutionary Anthropology*, 24 (2015), 111–126.

349. *On War*, p. 70.

350. Cited in Paret, *Clausewitz*, 210.

351. Ibid., 211.

352. Ibid., 267.

353. Vanya Eftimova Bellinger, *Marie von Clausewitz* (Oxford, 2016), 51.

354. Marie von Clausewitz, 'Preface', *On War*, p. 66.

355. Paret, *Clausewitz*, 210.

356. For R. Aron's well-known views on these matters, see esp. his *Peace and War: A Theory of International Relations* (New York, 1967), and 'What is a Theory of International Relations?', *Journal of International Affairs*, xxi (1967), 185–206. Also see Aron, *Clausewitz*, 17–20. Again, since the English edn. is substantially abridged, all references are made to the German version.

357. Aron, *Clausewitz*, 23.

358. C.B.A. Behrens, 'Which Side was Clausewitz On?' in *The New York Review of Books*, 14 (Oct. 1976); also, my *Origins of Military Thought*, 236–250; incorporated into my *History of Military Thought*, 238–252.

359. Michael Howard, 'Clausewitz *On War*: A History of the Howard-Paret Translation', in H. Strachan and A. Herberg-Rothe (eds.), *Clausewitz in the Twenty-First Century* (Oxford, 2007), p. v.

360. Michael Howard, 'Liddell Hart' (1970), and 'The British Way in Warfare: A Reappraisal' (1974), both reprinted in his *The Causes of War* (London, 1984), 189–207, 237–247.

361. Michael Howard, 'The Influence of Clausewitz', *On War*, 39–41, quotation from 41. See also my *History of Military Thought*, 692–695.

362. *On War*, p. 70.

363. Jan Willem Honig, 'Clausewitz's *On War*: Problems of Text and Translation', in *Clausewitz in the Twenty-First Century*, 57–73, quotation from 62.

364. Howard in *Clausewitz in the Twenty-First Century*, vi.

365. Sibylle Scheipers, *On Small War: Carl von Clausewitz and People's War* (Oxford, 2018), 8.

366. Antulio Echevarria II, *Clausewitz and Contemporary War* (Oxford, 2007), 4–5, 95–96.

367. Ibid., 154.

368. Ibid., 156.
369. Ibid.
370. Ibid., 168.
371. Ibid., 165.
372. Ibid., 157–162.
373. Palmgren, 'Clausewitz's Interweaving of *Krieg* and *Politik*', 50.
374. Palmgren, *Visions of Strategy*, 29.
375. Ibid., 31.
376. Ibid., 112–113.
377. *Visions of Strategy*, 18.
378. Ibid., 275.
379. See chap. 5, pp. 3–4, above, and the quotations there from Clausewitz's 'On Progress and Stagnation [*Stillstand* – standstill] in Military Activity' (1817).
380. *On War*, VIII, 3B, p. 593.
381. '*Krieg* and *Politik*', 65.
382. *Visions of Strategy*, 371.
383. Clausewitz, 'Aphorismen über den Krieg und die Kriegführung (Aus den hinterlassenen Schriften des Generals Carl von Clausewitz über Krieg und Kriegführung)', *Zeitschrift für Kunst, Wissenschaft und Geschichte des Krieges*, vol. 28:4 (1833), pp. 92–94; 28:5, 186–188; 28:6, 271–278; vol. 29:7 (1833), p. 102; 29:8, 196; 29:9, 276–278; vol. 30:1(1834), pp. 93–94; 30:2, 185–188; 30:3, 276–278; vol. 31:4 (1834), pp. 97–98; 31:5, 198–200; vol. 32:7 (1834), pp. 96–98; 32:9, 280–282; vol. 33:1, pp. 93–94; 33:2, 195–196; 33:3, 293–294; vol. 34:4, pp. 101–102; 34:6, 292–294; vol. 35:7 (1835), pp. 97–98. A digital copy of the journal can be found at: https://digital.slub-dresden.de/werkansicht/dlf/51104/1 Courtesy of Paul Donker.
384. Clausewitz, 'Author's Comment', *On War*, p. 63.

Index

CHRONOS
BOOKS

HISTORY

Chronos Books is an historical nonfiction imprint. Chronos publishes real history for real people, bringing to life people, places, and events in an imaginative, easy-to-digest and accessible way — histories that pass on their stories to a generation of new readers.
If you have enjoyed this book, why not tell other readers by posting a review on your preferred book site.

Recent bestsellers from Chronos Books are:

Lady Katherine Knollys
The Unacknowledged Daughter of King Henry VIII
Sarah-Beth Watkins
A comprehensive account of Katherine Knollys' questionable
paternity, her previously unexplored life in the Tudor court
and her intriguing relationship with Elizabeth I.
Paperback: 978-1-78279-585-8 ebook: 978-1-78279-584-1

Cromwell was Framed
Ireland 1649
Tom Reilly
Revealed: The definitive research that proves the Irish nation
owes Oliver Cromwell a huge posthumous apology for
wrongly convicting him of civilian atrocities in 1649.
Paperback: 978-1-78279-516-2 ebook: 978-1-78279-515-5

Why The CIA Killed JFK and Malcolm X
The Secret Drug Trade in Laos
John Koerner
A new groundbreaking work presenting evidence that the CIA
silenced JFK to protect its secret drug trade in Laos.
Paperback: 978-1-78279-701-2 ebook: 978-1-78279-700-5

The Disappearing Ninth Legion
A Popular History
Mark Olly
The Disappearing Ninth Legion examines hard evidence
for the foundation, development, mysterious disappearance,
or possible continuation of Rome's lost Legion.
Paperback: 978-1-84694-559-5 ebook: 978-1-84694-931-9

Beaten But Not Defeated

Siegfried Moos - A German anti-Nazi who settled in
Britain Merilyn Moos

Siegi Moos, an anti-Nazi and active member of the German
Communist Party, escaped Germany in 1933 and, exiled
in Britain, sought another route to the transformation of
capitalism.

Paperback: 978-1-78279-677-0 ebook: 978-1-78279-676-3

A Schoolboy's Wartime Letters

An evacuee's life in WWII — A Personal Memoir
Geoffrey Iley

A boy writes home during WWII, revealing his own
fascinating story, full of zest for life, information and humour.

Paperback: 978-1-78279-504-9 ebook: 978-1-78279-503-2

The Life & Times of the Real Robyn Hoode

Mark Olly

A journey of discovery. The chronicles of the genuine
historical character, Robyn Hoode, and how he became
one of England's greatest legends.

Paperback: 978-1-78535-059-7 ebook: 978-1-78535-060-3